T0340393

Public Interest Communication

Communication has become the technology of public interest, demanding a re-examination of the key concept of public in both public relations and communication theory. This book defines a new concept of public interest communication, combining the conflict, negotiation and adaptation inherent in public interest, with a critical approach to communication management and public relations.

Combining conceptual discussions about interest-forming practices and the fundamental role played by communication in constructing the public interest, the book uses case studies and theoretical modelling to explore the tensions and negotiation of conflicting interests. Public interest communication is identified within systems of governance at local, national and international levels, and across social and cultural contexts – such as health, community, media and the environment – each finding interest conflicts within the changing global environment.

Addressing the forces of fragmentation, inequality and individualisation that characterise the modern world, this thought-provoking volume will be of great interest to researchers and advanced students of communication, public relations, environmental communication, public communication, and public policy.

Jane Johnston is Associate Professor of Communication and Public Relations at The University of Queensland, Australia. Her book *Public Relations and the Public Interest* was published in 2016. Her other main research areas examine communication and open justice, and the changing media environment's impact on PR.

Magda Pieczka is Reader in Public Relations at Queen Margaret University in Edinburgh, UK, and Director of the university's Centre for Dialogue and Public Engagement. She is an Editor of *Public Relations Inquiry*, past Co-Editor of the *Journal of Communication Management*, and has served on the editorial boards of the *Journal of Public Relations Research* and *Prism*.

Routledge New Directions in Public Relations and Communications Research
Edited by Kevin Moloney

Current academic thinking about public relations (PR) and related communication is a lively, expanding marketplace of ideas and many scholars believe that it's time for its radical approach to be deepened. Routledge New Directions in PR & Communication Research is the forum of choice for this new thinking. Its key strength is its remit, publishing critical and challenging responses to continuities and fractures in contemporary PR thinking and practice, tracking its spread into new geographies and political economies. It questions its contested role in market-orientated, capitalist, liberal democracies around the world, and examines its invasion of all media spaces, old, new, and as yet unenvisaged. We actively invite new contributions and offer academics a welcoming place for the publication of their analyses of a universal, persuasive mind-set that lives comfortably in old and new media around the world.

Books in this series will be of interest to academics and researchers involved in these expanding fields of study, as well as students undertaking advanced studies in this area.

Public Interest Communication
Critical Debates and Global Contexts
Jane Johnston and Magda Pieczka

Public Relations in Japan
Evolution of Communication Management in a Culture of Lifetime Employment
Edited by Junichiro Miyabe, Yamamura Koichi and Tomoki Kunieda

Corporate Social Responsibility, Public Relations & Community Development
Emerging Perspectives from Southeast Asia
Marianne D. Sison and Zeny Sarabia-Panol

Social Media, Organizational Identity and Public Relations
The Challenge of Authenticity
Amy Thurlow

For more information about the series, please visit https://www.routledge.com/Routledge-New-Directions-in-Public-Relations–Communication-Research/book-series/RNDPRCR

Public Interest Communication
Critical Debates and Global Contexts

Edited by
Jane Johnston and Magda Pieczka

Routledge
Taylor & Francis Group

LONDON AND NEW YORK

First published 2019 by Routledge

2 Park Square, Milton Park, Abingdon, Oxfordshire OX14 4RN
52 Vanderbilt Avenue, New York, NY 10017

Routledge is an imprint of the Taylor & Francis Group, an informa business

First issued in paperback 2020

British Library Cataloguing in Publication Data
A catalogue record for this book is available from the British Library

Library of Congress Cataloging in Publication Data
A catalog record has been requested for this book

ISBN: 978-1-138-73711-2 (hbk)
ISBN: 978-0-367-66598-2 (pbk)

Typeset in Times New Roman
by Taylor & Francis Books

Contents

Tables

Contributors

Mhairi Aitken is a sociologist and Research Fellow in the Usher Institute of Population Health Sciences and Informatics at the University of Edinburgh, UK. Her research examines social dimensions of low carbon transitions and the role of members of the public in decision-making processes relating to climate change and energy policy.

Julieta Alejandra Brambila is an Assistant Professor in the Communication Department at the Universidad de las Américas, Mexico. She is a media scholar whose research includes journalism studies, comparative political communication, press freedom and violence against journalists. Her research has been published in English, Spanish and Japanese scholarly literature.

Nicholas Carah is a Senior Lecturer in media and communication at The University of Queensland, Australia. His research examines the intersections between branding, media platforms and cultural life. He is the author of *Brand Machines, Sensory Media and Calculative Culture* (with Sven Brodmerkel, 2016), *Media and Society: Production, Content and Participation* (with Eric Louw, 2015), and *Pop Brands: Branding, Popular Music and Young People* (2010).

Patricia A. Curtin, is Professor, Associate Dean for Undergraduate Affairs, and former Endowed Chair in Public Relations at the University of Oregon, United States. Her research interests centre on development of critical/postmodern approaches to public relations theory, particularly as applied to cross-cultural, marginalised and activist publics.

Scott Davidson researches and lectures on public relations and lobbying at the University of Leicester, UK. His recent work has focused on theorising the tensions between democratic norms and lobbying, and how public relations influences public participation in civic life more widely. Before becoming an academic he worked in campaign management and lobbying for 12 years.

Mohan J. Dutta is Provost's Chair Professor and Head of Communications and New Media at the National University of Singapore, and the founding

Director of the Center for Culture-Centered Approach to Research and Evaluation (CARE). His work examines grassroots politics of social change, research methods for radical democracies, and social justice activism in global contexts.

Susan Forde is Director of the Griffith Centre for Social and Cultural Research, and Professor of Journalism at Griffith University, Australia. Her research areas are alternative, community and Indigenous media. She worked as a journalist in the alternative and independent press prior to joining academia in 1998.

T. Kenn Gaither is a Professor and Associate Dean at Elon University, United States. He has more than nine years of professional public relations agency experience and most recently served as the president and chief executive officer of the Institute for Shipboard Education (Semester at Sea). He has written three public relations books and lived or taught in Brazil, China, Turkey and Ghana.

Robert L. Heath is Professor Emeritus, University of Houston, United States. He has written extensively on rhetorical theory, public relations, risk communication, crisis communication, issues management, narrative theory, and organisational communication. He is a reviewer and/or member of editorial boards for leading international journals on communication, public relations, health, crisis, and public safety.

Jenny Zhengye Hou is a Lecturer in Public Communication at the School of Communication, University of Technology Sydney, Australia. Prior to joining UTS, Jenny taught in Massey University, New Zealand. Her research interests include critical approaches to public relations, institutional sociology and strategic communication.

Jane Johnston is Associate Professor of Communication and Public Relations at The University of Queensland, Australia. Her book *Public Relations and the Public Interest* was published in 2016. Her other main research areas examine communication and open justice, and the changing media environment's impact on PR.

Jairo Lugo-Ocando, is an Associate Professor and Deputy Head of the School of Media and Communication at the University of Leeds, UK. His research deals with public relations, corporate social responsibility and humanitarian communication.

Magda Pieczka is Reader in Public Relations at Queen Margaret University in Edinburgh, UK, and Director of the university's Centre for Dialogue and Public Engagement. She is an Editor of *Public Relations Inquiry*, past Co-Editor of the *Journal of Communication Management*, and has served on the editorial boards of the *Journal of Public Relations Research* and *Prism*.

Boni Robertson is a Kabi Kabi Aboriginal woman, and a Professor at Griffith University, Australia. Her research interests are in the sociology of education, social justice and human rights as it applies to Indigenous Nations and families. She is a widely respected academic, researcher and advocate for human rights and education.

Ian Somerville is Reader in Communication at the University of Leicester, UK. His research has been published in a range of international communication and politics journals and his most recent book (as co-editor with O. Hargie, M. Taylor and M. Toledano) is *International Public Relations: Perspectives from Deeply Divided Societies* (Routledge, 2017).

Damion Waymer is Professor and Department Chair of Liberal Studies at North Carolina Agricultural and Technical State University, United States. His research centres on organisational discourse, particularly regarding PR, issues management, corporate social responsibility, branding, and strategic communication. His research addresses fundamental concerns about issues of power, race, class and gender.

Acknowledgements

We would like to acknowledge the editor of this book series, Kevin Moloney, who supported our approach to publish this book, recognising that the public interest provided an untapped field of potential for theoretical exploration by communication and public relations scholars. Together with Taylor & Francis editor Jacqueline Curthoys, Moloney encouraged this book from day one. In addition, we thank the anonymous reviewers who provided excellent feedback on the book proposal. We are very grateful for each of their contributions to the process, and think the book is stronger for their scrutiny and ideas. Finally, the book would not have occurred without the magnificent and tireless efforts of the chapter authors. Like the publishers, the stellar line-up of contributors showed great enthusiasm for the project from the start; a keenness to be part of the first published collection of public interest communication. Each brought rich and varied expertise to truly take this book into new territory.

Jane Johnston & Magda Pieczka

Public Interest Communication: Critical Debates and Global Contexts

An introduction

Jane Johnston and Magda Pieczka

When we embarked on this book, public interest communication was largely an uncharted territory. Our intention was to create a book that simultaneously expanded and challenged current theory in the fields of communication, public relations and the public interest. It needed to be open to critical and pragmatic perspectives, subaltern, alternative and mainstream communication, and media theory, and consider public/s and publicness from various cultural, socio-political, national and empirical viewpoints, while also incorporating an understanding of the complex and contested notions of public interest. The book needed to go beyond simplistic notions that the public interest was automatically antithetical to private interests and that it was necessarily aligned with equally mutable ideas of common good or community. Part of this process was to move beyond the dominant, largely Western democratic understanding of the public interest which has been widely examined (see, for example, Bozeman 2007; Douglass 1980; Flathman 1966; Goodin 2008; Goodin & Dryzek 2008; Johnston 2016), and explore how interest is contested in different socio-political environments. Crucially, it also needed to focus on an obvious gap in existing public interest literature and research – that is, the role played by communication in creating and serving shared public interests and interest conflicts. Theories of public interest acknowledge the role of communication but focus on the politics of *interest*; communication theory, instead, focuses on the question of the communicative existence of the *public*. In bringing these two together, and creating a space to examine these from multiple perspectives, *Public Interest Communication: Critical Debates and Global Contexts* was therefore positioned to take public interest and communication into new territory. Our argument for public interest communication was therefore based on the idea that the ontology of the public interest is communicative; that is, it comes into existence through acts of communication that allow for ideas to circulate, to be used, to be argued about and challenged, and finally, to be incorporated into social and political structures, such as regulation, legislation and codes of practice that give shape to human worlds but which are often contested.

A challenge of this book was to call to account expert communication practices that routinely work at the sharp edge of interest politics, and to support the scholars who are positioned to challenge the status quo in developing theory and interrogating practice environments. With this in mind, we approached the authors in this book to bring their expertise to contexts in which the public interest appears problematic, in which various appeals and challenges exist, where cooperation and settlement may or may not be achieved, and to examine ways in which undertakings are made possible by different communication forms and strategies. As such, the chapters – each written from a different critical, global, social or political perspective – interrogate interest conflicts and synergies and communication processes surrounding. The result is a rich and diverse collection of chapters that traverse topics such as climate change, media security, journalistic freedom, Indigenous and minority representation, located across North America, China, Europe, Australia and Africa. In ten chapters *Public Interest Communication: Critical Debates and Global Contexts* covers extensive ground as, through empirical investigation and theoretical critique, these leading scholars explore the idea of public interest communication through critical lenses. Each applies public interest communication to their own field of expertise, pushing the boundaries of this book into fascinating and new spaces of communication inquiry.

The book is divided into two parts: Part I interrogates theoretical intersections and conflicts, focusing on public interest issues in social, cultural and political contexts; Part II interrogates global perspectives of public interest and interest-conflicts, focusing on case studies within single or multiple nation-states.

Chapter run down

In Chapter 1, we provide a foundation for the book and a broad theoretical context for public interest communication. The chapter explores the widely interrogated field of the public interest as a largely political construct and continues in this line of inquiry to consider the ways in which communication and the public interest intersect. We introduce themes associated with process vs. outcome; the inquiry-driven dialectic; and questions of context, place and time as central considerations for public interest communication and inquiry. Our chapter examines why the public interest is so often understood as a paradox, drawing on the insightful works of John Dewey and Walter Lippmann; public sphere and communication intersections introduced by Habermas and critical theory; Castells's networked society and the public interest; and the work of public interest scholars from across a range of disciplines. The chapter is intended as a stand-alone public interest communication foundation which also sets up a framework that guides the rest of the book.

In Chapter 2 Robert Heath and Damion Waymer advance the theme that public interest is a contextualised and situated view of the benefits of collective choice and action. The chapter draws on Burke's sociological theory of language including his notion of terministic screens to explain how humans interpret their physical and social realms through terminological filters. The authors consider how discourse processes and outcomes lead to dominant (ultimate) terminologies that blend individual interests into shared (public) interests. Heath and Waymer examine discourse arenas – described as layered networks of interlocking relationships, interests and dialectically voiced viewpoints – which shape public understanding of the public interest. Focusing on the climate change debate, they examine how discourse is developed by corporate interests, for example by ExxonMobil, and how this affects the discourse arena in shaping corporate interests as public interests.

In Chapter 3 Mohan Dutta critically examines the ways in which strategic tools of engagement and participation are co-opted into the agendas of dominant structures. He examines how the language of public interest is deployed by public relations in serving the status quo, consolidating power in the hands of elite actors in global networks. He argues how, for instance, narratives of development and public good are used within efforts of community relations and corporate social responsibility to strategically achieve goals of organisational effectiveness. The chapter examines key issues surrounding the role of the private sector in redefining public interest through the framework of public-private partnerships and other strategies where voices of subaltern communities and their public interests are erased from the discursive space. Drawing upon a culture-centred approach to communication, he proposes the role of listening as an entry point for creating infrastructures of communication serving public interest.

In Chapter 4 Mhairi Aitken examines the public interest in the context of climate change communication, exploring the potential for deontic or dialogical approaches to the public interest and their implications for climate change-related planning and policy development. This chapter considers how invoking the public interest can conceal the range of interests and particular socio-political imaginaries, shaping and restricting how climate change is framed, focusing in particular on renewable energy. Aitken examines how communication problems are not about discovering 'scientific facts' or universal truths but rather of understanding and managing complex realities. She draws on Habermas's ideas of communicative action, proposing that dialogical approaches to the public interest, by focusing on processes rather than outcomes, emphasise the need for meaningful and open public engagement in decision-making processes, ensuring procedural and recognitional justice.

In Chapter 5 Nicholas Carah examines global media companies and their role in the public culture of capitalist liberal democratic societies. This chapter explores how media and communication platforms, notably Facebook and Google, represent engineering networks of production that illustrate an epochal shift in commercial media. Carah draws on a growing body of critical media theory (e.g. Andrejevic, Dahlberg, Smythe & Dinh, van Dijck) in challenging what it means for the public interest when media institutions do not produce content, but instead engineer data-processing infrastructures that draw from the continuous flow of public media activity to monitor and shape public life. He provides deep insights into how this ongoing interplay between human communicative capacities and the technical design and decision making of media platforms challenge many assumptions of the role of dominant media platforms in public interest communication.

In Chapter 6 T. Kenn Gaither and Patricia Curtin use critical/cultural and postcolonial theories to explicate the relationship between the public interest and communication practices by the state in emerging democracies, specifically in Ghana and Mozambique. They challenge notions of 'one-ness' or 'common Africanism', instead proposing the idea of *publics* over a more static notion of *a public*, and view of colonialism as a constitutive force that elevates some publics and abrogates others. The chapter draws on articulation theory as described by Barker, Hall and Laclau, which sees imagined communities connecting through the process of creating meaning around an identity, whether national, tribal or continental. Central to articulation theory are these relationships and the processes in which relationships form and are contextually articulated or broken apart through disarticulation. Gaither and Curtin argue that the public interest in these developing countries (and others) must be carefully scrutinised to examine how it is articulated and by whom.

In Chapter 7 Jane Johnston, Susan Forde and Boni Robertson examine public interest communication in Australia as it relates to government and media discourse, First Nations Australians and institutionalised understandings of what is in the public interest. The authors challenge how the public interest of Australia's Indigenous peoples is determined by and serves the expectations of decision makers – often white Australians – and the political interests of politicians, rather than those who are most affected. They argue that scant attention has been paid to the public interest as it relates to specific socio-political issues such as Australian Indigenous issues, especially from the voice of First Nations peoples. This chapter draws on two streams of theory – critical whiteness theory and mediatisation – to illustrate how white social constructs within settler societies such as Australia become the dominant discourse and how these feed into the political and media logics of news production.

In Chapter 8 Jenny Hou examines public interest communication in China, drawing on the Confucian concept of Great Harmony. Hou argues that China is distinguished from the West mainly in its authoritarianism, underpinned by Great Harmony thinking (*datong sixiang*), and the idea of obeying the hierarchy and authority to maintain political stability and social cohesion. The chapter reports the findings of Hou's empirical study of China's public relations industry in which she asks: *How does China's public relations as an industry interpret, articulate, or contest the public interest in practice as it interplays with the overarching Great Harmony context?* Hou's interviews with 46 practitioners provide deep insights and rich illustrations of harmony as a means of balance, counterbalance, and what is described as dynamic equilibrium. The chapter compares the Western focus on the tension between public and private interests, and the dominance of the Party-state as the major rival to, judge of and influencer of the public interest substance and process in China.

In Chapter 9 Ian Somerville and Scott Davidson examine how public interest communication is conceptualised and contested in divided communities. Two case studies are used to investigate and analyse the role of police public relations: the ethno-religious divisions in Northern Ireland; and the racially divided context of Ferguson, Missouri, United States. Their chapter interrogates the meta-discursive framing that surrounds the idea of human problems being caused by poor communication, with models for democratic peace building and conflict resolution (deliberative democracy and agonistic pluralism) explored in relation to how the public interest may be understood in divided societies. Somerville and Davidson point to the need to recognise that it is often lack of trust, disappointment or dissensus that prompts participation and engagement within divided communities. The chapter suggests that communication in these contexts cannot rely on consensus or top-down approaches, urging neighbourhood-level communication and a willingness by institutional communicators to cede control of the dialogue and not fear the enactment of passionate disagreement.

In Chapter 10 Julieta Brambila and Jairo Lugo-Ocando investigate the relationship between civic networking coalitions and public interest communication by examining lobbying and campaigning in Mexico. The chapter explores two civic networking coalitions which were established in order to resist and denounce anti-press violence in two time frames: 2006 and 2010. The authors examine the idea of public interest-forming practices, as outlined in Chapter 1, to see how these civic coalitions could positively impact on journalistic safety. They draw on Castells's ideas of the power within networked societies, and the social and media movements that can emerge, and raise awareness, bringing public support and influencing policy making. While they argue that these civic networking coalitions can have success, they also note how, against a background of corruption, violence and collusion, these public interest-forming practices alone are insufficient for effecting meaningful change.

In conclusion

These ten chapters, individually and collectively, make a highly original contribution to the growing critical scholarship in public relations and communication. Importantly, they also provide the *first collection of critiques of public interest communication* within the one volume, interrogating some of the biggest issues of contemporary society, providing insights across cultures, politics and continents.

We believe the book is inherently about dialectic, where thesis is met by antithesis, and continues to move forward. In this dynamic state, *public interest communication* is not a static concept, but rather is organic and contingent on factors such as process, context, social and cultural norms, and agency. This is a central theme throughout the book expressed both explicitly and implicitly along with other themes such as minority and subaltern communication, and bottom-up, localised communicative practice.

We hope you find the following chapters challenge you to rethink the connections between communication and private, corporate, national and public interests. If we accomplish this, the book has achieved its aim.

References

Bozeman, B 2007, *Public Values and Public Interest: Counterbalancing Economic Individualism*, Georgetown University Press, Washington, DC.

Douglass, B 1980, 'The common good and the public interest', *Political Theory*, vol. 8, no. 1, pp. 103–117.

Dryzek, J 2002, *Deliberative Theory and Beyond: Liberals, Critics and Contestations*, Oxford University Press, Oxford.

Flathman, R 1966, *The Public Interest*, John Wiley & Sons, New York.

Goodin, R & Dryzek, J 2008, 'Making use of mini-publics', in R Goodin, *Innovating Democracy: Democratic Theory and Practice after the Deliberative Turn*, Oxford University Press, Oxford.

Goodin, RE 2008, *Innovating Democracy: Democratic Theory and Practice after the Deliberative Turn*, Oxford University Press, Oxford.

Johnston, J 2016, *Public Relations and the Public Interest*, Routledge, New York.

Part I
Critical debates

1 Public interest communication
A framework for systemic inquiry

Jane Johnston and Magda Pieczka

Introduction

Public interest as a concept is a cornerstone of democratic governance, a touchstone for public policy and a matter of practical consequence and activity. *Public interest* belongs to the field of political reflection on how the relationship between the individual and the state should be managed in order to produce a fair, lasting democratic system of governance. Thus, it shares some territory with *the public, public sphere, common good, public opinion* and the debates about how these concepts can be defined, and how they can be pursued in practice. Public interest is a powerful political idea. Its sovereignty is demonstrated by a commonly used English phrase 'to *serve* the public interest' and its importance demands that it be protected. We are thus accustomed to think of public interest as real and about our activities in relation to it as comparable to the function of a light dimmer, lowering or enhancing the brightness with which the public interest light shines on our lives.

This book, *Public Interest Communication: Critical Debates and Global Contexts* enters this vast political field with an assumption that communication does not only serve the public interest, but that it is also in a dialectical relationship with all public interest-forming practices, whether enacted through the institutions of the state, such as the legislature or the judiciary, or through civil society. This leads us to ask about the ways in which communication and the public interest intersect and interact. We do so with the aim of articulating a framework for understanding the phenomenon of public interest communication as distinct from communication *in* the public interest. Thus we shift the focus away from communication as a function of the public interest, whose definition could be seen as extraneous to communication, to communication as constructive of the public interest. In other words, we ask if it is possible to look beyond *instances* of applied communication that in some way address or invoke the public interest in order to find a *pattern* of greater coherence across both the different approaches to communication, i.e. deliberation and advocacy, and the different field-specific articulations of the public interest – for example, sustainability in the field of the environment, or harmony, in Chinese politics. In this sense, public interest communication contributes to research that has engaged with the idea of *the public* (Dewey 1927; Habermas 1989, 1984, 1987; Lee 2015; Lippmann 1927) and, through it, is embedded in the nature of social change that has enfolded in and out of the first world countries for over a century.

This chapter confronts the public interest (following Lippmann 1955, p. 42) showing it to be challenging both conceptually and practically. The discussion starts with an overview of political theories of public interest and approaches which have emerged since the 1920s, bringing the public interest literature into dialogue with research in communication and public relations (PR). We pursue the idea of the public interest by discussing the key themes and arguments in the debate between Walter Lippmann and John Dewey, described as 'a staple of American political thought' (Rogers 2012, p. 5) and, given its specific historical and political place, also a staple of modern democratic thought. The chapter then turns to communication theory, drawing on the work of Habermas, on some of the critiques of the public sphere, on the deliberative democracy literature (Dryzek 2002; Gastil 2007; Fischer 2009), and on the work of Castells (2009), thus placing the public interest in the context of communication networks and the network society. Out of this discussion, the chapter articulates *public interest communication* offered as an analytical framework intended to support a comparative approach that goes beyond normative commitments to consensus or dissensus, and instead takes a pragmatic approach to communication as 'coordination of practical activities through discourse and reflexive inquiry' focusing on key problems for communication defined as 'incommensurability, nonparticipation, nonreflexivity or dogmatism, [and] defective discourse practices' (Craig 2007, p. 136).

Public interest – a political idea

The public interest is understood both as a simple and a complex concept. On the one hand, it is often aligned with utilitarian thinking, frequently invoked and understood as representing a benchmark for effective governance, providing an 'antidote to fractional and divisive politics of interest' (Cochran 1973, in Bozeman 2007, p. 87; Goodin 1996). Historically, this tendency prevailed in the development of policy and legislative frameworks where new democracies were being created and developed. Goodin (1996, p. 332) explains how the founders of the American Constitution:

> tended to employ the phrase 'public interest' with relatively little reflection. Assuming as they did that the term's meaning was relatively transparent, writers of this period tended to devote little care or attention to its precise elaboration.

The dominance of the concept expressed in the American government's framing documents was seen to be 'unrivalled' by any other period (Sandel 1996, p. 86). Downs argued that early use of the expression assumed certain knowledge: 'everyone who uses such a concept has a notion of what is means, and employs that notion to order the events he encounters and to communicate his thoughts to others' (Downs 1962, p. 2). As such, the public interest was a taken-for-granted concept, employed without definition. Johnston (2016) notes that the term continues to be so used today in law, public policy and public administration, typically invoked without definition or terms of reference, but often with examples; cited as a process or outcome where interests compete. It is described as one of the most used, least defined and least understood terms in the lexicon of public administration (Wheeler 2013).

Paradoxically, however, the public interest is also much interrogated and described as complex, mutable, context-bound and ambiguous (Johnston 2016). For example, Mansbridge (1998) argues that the public interest can have differing relationships with private or sectional interests: relations of congruity, contrast or compatibility. Consequently, the public interest does not necessarily present as a binary of public vs. private interests – indeed, where they are compatible, 'one nests inside the other' (Mansbridge 1998, p. 17). Public interest scholars Campbell and Marshall (2002) speak to the postmodern turn which sees a plurality of thinking about the public interest, and they reflect on how this broader view has liberated theorising from 'the straitjacket of neutrality and impartiality' previously considered the norm (Campbell & Marshall 2002, p. 173). They argue against the universalising term of *the* public interest, for two reasons: firstly, the shift to a greater plurality and heterogeneity that lies at the heart of postmodern and other contemporary critiques; secondly, the acceptance that agents in all fields bring with them their own ethical judgements, which renders universalised answers problematic (Johnston 2016).

As the possibility of a single definition recedes, scholars point out that governments nevertheless provide mechanisms to serve *the* public interest practically:

> the real service that each of the mechanisms … performs is … not so much to *make* politicians and the voters they represent respect the public interest as it is to *remind* them to do so.
>
> (Goodin 1996, p. 340, emphasis in original)

Indeed, Goodin continues: 'Anyone determined to flout such duties can always work around such mechanisms. Still, having to do so will discomfort any who harbor even minimal respect for their public responsibilities' (Goodin 1996, p. 340). In much the same way, the public interest is described as having a 'hair shirt' quality – intended to remind decision makers about interests other than their own (Sorauf 1957, p. 639). Sorauf argues how those tasked with major decision-making roles should identify and consult the interests of the 'unorganized, unrepresented or underrepresented' (Sorauf 1957, p. 639) in order to locate the public interest.

The lack of a consistent, clear definition of the public interest has led to the development of discipline-specific discourses – including law, regulation, planning, media, accounting, economics, and psychology – that have critiqued the public interest as it applies to their particular field (Johnston 2017). Within its political origins, the concept has evolved around a range of theoretical categories and approaches: the abolitionist, normative, communitarian/consensualist, and process theories, inclusive of aggregative, procedural and pluralist (see Flathman 1966; Cochran 1974; Bozeman 2007; Johnston 2016). Mansbridge also identified the category of 'functional' (Mansbridge 1998, p. 17), which we absorb into Bozeman's pragmatic approach (2007), in which he draws on Dewey. Based on Johnston's 2016 study of the public interest, we also include a critical approach to provide 'an alternate dimension for viewing the public interest, especially when considering resource and access inequalities and the dialectic that is so often inherent in interest conflicts' (Johnston 2016, p. 204). Briefly, the *abolitionist* approach proposes ignoring or removing the public interest due to its vague nature and non-scientific thinking. The *normative* approach sees the public interest as synonymous with the common good or pursuit of a substantive value. The *communitarian/consensualist* approach highlights consensus found in certain types of societies which are more community oriented and less individualist. The *process* approach sees the public interest derived through procedural paths or as more accommodating of pluralism, or as an aggregate of many individual interests. The *pragmatic* approach accentuates the role of judgement and discretion required by decision makers in determining concrete decisions and outcomes. The *critical* approach argues for the need to pay fuller attention to power, access, equality and agency. We see examples of many of these approaches within this book (sometimes two or more combined), as authors examine the public interest as a territory of conflict and cooperation between various interests.

At the root of some of these typologies lie the liberal and utilitarian conceptions of the public interest, derived from Rousseau: something is in the public interest 'if the general will wills it' (Rousseau, in Benditt 1973, p. 293); and from Bentham: the public interest is served 'when the tendency it has to augment the happiness of the community is greater than any it has to diminish it' (Bentham, in Benditt 1973, p. 292). Campbell and Marshall make sense of the differences between the various categories identified in the literature with reference to the dimensions of the interest base: *collective* or *individual; subjective* or *objective.* They note:

> In general, the subjective categorizations involve variants of utilitarianism and are individualistic in the sense that they assume that judgments in the end are dependent on individual evaluations of good or bad, better or worse. In contrast, objective categories emphasize collective values either in the sense of interests generally shared by everyone or in terms of a normative standard against which judgments are made concerning collective interests or the common good.
>
> (Campbell & Marshall 2002, pp. 173–174)

Importantly for our discussion, a preponderance of literature has also given rise to the widely held view that public interest is given shape *contextually*, on a *case-by-case* basis (see, for example, Flathman 1966; Ho 2011; Leveson 2012; Bozeman 2007; Johnston 2016).

Though the public interest, thus comprising many theories, has ebbed and flowed in both popularity and acceptability for many decades, it has nevertheless grown in theoretical understanding and scope. Sorauf's (1957, p. 639) advice from the 1950s has been well heeded: 'the very lack of consensus on a theory of the public interest emphasizes the need for expanding the debate on a concept so crucial and central to political science'. Following Johnston (2016, 2017), we argue for communication and public relations to make a contribution to this discussion.

Public interest and communication: foundations

In approaching the public interest from the disciplinary perspective of communication, we choose as the starting point the well-known debate between two thinkers passionate about the state of democracy in the early 20th century who each engaged in public interest thinking, oftentimes in very different ways. This allows us to identify a number of dilemmas and practical difficulties – notably, the existence and nature of the public and its relationship with the state. Walter Lippmann and his contemporary John Dewey are among those best known to have interrogated the public interest at greatest length and advanced the general understanding of how it has applied within evolving democracies. Their work is richly contrasting as it relates to the adequacies and inadequacies of democratic society, the public, and interest politics, in a sense presenting a dialogue about the public interest and its constituent parts, focusing in particular on the American public. In questioning the public interest, Lippmann posited that if it *did* exist it would be 'what men would choose if they saw clearly, thought rationally, [and] acted disinterestedly and benevolently' (Lippmann 1955, p. 42). Over time, in the absence of other definitions, Lippmann's has become arguably the most popular of all scholarly definitions of the public interest. Lippmann doubted individuals' capacity for determining the pressing issues of the time, questioning the existence of any single public, arguing that because people hold situational, operational and *ad hoc* connections to an interest, 'the public' at large was 'a phantom' to the extent that there was such a thing as 'a genuine and effective public' (McClay 1993, p. xxvi).

In contrast, Dewey argued for the existence of the public and government responsiveness to its citizens. Unlike Lippmann, he proposed that publicly accessible information could have a regulative effect within a democracy, first because of its availability to the public and, also, because individuals would be predisposed to locate it. Dewey argued that the 'collective intelligence' of democracy can bring issues into the open where special claims to interest can then be examined and appraised: 'where they can be discussed and judged in the light of more inclusive interests than represented by either of them separately' (Dewey 1991, p. 81). This provided a means for working through interest conflicts, as he outlines in the following example:

> There is, for example, a clash of interests between munition manufacturers and most of the rest of the population. The more the respective claims of the two are publicly and scientifically weighed the more likely it is that the public interest will be weighed and will be made effective.
>
> (Dewey 1991, p. 81)

Thus while both Lippmann and Dewey acknowledge the fundamental presence of the public interest in society, they offer different routes to ensuring its articulation. For Lippmann the public interest exists as an ideal accessible to experts. While in principle all human beings possess the rational capacity to grapple with the question of the public interest, in modern societies the complexity and speed of life and the institutionalised mediation of knowledge (through mass media) together have changed the political application of reason into expert preoccupation. Consequently, this position delimits the scope of action that the public and the experts are granted in relation to public interest: the public is limited, even in its agreement on procedural matters, while the experts make substantive decisions. Dewey, in his careful inquiry into the relationships between the state, the individual and community, suggested that public interest is an outcome of a community's self-reflection on the nature, including moral nature, of its shared life (Dewey 1927). The self-reflection is enacted sporadically through public deliberation conducted by a public and managed on a daily basis by public officials, who act as agents of the public interest. The public interest is, therefore, premised on the existence of a reflexive public and is a process as much as it is its product. In the end, the difference between the two authors in their treatment of the public interest arguably comes down to the question of reason. For Lippmann, reason is primarily an individual capacity to inquire and form judgements influenced by a set of circumstances, such as individuals' interest and engagement in public affairs, education, access to information, media systems, or more broadly public communication systems, together with the content they produce and circulate. For Dewey, reason is fundamentally social in nature; judgements about the public interest integrate an assessment of the soundness of scientific knowledge with the knowledge built on personal ties, out of direct association, communication and commitment to others.

'The phantom public', 'The Public' and 'many publics'

Lippmann's scepticism about the practical possibility of the existence of the public – characterised as informed, attentive and reasoning about public issues – is aptly summarised by the term 'phantom public'. The consequence of this view is, as we have seen, technocratically defined public interest. For

Dewey, the public is real as a collaboration between private persons who come together through a common need or interest. Shared interests derive from the bringing together of consequences that apply beyond the individual, whereby the 'nature of the interconnected behaviour is ... transformed' (Dewey 1927, p. 27). It is through the shared conditions and interests that Dewey argues: 'Those ... affected for good or for evil form a group distinctive enough to require recognition and a name. The name selected is The Public' (Dewey 1927, p. 35). In turn, the public is made effective by legislators, executives, judges and other agents. Importantly, Dewey also raises crucial conditions for determining the public interest as it applies within the state-public nexus:

> there is no *a priori* rule which can be laid down by which when it is followed a good state will be brought into existence. In no two ages or places is there the same public. Conditions make the consequences of associated action and the knowledge of them different.
>
> (Dewey 1927, p. 33, original emphasis)

What is essential is that experimentation and experience should provide the opportunity to move forward in decision making so that 'men may learn from their errors and profit by their successes' (Dewey 1927, p. 34). Thus what is key to Dewey's conceptualisation of the public is that it is based on the shared orientation to 'consequences' that apply to all members of the public, that it is a collaborative effort of inquiry and decision making dependent on communication, and that the public thus formed supplies the logic that powers the state and its institutions.

Both the idea of the public, and later Habermas's *public sphere* are offered explicitly to search for the post-Enlightenment solution to legitimate, democratic government in large-scale industrial societies. The account they offer centres on 'the interest of all' (Habermas 1989, p. 83), arguably, the public interest. Habermas like Dewey reflects on how in pluralist societies politics can 'remain sensitive to a broad spectrum of values and interests' (Habermas 1996, cited in Johnston 2016, p. 35). To this end,

> [p]ublic debate was supposed to transform *voluntas* [will] into a *ratio* [reason] that in the public competition of private arguments came into being as the consensus about what was practically necessary *in the interest of all*.
>
> (Habermas 1989, p. 83, emphasis added)

To create political legitimacy, the many spaces of free discussion within civil society are seen to be in a collaborative relationship with the institutions of the state, the *lifeworld* can be meaningfully, substantively and practically connected to the *system*. In this we find support for Dewey's insistence on the intelligence of the citizens, their ability to transcend individual interests, and the need to find a way of curating the public interest in the formal spaces of the state administration. The more recent elaboration of the idea of *the public* that has come about notably as a feminist critique of the exclusionary nature of the bourgeois public sphere (Fraser 1992, 2002) points to the existence of many publics, including subaltern counter-publics and, consequently, draws attention to the difficulty of conceptualising the public interest in the absence of the public understood with an unproblematic 'sense of totality' (Warner 2002, p. 65).

Deliberative praxis and the public interest

Habermas's work on the public sphere and discursive rationality has been continued by the deliberative theory of democracy starting in the late 1980s (Talisse 2012; Dryzek 2002; Goodin 2008). Political scientists were drawn to the idea of deliberation as a way of reinvigorating democracy (Della Porta 2013; Fischer 2009), and produced both theoretical analysis and empirical experimentation with deliberative practices.[1] This body of work is of relevance here for four reasons: first, it shows that the recognition of *interest* is both explicit in and fundamental to deliberative democracy; secondly, it develops a practical acknowledgment of the social architecture of spaces for deliberative practice crucial to contemporary public interest praxis; thirdly, it deals with the role of experts; and finally, it provides empirical evidence for further theoretical thinking.

Our starting point here is well summarised by the two quotations used in Steiner's *The Foundations of Deliberative Democracy* at the beginning of the chapter devoted to the role of self-interest in democratic deliberation:

> Deliberative democracy is well placed to deliver the public interest ...
> (O'Flynn 2010, p. 301, cited in Steiner 2012, p. 88)

> Deliberative democracy has traditionally been defined in opposition to self-interest.
> (Mansbridge et al. 2010, p. 64, cited in Steiner 2012, p. 89)

Habermas, and Dewey before him, excluded self-interest from the public domain, yet now Mansbridge et al. (2010) argue for its inclusion on two counts: it offers a direct connection to citizens' experiences, and it acts as a safeguard against the domination of the public interest by the powerful. Steiner draws further on O'Flynn's work in warning that 'although deliberation is helpful to find the public interest, it would be too easy to say that the public interest is whatever results from deliberation' (Steiner 2012, p. 89). Despite this doubt, deliberative democracy works most clearly as the process approach to the public interest. More recently, deliberative scholarship has taken its own 'systemic turn' (Hendriks 2016, p. 47) in moving away from a fascination with the multiplicity of formats for citizen deliberation, referred to as mini-publics – such as deliberative polls, consensus conferences, citizens' juries, planning cells (Gastil & Levine 2005; Goodin & Dryzek 2008) – to a more focused exploration of the design of deliberative systems. Hendriks talks about a shift in conceptualisation from *transmission* between different parts of deliberative systems, to the preoccupation with *coupling* of its different parts, thus suggesting what might be termed 'system design approach' to public interest.

> In Habermas' (1996) two-track model ... public opinion is formed in the public sphere (first track) which is then transmitted through the media, elections and social movements to empowered sites, such as parliament (second track) ... Mansbridge et al. (2012, p. 22) define a deliberative system as 'a loosely coupled group of institutions and practices that together perform three functions ... seeking truth, establishing mutual respect and generating inclusive, egalitarian decision making'.
>
> (Hendriks 2016, p. 45)

Thus what we see is, firstly, an expression of caution about the extent to which deliberation works unfailingly as a mechanism for the public to exist and for the public interest to emerge. This boils down to the question about the extent to which power seeps into deliberation. Secondly, at the large-scale institutional level of discussion, we see some loosening of the formal demands (such as apply to the design of deliberative mini-publics) as the emphasis appears to be shifting from deliberative events to deliberative values – of truth, respect and inclusivity. However, as these can, at least partly, be achieved through advocacy or a trade-based technique of negotiation, it is reasonable to propose that deliberative systems may be open to non-deliberative forms of communication (Edwards 2016), thus further complicating the relationship between deliberation and the public interest.

Deliberative democracy elaborates also the role of experts and technical expertise in governance, highlighted earlier as an important theme in the Lippmann-Dewey debate. Fischer (2009, p. 28) starts by reprising Dewey's view of experts contributing to public deliberation 'as teachers and interpreters, [who] could decipher the technological world for citizens in ways that enabled them to make intelligent political judgments', and then conceptualises the role of the expert from the constructivist position as argument based. He turns to the Aristotelian conception of practical reason, *phronesis* and concludes:

> From this perspective, the role of the postempiricist expert is that of an interpretive mediator operating between the available analytical frameworks of social science and competing *local perspectives*. In the process, a set of criteria is consensually derived from the confrontation of views (Innes 1990). Such criteria are used to organize a dialectical exchange

that can be likened to a conversation in which the understandings of both the policy analyst [i.e. the expert] and the citizens are extended through discursive interactions.

(Fischer 2009, p. 125, emphasis added)

We can interpret this position as the move away from the transmission model of the expert role – defined as transferring scientifically created knowledge and facts into the public discussion – to a dialogic model of the interaction between scientific and lay epistemologies through which both may be changed. Extending this thinking to the public interest reframes it as *articulation*, an idea used in cultural studies (see Gaither and Curtin's Chapter 6 in this book): the public interest thus can be understood as a meaning that emerges out of a pattern of possibilities, involving local dynamics of power and agency in the process.

As we have shown, deliberation is viewed first and foremost as the practice of 'dialogic rationalism' (Myerson 1994), where reason is understood as intersubjective and can be treated analytically as justification, or reason giving in communication. Let us start with an observation that the public interest in deliberative practice is often folded into substantive details of subject-specific and often place-specific issues (environmental communication and planning offer plentiful evidence). Thus while the public interest serves as justification for a specific course of action, the way in which it is invoked deserves some further consideration.

A rich account of deliberative praxis, offered in a report on citizen juries deliberating about onshore windfarm development in Scotland (Roberts & Escobar 2015), contains a good illustration of the embeddedness of the public interest in specific policy recommendations. Reporting on deliberative outcomes from the three juries (pp. 128–145), the authors display the actual formulations produced by the jurors, such as:

> Local community should be surveyed, listened to and involved in the decision-making.
>
> (Roberts & Escobar 2015, p. 124)

> Windfarm development should be funded from private investment only, with all future 'restoration' costs fully funded by developers up front.
>
> (Roberts & Escobar 2015, p. 127)

These statements of agreed views on how policy and planning decisions should be made do not include their justification, i.e. they do not articulate the public interest in each case. In these two examples, however, it is not difficult to reconstruct their justifications. The first statement is premised on the recognition of the principle of subsidiarity and its complexity in this case: decisions should be made closest to where their effects will be felt, but energy generation always combines different levels of subsidiary, for example local and national. It is in the public interest to recognise the complexity of subsidiarity involved. The second statement is offered in the context of the privatised energy generation sector in the UK and it reduces the public interest to the consideration of the economic benefits and costs. It is in the public interest that developers who benefit economically from windfarms are obliged to cover the costs associated with the operation, including decommissioning.

Steiner's (2012) work sheds more light on some of the dynamics of justification, or reason giving, in his research on deliberation conducted in a number of European parliaments as well as citizen fora not constrained by such institutional settings. The analysis shows (pp. 94–103) that the way in which the public interest features at the discursive level appears to be linked to social norms of public life, specific institutional norms, or deliberative pragmatics. For example, expressions of self-interest were relatively rare in public deliberation; appeals to common interest were found more often in the European rather than national parliaments; the balance of appeals to common or group interest may be connected to the public openness of the deliberative forum (roughly, the wider the forum, the wider the justification used). Practical considerations are also found to be a factor: balancing scrupulous repetitions of the interest at play with the liveliness of the discussion may lead to deliberative shortcuts or omissions. While acknowledging these practical factors, Steiner also argues that 'to be useful in a deliberative discourse, common-good arguments must be expressed in very specific ways. It is only under this condition that other discussants can react to such arguments' (Steiner 2012, p. 103). There are two implications for research and analysis that suggest themselves here: firstly, the need to distinguish between a practical solution/decision taken in the public interest and its ultimate articulation and orientation to the specific principle and value; and secondly, the need to develop a more systematic understanding of public interest pragmatics, that is the way in which communication contexts produce the meanings of the public interest.

Public interest and public relations

The treatment of public interest in the academic field of public relations reflects the development of the public relations professional project, including its claim to legitimacy made on the basis of serving the public interest, and the way in which it may be connected to and interrogated from positions articulated by communication theory. Public relations and professionalised communication have dealt with the notion of the public interest in both explicit and implicit ways. Firstly, strong statements have been made about the ultimate orientation of public relations towards the public interest and they have been questioned in critical scholarship (Bivins 1993; Edwards 2011; Johnston 2016; McKie & Munshi 2007; Messina 2007; Moloney 2006; Stoker & Stoker 2012). Secondly, there is a body of scholarship that orients itself to notions of common good, social justice and democracy, and follows either a liberal pluralist conception of society (JE Grunig 2001; LA Grunig 1992; Heath 1992, 2001), communitarian approach (Kruckeberg & Stark 1988), or speaks from specific critical positions such as diversity (Munshi & Edwards 2011), gender (Aldoory 2005; Daymon & Demetrious 2014), subaltern perspectives (Dutta 2011), or activism (Demetrious 2013; Holtzhausen 2012). It is important to identify here also a line of thinking that continues the Habermasian tradition either directly (Burkart 2004, 2009), or by framing the role of public relations explicitly with reference to deliberative systems (Edwards 2016), public communication (Demetrious 2013) or civil society (Sommerfeldt 2013; Taylor 2010). The link between public relations and the public interest is thus constituted through critical publicity, plurality and inclusiveness, and their contribution to the strengthening of social bonds and trust. In critical terms, it responds to the concerns raised by Habermas's view of public relations as self-interested opinion management (Cronin 2018; Ramsey 2016).

As we have shown, a discussion about the public interest inevitably involves a discussion about what is to be understood as the public. Public relations scholarship has engaged with the concept of the public in a number of ways. Similarly to the discussion about the public interest in political theory, public relations also arrived at something of an impasse and acknowledged inadequacy of its own understanding of the public and the ambiguity of the concept (Leitch & Neilson 2001; Vasquez & Taylor 2001). As a social-psychological concept, *the* public is a generalisation of *a* public, and it offers a way to understand the behaviour and formation of such groups (publics) in relation to organisational activity (e.g. situational theory of publics). This approach is extended to the political field, where publics become political actors involved in agenda building. While Vasquez and Taylor (2001) highlight the link between agenda building as part of mass communication and democratic governance, Leitch and Neilson (2001) largely focus on the issue of 'multiplicity' of publics (see also Jahansoozie 2006; Springston & Keyton 2001) as standard in organisational practice and as a deficiency in public relations theory showing its poor understanding of the plurality of positions and ways of acting available to individuals who form publics. Both discussions compared here acknowledge also the cultural, language-based approach to the phenomenon of the public: Vasquez and Taylor do so from the rhetorical point of view, Leitch and Neilson reach to the concept of discourse.

Public relations, thus, shares its approaches to the idea of the public with the wider field of communication theory where the focus can be on group dynamics and interactions at the organisational/institutional level, or on the public as a political imaginary. Warner (2002) argues for a public as a social imaginary, a kind of discourse public, which is self-organised and defined by its shared attention to a specific text (i.e. communication content or event), rather than by interaction. A public in this sense is constructed subjectively, rather than inter-subjectively: it is the recognition of the public self that we as individuals adopt in response to public discourse, rather than a dialogic recognition of the self in the other. The discourse perspective thus resonates with the emerging line of reflection on the role of public relations not only in democracy but also at a deeper level of the social change taking shape in late modernity. In this context, Cronin argues that the discursive basis of democratic value is being altered through communication. She uses the term of 'commercial democracy' to signal this change and states that public relations

> appears to mirror the contract or bond of representative democracy by offering multiple promises to the public: in mediating between a corporation or institution and the public PR promises representation; it promises public 'voice' through their engagement as consumers or stakeholders; it provides a media forum and stages debate. It is part of, and attempts to shape, the realm in which the public witnesses itself as a collective entity. This collective witnessing is a form of 'publicity' as described by Michael Warner ...
>
> (Cronin 2018, p. 4)

To conclude, in terms of communication, the public interest is understood mostly as a form of public argument. It can take the persuasive form offered by Lippmann, where experts are expected to carry the public opinion with them, but more importantly, it has come to be defined as deliberative reasoning (by Dewey and Habermas). On the other hand, the performative approach to the public, and by extension to the public interest, underscores the importance of public discourses, and thus goes beyond the normative boundaries of deliberation towards the pragmatic engagement with the content of what comes into the public view through publicity.

Power, communication and the public interest

Although public interest is largely implicit in Castells's *Communication Power* (2009), we turn to his theoretical approach because it focuses on power as integral to interests. Castells investigates power and domination to propose how a society, where the individual's freedom is the real basis of the political structure, can be achieved. Castells's starting point is that power cannot be peeled off any aspect of social and political life because it is in the fabric of its institutions and in the language people use: 'Power is the most fundamental process in society, ... since society is defined around values and institutions, and what is valued and institutionalized is defined by power relationships' (Castells 2009, pp. 10, 14). Power, and domination, thus can be seen as an inherent element of the social world. In working towards his model of the network society, Castells builds on Mulgan's reflection on the sources of power:

> Of the three sources of power the most important for sovereignty is the power over the thoughts that give rise to trust. Violence can only be used

negatively; money can only be used in two dimensions, giving and taking away. But knowledge and thoughts can transform things, move mountains and make ephemeral power appear permanent.

(Mulgan 2007, p. 27, cited in Castells 2009, p. 16)

While the symbiosis of 'violence and discourse, coercion and persuasion, political domination and cultural framing' (Castells 2009, p. 50) is not new, the way in which it plays out in the network society is different. The essence of Castells's work is to identify and reflect on communication networks, which he sees as dominating the 'programming' of the human mind, i.e. creating meaning and value.

The second point on which we follow Castells's work concerns his thinking about the structural organisation of contemporary societies, and consequently about the political structures within which the public interest might be considered. We have given primacy in our discussion until now to the conception of the public interest built within Habermas's 'state-centric conception of democracy', which Bohman critiqued in relation to global governance (Brassett & Smith 2010, p. 415). Castells offers a more complex account of contemporary society and argues that it should be understood as a network society,

a society whose social structure is made around networks activated by microelectronics-based, digitally processed information and communication technologies. I understand social structures to be the organizational arrangements of humans in relationships of production, consumption, reproduction, experience, and power expressed in meaningful communication coded by culture.

(Castells 2009, p. 24)

Networks are constructed by flows of communication, held together by values, and operating across all 'core activities that shape and control human life in every corner of the planet' (Castells 2009, p. 25). Networks, moreover, operate on a global scale but at the same time they are fragmented, with simultaneous interactions taking place between 'national, supranational, international, co-national, regional, and local institutions, while also reaching out to the organizations of civil society' (p. 40). Different networks, for example global financial networks or global media networks, can and do interlink through sharing communication, values, and having points of connection. Against this backdrop, the nation-state, Castells argues, does not disappear, but 'the national boundaries of power relationships are just one of the dimensions in which power and counterpower operate' (p. 18). The new form of power, network power, can only be resisted in organised, counternetwork ways in order to challenge and change the values around which networks exist. By extension, thus, the public interest demands discursive vigilance and challenge in relation to the values of various networks as they become accessible through communication. On this logic, agonism (Davidson 2016; Mouffe 2000), not consensus, is the path towards the public interest. To this, we can add two more implications for the public interest. First, if, as Castells argues, networks exercise power through their binary logic of inclusion/exclusion, the presence or absence of a 'voice' has to be taken analytically into account. Secondly, there is also a need for the appreciation of the multidimensional nature of interests that enter into communication. For example, where a local decision needs to be made it is important to ask whether the interests (networks) present in the process extend beyond the declared participants and content of the public discourse. These elements are now further explored in our public interest communication framework which follows.

Defining and analysing public interest communication

John Durham Peters proposes that understanding communication allows us 'to understand much more' (Peters 1999, p. 2) – in our case, this means the public interest. Like Peters, we treat communication as an ongoing 'project of reconciling self and others' (p. 9), conducted in structured social spaces. We thus see public interest communication not as a single normatively defined phenomenon but as contextually shaped practices of public discursive actions aimed at regulating specific aspects of the social world. Public interest communication is understood here as an interplay between communication and other public-interest practices, such as regulation, decision making, circulation of knowledge, formation of opinions, attitudes and routines/scripts for performing the public interest in public.

Our contribution focuses on taking the question of the public interest as an explicit focus and aims to theorise public interest communication from a critical perspective, thus including greater attention to issues such as power, access, debate and agency. In order to do so, we have learned from a range of scholars who reflect on communication to reflect on society. The starting point for our framework is to claim that public interest is communicative, i.e. it comes into being through acts of communication that allow for the idea to circulate, to be used, to be argued and challenged, and incorporated into laws, regulation, policies and practices. Secondly, we propose that to understand, study and practise public interest communication it should be treated as a dialectic, as inquiry driven, i.e. its primary orientation is to ask questions, to reflect and respond. Based on the discussion so far, we propose public interest communication as an analytical framework based on six dimensions: publicness, accessibility, substantive anchoring, rationality, inter-subjectivity and connectedness, or links to other forms of action. Each of these will be now discussed briefly.

Our understanding of the *publicness* of public interest communication is inspired particularly by Habermas, Dewey and Castells as we have interpreted them in this discussion. We draw on the idea of the public sphere understood as a multiplicity of spaces open to participation of various actors, both individual and collective, in which direct interaction with others can occur or where consumption of publicly available communication content takes place involving a degree of critical reflection and response. In this way we acknowledge both the need for dialogue and reflexivity, and also the influence of the media and communication networks in the shaping of 'the public mind' (Castells 2009). As a consequence of the co-presence of different types of communication and actors, reflecting on the nature of the public space constituted in this way may be seen as the first analytical step, driven by questions such as: Whose interests are present? What values are present? How is power exercised? It is also helpful to inquire into the social/institutional norms of these public spaces: for example, a televised debate, a radio chat show, Twitter interaction, a town hall meeting, or a meeting of volunteers working on a neighbourhood project all have their own social and communication architectures. While conventions and norms can be challenged and changed, they also have to be acknowledged as the actual context in which public interest communication operates. Finally, the public character of public interest communication should be understood as multidimensional, i.e. with links going beyond the level of the actual spaces and participants.

Accessibility is linked to the dimension of publicness. Here we understand it as both physical and semiotic. If we approach public interest communication as a public dialectic, then the question of actors' ability to participate in such communication deserves systematic analytical attention. Physical accessibility refers to presence and participation in the public spaces. Semiotic accessibility is defined as the ability to engage in the meaning-making processes, as a minimum condition. This refers to the ability to understand the use of symbols of communication at a literal level (denotation) and extends to the mastery of non-literal levels of meaning (connotation and myth) related to practices of framing, discursive control and (communication) genres as way of acting (Fairclough 2003). Both kinds of accessibility, physical and semiotic, can be investigated in terms of inclusion or exclusion.

Substantive anchoring as a dimension focuses on field-specific characteristics of argumentation, such as economic, technological, environmental, cultural, political and military spheres of activity and impact (Castells 2009). Here we refer to the body of work in policy analysis that considers discourse as an ordering device, a way of understanding 'reality' (Hajer & Laws 2006, p. 252); as 'the third dimension of power' (Lukes 1974) exercised by shaping the individual consciousness (Carter 2007, pp. 184–185); and as a networking mechanism of 'discourse coalitions' based on the adherence to particular storylines, such as human rights or sustainability. In this sense, substantive anchoring in public interest communication deals with the question of knowledge, its production, circulation and distribution across the public space.

The rational character of public interest communication means that communication encompasses explicit reason giving: Why is this good or right for us to do? Theoretically, this dimension responds both to the classical liberal recognition of the role of reason as 'an instrument of political action' (Carey 1989, p. 35) and particularly to Habermas's elaboration of the inter-subjective rationality (Habermas 1984, 1987). However, we also acknowledge rationality as connected to other discursive dimensions, for example: to performance of a particular identity (being a member of the public); or to the recognition of the link between reason as justification and tradition, understood as an historical sense of society's moral narratives (cf MacIntyre 1981). The public interest communication framework pays particular attention to inter-subjectivity, a close partner dimension to rationality, as a way to investigate how 'the third perspective' (Russill 2004, p. 105), a standpoint that represents the shared rather than individual interests, emerges in the relevant public interest practices.

This leads us to the final element in the framework, namely the connection of public interest communication to other types of action. The whole point of eliciting a shared sense of where the public interest lies in any given case is to make it possible for practical action to follow legitimately, be it policy or specific practices. In this context, questions that can be asked here are: What actions are taken, or excluded, by those participating in public interest communication? What practical consequences follow, or can be expected to follow, from these actions?

Emerging themes

This final section of the chapter attempts to push beyond the public interest communication framework articulated as a way of sustaining systematic analysis and comparison, and identify some early themes emerging from the dialogue between these ideas and some of the case studies and reflections presented by the authors included in this book.

Let us begin with the idea of the public interest arena inspired by that of the 'discourse arena' brought into the discussion by Heath and Waymer's chapter on terministic dialectics, to draw attention to the way in which public discourse is filled with what Castells would refer to as networks' voices. Extending this analogy to the public interest has a number of implications. We argue that the public interest arena should be understood as synonymous with the public interest communication arena, demanding that all communication offered in this arena is analytically relevant. Treating the arena as a metaphor draws our attention further to the distinction between performers and the audience. While the deliberativist position is that only the performers can actively shape the public interest, audience theory (confirmed by anyone with an experience of performing in front of audiences) recognises that audiences have agency, even their absence is meaningful and leads to definite outcomes. As Peters points out, '[t]he other, not the self, should be the center of whatever "communication" might mean' (Peters 1999, p. 265). Following this logic, the need to understand the relationship between the actors and their audience in the public interest communication arena emerges as a new, useful line of inquiry.

Finally, turning to the arena inspires other questions – about staging and production. While in deliberative praxis, what is expected is a kind of improvisation within predetermined boundaries for the benefit of the other performers, the arena makes us inquire, for example, into the relationship between the out-front and backstage activities, and indeed the extent to which public interest communication as performance is/can be scripted.

A related methodological issue is that of how to define or delimit the public interest communication arena. We can see that these arenas might be reasonably tightly defined around an event (for example, around specific planning decisions), or become very extensive cases of discourses in public use, or even extend to historical analysis of nation building. We shall pose this as a question, rather than attempt to offer any answers; however, we alert the reader to how nation building and representation is a central focus of several chapters in this book and thus some insightful further exploration on this theme is provided.

Another emerging theme we suggest here is the culture-dependent nature of the idea of the public interest and, therefore, public interest communication. Firstly, as the experiences of the Chinese public relations practitioners discussed by Hou demonstrate, the public interest finds a specific focus within the Confucian tradition, which can be problematic within Marxist state ideology. It has nevertheless achieved a limited (though perhaps growing) recognition, illustrating elements of communitarian and pragmatic public interest approaches outlined earlier in this chapter. This prompts us to suggest that the public interest can be understood as an imaginary and, consequently, that public interest communication can be approached, at least partly, as the study of the diffusion of innovation (Rogers 1995). A different point of relevance to the cultural approach discussed here relates to the limits of the public interest debate – that is the limit of what can and cannot be said, what can be questioned within the boundaries of a culture. The work related to press freedom and human rights abuses presented in this book suggests that there are cultural boundaries that define the limits of the public interest, such as natural and human rights. At such points, public interest communication turns from inquiry to campaigning for the appropriate institutional mechanism of protection of these rights.

Finally, in our earlier discussion we pointed to the lack of conceptual clarity of 'the public'. In some contexts authors talk about a public (a group), sometimes the public is a political imaginary, sometimes it is a cultural or social imaginary. On reflection, we argue that this lack of clarity can instead be seen as *a conceptual range* and that in analytical practice of public interest communication it may be helpful to acknowledge how these particular meanings shade into one another to offer an enriched interpretation of complex phenomena. Consequently, we propose an openness to these various definitions of the public as a group, as an imaginary, or as an enactment of a 'public subject' position. The final point of reflection here is to ask whether we should be prepared to extend this concept to non-human participants in public discourse arenas: What happens to public interest communication arenas shaped by data-processing infrastructure outside public scrutiny? This theme, central to Carah's chapter on media and surveillance, illustrates one of the challenges for public interest communication now and in the future; as Peters sums up, '[c]ommunication is a risky adventure without guarantees' (Peters 1999, p. 267). Public interest communication simply provides a new tool for navigating the adventure.

Note

1 Deliberative democracy is defined 'as a form of government in which free and equal citizens (and their representatives), justify decisions in a process in which they give one another reasons that are mutually acceptable and generally accessible, with the aim of reaching conclusions that are binding in the present on all citizens but open to challenges in the future' (Gutmann & Thompson 2004, p. 7).

References

Aldoory, L 2005, 'A (re)conceived feminist paradigm for public relations: A case for substantial improvement', *Journal of Communication*, vol. 55, no. 4, pp. 668–684.

Alexander, JC 2006, *The Civil Sphere*, Oxford University Press, New York.

Benditt, TM 1973, 'The public interest', *Philosophy and Public Affairs*, vol. 2, no. 3, pp. 291–311.

Bivins, TH 1993, 'Public relations, professionalism, and the public interest', *Journal of Business Ethics*, vol. 12, no. 2, pp. 117–126.

Bohman, J 2007, *Democracy Across Borders: From Demos to Demoi*, MIT Press, Cambridge, MA.

Bozeman, B 2007, *Public Values and Public Interest: Counterbalancing Economic Individualism*, Georgetown University Press, Washington, DC.

Brassett, J & Smith, W 2010, 'Deliberation and global civil society: Agency, arena, affect', *Review of International Studies*, no. 36, pp. 413–430.

Burkart, R 2004, 'Consensus-oriented public relations (COPR): A conception for planning and evaluation of public relations', in B van Ruler & D Vercic (eds), *Public Relations and Communication Management*, Mouton de Gruyter, Berlin, pp. 446–525.

Burkart, R 2009, 'On Habermas: Understanding and public relations', in Ø Ihlen, B van Ruler & M Fredriksson (eds), *Public Relations and Social Theory: Key Thinkers and Concepts*, Routledge, London, pp. 141–165.

Campbell, H & Marshall, R 2002, 'Utilitarianism's bad breath? A re-evaluation of the public interest justification for planning', *Planning Theory*, vol. 1, no. 2, pp. 163–187.

Carey, JW 1989, *Communication as Culture: Essays on Media and Society*, Unwin Hyman, Winchester, MA.

Carter, N 2007, *The Politics of the Environment*, 2nd edn, Cambridge University Press, Cambridge.

Castells, M 2009, *Communication Power*, Oxford University Press, Oxford.

Cochran, CE 1974, 'Political science and the public interest', *The Journal of Politics*, vol. 36, no. 2, pp. 327–355.

Craig, RT 2007, 'Pragmatism in the field of communication theory', *Communication Theory*, no. 17, pp. 125–145.

Cronin, A 2018, *Public Relations Capitalism: Promotional Culture, Publics and Commercial Democracy*, Palgrave, London.

Dahl, R, Shapiro, I, & Cheibub, JA (eds) 2003, *The Democracy Sourcebook*, MIT, Cambridge.

Davidson, S 2016, 'An agonistic critique of the turns to dialogue and symmetry', *Public Relations Inquiry*, vol. 5, no. 2, pp. 145–167.

Daymon, C & Demetrious, K (eds) 2010, *Gender and Public Relations*, Routledge, London.

Della Porta, D 2013, *Can Democracy Be Saved? Participation, Deliberation and Social Movements*, Polity, Cambridge.

Demetrious, K 2013, *Public Relations, Activism and Social Change: Speaking Up*, Routledge, London.

Dewey, J 1927, *The Public and its Problems*, Swallow Press, Athens.

Dewey, J 1991, *Liberalism and Social Action*, Prometheus Books, New York.

Downs, A 1962, 'The public interest: Its meaning in a democracy', *Social Research*, Spring, vol. 29, no. 1, pp. 1–36.

Dryzek, J 2002, *Deliberative Theory and Beyond: Liberals, Critics and Contestations*, Oxford University Press, Oxford.

Dutta, MJ 2011, *Communicating Social Change*, Routledge, New York.

Edwards, L 2011, 'Questions of self-interest, agency and the rhetor', *Management Communication Quarterly*, vol. 25, no. 3, pp. 531–540.

Edwards, L 2016, 'The role of public relations in deliberative systems', *Journal of Communication*, vol. 66, no. 1, pp. 60–81.

Fairclough, N 2003, *Analysing Discourse*, Routledge, London.

Fischer, F 2009, *Democracy and Expertise: Reorienting Policy Inquiry*, Oxford University Press, Oxford.

Flathman, R 1966, *The Public Interest*, John Wiley & Sons, New York.

Fraser, N 1992, 'Rethinking the public sphere: A contribution to the critique of actually existing democracy', in C Calhoun (ed.), *Habermas and the Public Sphere*, MIT Press, Cambridge, MA, pp. 109–142.

Fraser, N 2002, 'What's critical about Critical Theory. The case of Habermas and gender', in D Rasmussen & J Swindal (eds), *Jurgen Habermas*, Sage Masters of Modern Thought, vol. III, Sage, London, pp. 55–84.

Gastil, J & Levine, P (eds) 2005, *The Deliberative Democracy Handbook*, Jossey Bass, San Francisco, CA.

Gastil, J 2007, *Political Communication and Deliberation*, Sage, Thousand Oaks, CA.

Goodin, R & Dryzek, J 2008, 'Making use of mini-publics', in R Goodin, *Innovating Democracy: Democratic Theory and Practice after the Deliberative Turn*, Oxford University Press, Oxford, pp. 11–37.

Goodin, RE 1996, 'Institutionalizing the public interest: The defense of deadlock and beyond', *The American Political Science Review*, June, vol. 90, no. 2, pp. 313–343.

Goodin, RE 2008, *Innovating Democracy: Democratic Theory and Practice after the Deliberative Turn*, Oxford University Press, Oxford.

Grunig, JE 2001, 'Two-way symmetrical public relations: Past, present, and future', in RL Heath & G Vasquez (eds), *Handbook of Public Relations*, Sage, Thousand Oaks, CA.

Grunig, LA 1992, 'How public relations/communication departments should adapt to the structure and environment of an organization ... and what they actually do', in JE Grunig (ed.), *Excellence in Public Relations and Communication Management*, Lawrence Erlbaum Associates, Mahwah, NJ.

Gutmann, A & Thompson, D 2004, *Why Deliberative Democracy?* Princeton University Press, Princeton, NJ.

Habermas, J 1984, *The Theory of Communicative Action*, vol. 1. Polity Press, Cambridge.

Habermas, J 1987, *The Theory of Communicative Action*, vol. 2. Polity Press, Cambridge.

Habermas, J 1989, *The Structural Transformation of the Public Sphere: An Inquiry into a Category of Bourgeois Society*, MIT Press, Cambridge, MA.

Habermas, J 1996, *Between Facts and Norms: Contribution to a Discourse Theory of Law and Democracy*, MIT Press, Cambridge.

Hajer, MA & Laws, D 2006, 'Ordering through discourse', in M Moran, M Rein & RE Goodin (eds), *The Oxford Handbook of Public Policy*, Oxford University Press, New York.

Heath, RL 1992, 'Visions of critical studies in public relations', in EL Toth & RL Heath (eds), *Rhetorical and Critical Approaches to Public Relations*, Lawrence Erlbaum Associates, Mahwah, NJ, pp. 317–318.

Hendriks, C 2016, 'Coupling citizens and elites in deliberative systems: The role of institutional design', *European Journal of Political Research*, no. 55, pp. 43–60.

Hill, JW 1958, *Corporate Public Relations: Arm of Modern Management*, Harper & Bros, New York.

Ho, L-S 2011, *Public Policy and the Public Interest*, Routledge, London.

Holtzhausen, D 2012, *Public Relations as Activism: Postmodern Approaches to Theory and Practice*, Routledge, New York.

Jahansoozi, J 2006, 'Relationships, transparency, and evaluation: The implications for public relations', in J L'Etang & M Pieczka, *Public Relations: Critical Debates and Contemporary Practice*, Lawrence Erlbaum, Mahwah, NJ, pp. 61–92.

Johnson, P 2006, *Habermas: Rescuing the Public Sphere*, Routledge, London.

Johnston, J 2016, *Public Relations and the Public Interest*, Routledge, New York.

Johnston, J 2017, 'The public interest: A new way of thinking for public relations?', *Public Relations Inquiry*, vol. 6, no. 1, pp. 5–22.

Kruckeberg, D & Stark, K 1988, *Public Relations and Community: A Reconstructed Theory*, Praeger, New York.

Lee, CW 2015, *Do-it-yourself Democracy: The Rise of the Public Engagement Industry*, Oxford University Press, Oxford.

Leitch, S & Neilson, D 2001, 'Bringing publics into public relations', in R Heath (ed.), *Handbook of Public Relations*, Sage, Thousand Oaks, CA, pp. 127–138.

Lippmann, W 1993 [1927], *The Phantom Public*, reprinted by Transaction Publishers, New Brunswick.

Leveson, Lord Justice 2012, *An Inquiry into the Culture, Practice and Ethics of the Press*, 29 November, viewed 29 May 2013, www.levesoninquiry.org.uk

Lippmann, W 1989 [1955], *The Public Philosophy*, reprinted with new introduction by Transaction Publishers, New Brunswick.

Lukes, S 1974, *Power: A Radical View*, Macmillan, Basingstoke.

MacIntyre, A 1981, *After Virtue*, University of Notre Dame Press, Notre Dame, IN.

Mansbridge, J 1998, 'On the contested nature of the public good', in WW Powell & ES Clemens (eds), *Private Action and the Public Good*, Yale University Press, New Haven, CT, pp. 3–19.

Mansbridge, J, Bohman, J, Chambers, S, Christiano, T, Fung, A, Parkinson, J, Thompson, D & Warren, M 2012, 'A systemic approach to deliberative democracy', in J Parkinson & J Mansbridge (eds), *Deliberative Systems: Deliberative Democracy at the Large Scale*, Cambridge University Press, Cambridge, pp. 1–26.

Mansbridge, J, Bohman, J, Chambers, S, Estlund, D, Follesdal, A, Fung, A, Lafont, C, Manin, B & Marti, J 2010, 'The Place of Self-Interest and the Role of Power in Deliberative Democracy', *Journal of Political Philosophy*, vol. 18, pp. 64–75.

McClay, WM 1993 [1927], 'Introduction to the transaction edition', in W Lippmann, *The Phantom Public*, Transaction Publishers, New Brunswick, pp. xi–xiviii.

McKie, D & Munshi, D 2007, *Reconfiguring Public Relations: Ecology, Equity and Enterprise*, Routledge, New York.

Messina, A 2007, 'Public relations, the public interest and persuasion: An ethical approach', *Journal of Communication Management*, vol. 11, no. 1, pp. 29–52.

Moloney, K 2006, *Rethinking Public Relations*, 2nd edn, Routledge, London.

Mouffe, C 2000, *The Democratic Paradox*, Verso, New York, NY.

Munshi, D & Edwards, L 2011, 'Understanding 'Race' in/and public relations: Where do we start from and where should we go?', *Journal of Public Relations Research*, vol. 23, no. 4, pp. 349–367.

Myerson, G 1994, *Rhetoric, Reasons and Society: Rationality as Dialogue*, Sage, London.

O'Flynn, I 2010, 'Deliberating about the Public Interest', *Res Publica*, vol. 16, pp. 299–315.

Peters, JD 1999, *Speaking into the Air: A History of the Idea of Communication*, Chicago University Press, Chicago, IL.

Ramsey, P 2016, 'The public sphere and PR: Deliberative democracy and agonistic pluralism', in J L'Etang, D McKie, N Snow & J Xifra (eds), *Routledge Handbook of Critical Public Relations*, Routledge, London, pp. 65–75.

Roberts, J & Escobar, O, 2015, *Involving Communities in Deliberation: A Study of 3 Citizens' Juries on Onshore Wind Farms in Scotland*, viewed 20 June 2016, www.climatexchange.org.uk/files/5614/3213/1663/Citizens_Juries_-_Full_Report.pdf.

Rogers, EM 1995, *Diffusion of Innovations*, 4th edn, The Free Press, New York.

Rogers, ML 2012, 'Introduction', in J Dewey, *The Public and Its Problems*, The Pennsylvania State University, University Park, PA.

Russill, C 2004, *Toward a Pragmatist Theory of Communication*, Doctoral dissertation, The Pennsylvania State University, Park, PA.

Sandel, MJ 1996, *Democracy's Discontent: America in Search of a Public Philosophy*, Harvard University Press, Cambridge, MA.

Sommerfeldt, E 2013, 'The civility of social capital: Public relations in the public sphere, civil society, and democracy', *Public Relations Review*, vol. 39, no. 4, pp. 280–289.

Sorauf, FJ 1957, 'The public interest reconsidered', *The Journal of Politics*, vol. 19, no. 4, pp. 616–639.

Springston, JK & Keyton, J 2001, 'Public relations field dynamics', in R Heath (ed.), *Handbook of Public Relations*, Sage, London, pp. 115–126.

Steiner, J 2012, *The Foundations of Deliberative Democracy: Empirical Research and Normative Implications*, Cambridge University Press, Cambridge.

Stoker, K & Stoker, M 2012, 'The paradox of public interest: How serving individual superior interests fulfil public relations' obligation to the public interest', *Journal of Mass Media Ethics*, no. 27, pp. 31–45.

Talisse, R 2012, 'Deliberation', in D Estlund (ed.), *The Oxford Handbook of Political Philosophy*, Oxford University Press, Oxford.

Taylor, M 2010, 'Public relations in the enactment of civil society', in R Heath (ed.), *Sage Handbook of Public Relations*, Sage, Thousand Oaks, CA, pp. 5–16.

Vasquez, MG & Taylor, M 2001, 'Research perspectives on "the public"', in R Heath (ed.), *Handbook of Public Relations*, Sage, Thousand Oaks, CA, pp. 139–154.

Warner, M 2002, *Publics and Counter Publics*, Zone Books, New York.

Wheeler, C 2013, 'The public interest: We know it's important, but do we know what it means', *AIAL Forum*, no. 72, pp. 34–49, viewed 31 December 2017, https://search.informit.com.au/documentSummary;dn=201218122;res=IELAPA.

2 Terministic dialectics of individual and community agency

Co-creating and co-enacting public interest

Robert L. Heath and Damion Waymer

Introduction

Public interest is a contextually relevant, situationally preferred view of the benefits of collective choice and action in a given society at a moment in time. Ideally, it is the win-win amalgamation of many individual interests, but consensus is more aspirational than realistic. Expressions of public interest are dynamic, not static – a matter of participatory engagement (Jian 2007). Deliberation, the essence of public interest communication, consists of individual statements that employ the power and suffer the weaknesses of language. To unlock the content of public interest communication requires understanding the motives behind such discourse, especially whether it serves self-interest as the public interest.

Public interest discussions arise from and reveal context-specific tensions between interests. Tensions lead to debate; they force dialectic, contextually (by topic). As such, public interest debates provide both fuel for and braking systems against the enactment of individual preferences of self-interest as public interest. This conception of public interest means that instead of thinking of it as the sum of all relevant individual and organisational interests, it is better viewed as motivating and encountering issue discussions that both foster and impede public interest decision making, always a work in process. Such discussions co-express interests that result from multiple stakeholders' searches for common interests that can be synthesised as public interest, but can end up being the expressed interest of one dominant voice or multiple dominant voices.

Public interest is expressed as both the substance and outcome of dialectical discourse created when interests collide. This dialectic approach presumes that organisations, which are empowered and constrained by public interest(s), have a community obligation, however motivated by 'self-interest', to help create the standards of legitimacy that are enacted in the public interest. Such engagement can truly serve the public interest or misshape and inappropriately structure it to serve self-interest in the name of public interest.

The purpose of this chapter is to explore the discursive nature of public interest as dialectical tensions that enact and test discourse arena integrity where intellectual space co-creates and co-enacts public interest. Central to such discourse is the scientific battle regarding the existence, harm and causes of climate change. Scientists working in the public interest investigate climate change and report their findings. However important that controversy is among scientists, the purpose of this chapter is not to critique the science per se but to investigate how an organisation, ExxonMobil in this case, can alter the discourse quality of the arena so that it could bend the discourse of public interest to serve its corporate interest.

Public interest as dialectical tensions

Dialectical analysis 'focuses less on identifying the meaning of particular discourses, and more on the interpretive struggles among discourses and practices' (Mumby 2005, p. 24). This insight is compelling because dialectic can occur on any and within multiple issue and terministic levels simultaneously (Burke 1968). For example, a dialectic can be as specific as the tensions between one family member and others in the family (micro-level), or as complicated and perplexing as global tensions between the hydrocarbon industry and the scientific community (macro-level) regarding climate change. Discourse process can result from tensions between one of the giants of that industry and environmental quality interests (meso-level), and even between one of the giants of the industry and other giants of the industry (potentially interdependent layers of meso- and macro-level tensions). As such, public interest (and for that matter private/personal interest) contests seek to know and express conditions of legitimacy by which actions are judged morally and pragmatically, and resources are granted or denied based on whether they are deemed to be legitimately deserved, in the public interest.

As advocacy and counter-advocacy, dialectic is a discursive means for achieving the lesson learned from each encounter. If ideas/arguments push against one another, they should refine each other so that the best survive as wheat is separated from chaff.

As well as ideas, dialectic results from tensions between identities and within relationships. This tension can be parsed as I/Thou, however specific 'I' is and generalised 'Thou' is. Challenged by such wrangles, George Herbert Mead's (1934) work informed Kenneth Burke's (1950/1969) understanding of how individuals blend their sense of self and others (e.g. I as me, and I with thou), and encouraged the I/Thou analysis of scholars such as Martin Buber (1965). In more contemporary scholarship, Cheney (1992, p. 179) noted the paradoxes of I/Thou as (re)presentation: 'Individual organisations both reflect and contribute to the society of which they are constitutive parts'. As such, successful organisations manage the tensions and accomplish a relational balance between individual (I) and public interest (Thou). That is not to say that organisations cannot advance the public interest as they advance their own, but the problematic, as we explain later in this chapter, occurs when organisations advance their self-interest as the public interest.

Our analysis explores the manner in which organisations terministically and functionally act self-interestedly by cloaking themselves in the public interest. This consideration is paramount because public interest can be shaped to justify the functional/pragmatic and normative/moral conditions of corporate social responsibility (Golant & Sillince 2007) and the criteria-based reasoning by which organisational legitimacy is determined (Suddaby & Greenwood 2005). Since legitimacy is terministically constructed and functionally achieved, the challenge to organisational communicators and observant critics is to demonstrate 'how rhetoric can be used to expose and manipulate dominant and subordinate institutional logics and create the impetus for institutional change' (Suddaby & Greenwood 2005, p. 36).

Legitimacy occurs because of the interdependence of rhetorical positioning (descriptive and evaluative) and functional operations. If the latter lacks legitimacy, repositioning and redefinition can remediate that problem. By this logic, public interest is a standard against which to judge operational legitimacy and is a terministic logic by which to justify such legitimacy. If corporate actions, for instance, are not 'in the public interest', they are motivated to change their operations, to change 'public interest', or to demonstrate that in fact they are in the public interest, or can be made to appear so.

Given that public interest is asserted and contested as co-created amalgamations of individual interests, it can be hypothesised that public interest is (or has the capability of being) self-correcting. If individual interests struggle against one another to express public interest, such tensions call for resolution, concurrence, and even consensus. But, given power/knowledge disparities and the ability of some voices to reshape not only the arenas of public interest discussion but also the outcomes of discourse, then public interest is capable of becoming the expression of some dominant individual interest in (or as) the public good. The paradox is whether one or a few voices dominate the discussion of public interest, or whether public interest is the result of polyvocal deliberate democracy.

After discussing public interest as critical debate to guide strategic management, this chapter explains the nature of dialectic and applies that analysis to critique the role that ExxonMobil has played in the discussion of climate change as public interest. Arguably, ExxonMobil worked to protect its material/financial assets by asserting its legitimacy as public interest while quietly working to morph public interest to serve its self-interest. Corporate strategic management and communication reflect dialectical relationships of interacting, competing and conflicting interests that ultimately can be bent to serve one interest as public interest, or can bend individual interest to the public interest.

Public interest's critical legitimacy debates

The interdependence of public interest definitions and strategic management choices was framed normatively and strategically by John Hill (co-founder of

Hill & Knowlton). Hill believed that no organisation could long prosper, serve its own interests, let alone those of society, if its operations were misaligned with the public interest.

> It is the job of public relations to help management find ways of identifying its own interests with the public interest – ways so clear that the profit earned by the company may be viewed as contributing to the progress of everybody in the American economy.
>
> (Hill 1958, p. 21)

Relevant to the I/Thou theme of this chapter, Hill (1963) emphasised, 'no one person, and no one group, is entitled to determine arbitrarily what is in the public interest' (p. 253).

Public interest legitimacy reflects the moral and pragmatic ability of any organisation to switch strategic perspectives in such a way as to reframe accounts of corporate responsibility (Sillince & Mueller 2007). Legitimacy battles become shaped and reshaped as perspectives shift and compete. For instance, citizens may oppose welfare in the abstract but support policies intended to help needy children. People may oppose government assistance in the abstract but seek it in times of personal need. They demand lower prices for what they buy and higher prices for what they sell (Stone 2012).

Fascinated by such terministic entanglements, Kenneth Burke (1968) based his theory of language on his notion that terministic screens explain how humans interpret their physical and social realms. In essence, the concept of terministic screens reasons that instead of assuming that things define words, humans create terminologies (idioms) to define and judge their physical and social worlds. Instead of reality informing meaning, words name, evaluate and attitudinise reality. Words are the root of misjudgements.

Flaws in language manifest themselves as flaws of society. To justify that conclusion, Burke (1968) pointed to the dialectical hierarchy of terms which moved away from a preference for positivism to one that featured idealism: *positive* (words that name things), *dialectical* (words of opposition – abundance-scarcity, democracy-tyranny), *ultimate* (god and devil terms that by transcending others become uniquely propositional). Such hierarchy, as inherent to language, necessarily layers categories of public interests that correspond to each of these categories. That critical, practical discussion is further grounded by narrative theory (Fisher 1985; Heath 1994), and Mead's (1934) conception of the three pillars (mind, self and society) of the human condition. How Burke's and Mead's works inform a narrative conceptualisation of public interests is important.

Public interest is a contextual and situational narrative of the benefits of collective choice and action. Public interests ostensibly express the win-win amalgamation of many interests as one collective interest. That logic applies to the theoretical, critical and practical discussion of energy and environmental issues, including sustainability, lifestyle choices, market systems, national identity, and health and safety. Humans' words bracket experiences and interests in various degrees of terministic tension. Positive terms refer to energy sources: fossil, solar or wind, for instance. Dialectical terms contrast comfort with discomfort, mobility with immobility, and sustainability with unsustainability. At the penultimate level, energy is power (personal, community, national and global). Humans act in the name of energy as they compete for dominance (locally and globally).

In a slightly different articulation, Mead (1934) proposed that individual thoughts are reflexively influenced by others' statements and refined by experienced reality. Minds conceptualise physical and social realities as a rationale for collective action to facilitate individual-collective interests. Such enactments are narrativised by script, role, purpose, theme and action as terministic frames by which individuals and collectivities deal with the universal challenges, such as risk assessment as uncertainty. Individuals' interests (dialectics of individual and collective interests) manifest themselves into thought and action to satisfy (individual and public) interests in the face of risk and uncertainty, knowing that individuals are more agentic together than alone.

Agency resides at the boundary of efficacy: self-efficacy and/or collective efficacy, thus public interest. Organisations engage in public discourse to create operating environments that rationalise and legitimatise their self-interested business plans. As large organisations encounter resistance to the operationalisation of their missions and visions, they 'change their behavior, not so much out of rationality or a need for effectiveness, but because of their search for legitimacy' (Frandsen & Johansen 2013, p. 602). Dialectically, strategic management shifts from organising to communicate, to communicating to organise (Christensen & Cornelissen 2011).

Agency consists of the individual's ability to achieve self-interest as amplified by the ability of the whole, society or community to achieve agency. This tension between self and society reasons that individuals cannot be agentic without, or are more agentic when, collaborating rather than going alone. As Spoel and Den Hoed (2014, p. 167) opined, 'rhetorical analysis of "community" suggests a generative method for understanding the complex relations animating specific risk communication contexts as well as potentially reinventing "community" in terms more conducive to meaningful citizen engagement'. The lone actor needs the ensemble; the interests of the ensemble constrain and empower the individual. The self can be agentic in the whole but only by how it serves the whole, while serving the self. So, as multiple interests engage, the public interest becomes contextually defined and affirmed as more than the sum of individual interests because interests necessarily compete with one another.

The agency of society requires terminological glue. Acts reinforce and define terms, such as just actions affirm the term, justice. But as that is the case for individuals, others may act in ways that disaffirm the term. One of the tensions of self and society is the dialectical truth as Burke (1937/1968, pp. 78–79) reasoned 'that two people of totally different experiences must totally fail to communicate'; however, such is the case, that 'there are no two such people, the "margin of overlap" always being considerable (due, if to nothing else, to the fact that man's biologic functions are uniform)'. And, thus, Burke (1968) reasoned, humans' words bracket their experiences and interests in various degrees of tension which nevertheless allows for cooperation. Then, 'as we communicate approximately though "imprisoned within the walls of our personality," so we communicate approximately though imprisoned within the walls of our age' (Burke 1968, pp. 78–79). Tensions are produced by terministically defined experiences, interests, estrangements and alignments of individuals as they aspire to be agentic in the company of others while realising that their imprisonment could defy the aspirations of collective (and therefore individual) agency. Burke (1939) emphasised how terminological constraints result when words are neither material reality (but mindful conception), self or society, but expressions of them.

Terministic screens define and amalgamate interests. Apropos to the case to be examined later, societal/community narratives specific to the case of global warming are co-constructed by dialectical tensions arising from the collective resource management of environmental risk and uncertainty. Considered in light of Burke's (1968) hierarchy of terms, the positive level expresses scientific investigation (and lay observation), terms of scientific description and probabilistic assessment. The dialectical level presumes such themes as bad and good science, or science and no science, as well as corporate hydrocarbon interest and constraining public interest: free enterprise/regulated enterprise and comfort/discomfort. Ultimate level terminologies invoke 'science-based climate change assessment' which can collide with 'God's will' and 'free enterprise'. Ultimate terministic levels subsume lower levels; ultimate terms prescribe the enactment of public interest as science, faith (God's will), or free enterprise, but do these lines of analysis lead to one coherent functional and moral sense of the public interest?

In summary, individuals aspire to have public interest give agency to their self-interests. Corporations may reason that what serves their interests serves the public interest. But, since individuals argue for the definition and enactment of their interests, such discourses are necessarily a slippery slope. Public interest is co-created and co-enacted and thus can be analysed by understanding the dialectics of mind (analytical dispute), self (I/Thou), and society (We). In the case of public interest communication regarding climate change, scientists argue, in the public interest, that hydrocarbons and therefore specific businesses cause climate change; corporations have resisted, to various degrees and in various ways. The following case analysis addresses the question of whether discourse locates the agency of public interest in the public good, or whether the enlightened engine of public interest discourse is distorted by grit rather than facilitated by grease as, for instance, a major corporation narratively increases decision uncertainty by promoting alternative (even dysfunctional) scientific conclusions and interpretations of climate change based on faith – God's will.

Hydrocarbons as public interest political discourse

The global Industrial Revolution was given a jump-start in the 19th century when hydrocarbons were bent to serve the public interest as energy facilitated mass production/mass consumption. Has that dialectic changed?

Energy-based public policy battles have increased over the past 60 years as scientific evidence (and lay observation) documented changes in weather, climate, crops, animal populations and behaviour, and health-related issues of species that include humans. Discourse constitutes a public battleground to justify the functional/pragmatic and normative/moral conditions of corporate social responsibility as expressions of public interest (Heath et al. 2012). However, public participation should not be romanticised to presume that engagement inherently and easily propels decision making forward rather than sends it into a stalemating swirl.

Companies that emit waste by-product argue that higher levels of water toxicity, rising oceans, and noticeably more frequent and dramatic weather events are tolerable given that desirable products and jobs 'created' serve the public interest. Conversely, environmentalists argue that water toxicity and temperature change levels should be minimal because preserving water quality for marine wildlife and human use serves the public interest. Agricultural production and public health can be observed to relate to climate change. If science actually determines whether the climate is changing, can it identify the causes of change? If climate change is real, is its cause humans' actions, natural processes, or the will of God? As the enactment of free enterprise, does private interest trump (and therefore define) community interests?

Within the climate discussion in the United States, jobs are defended as combining individual/community and organisational interests framed in the public interest: the functional/pragmatic and normative/moral conditions of corporate social responsibility legitimacy. Climate change deniers reason: 'Regulation kills jobs, so to grow jobs, kill regulation.' Thus, is private, corporate interest merely the servant of public interest? Interests, both individual and public, are expressions of quality of life and quality of the environment. The 'public interest' is an I/Thou dialectic regarding terministic interpretations of reality (mind/cognition), self (I/Thou), and society (We versus Them). Such questions need to be addressed as argumentative processes that occur in discourse/issue arenas that are supposed to be level playing fields. Can they be tipped to advantage individual interest masked as public interest legitimation?

A community is enriched when relevant and deserving voices participate robustly in public interest debates. Communities are harmed when voices are encouraged to participate not for what they contribute to the substance of discourse but rather to contravene and even confuse dominant logics needed to inspire and guide management policies. Apropos to climate change dialectics of decision making, tensions at the positive level of discussion can be elevated, first to the level of competing interest (dialectical terms) and can be confounded if ultimate terms win in discussion. Deliberative democracy works best when thoughts survive on merit not by distorting the quality of relevant discourse arena.

Climate change, as public interest, is co-created and co-enacted through environmental discourse that ostensibly is collaborative (Brulle 2010; Wittneben et al. 2012; Wright & Nyberg 2014). Discussants of climate science express incentives and seek discourse means to avert pending disaster. Public participation is enacted through evidence, probabilistic assessment, and value judgements to examine strains between the physical world and social constructions (Peterson et al. 2007; Walker 2007). However, as Simmons (2007) emphasised, large enterprises and governmental agencies often determine what citizens say and how, if at all, on matters of environmental quality.

The battle to scientifically ground climate change discussion, coupled with the morality of environmental protection, came to a major juncture during the 2015 United Nations Climate Conference in Paris (from which President Trump withdrew the United States in 2017). By April 2014, leading climate scientists, the Intergovernmental Panel on Climate Change (IPCC), had reached consensus and issued another joint warning about climate change. This statement was endorsed by 1,250 international scientists and approved by nearly 200 governments. The challenge was to reduce carbon emissions and even decarbonise the environment (Rowell 2014).

Environmental discourse: public interest communication

Climate change scientists developed the working probabilistic hypothesis that carbon emissions can increase the rate of climate change and exacerbate its harmful consequences. Discussions of environmental quality can both empower and delegitimise management preferences through language resources that allow humans to smooth or obstruct pathways to organisational and societal agency (Harris et al. 2013). Scientific evidence and reasoning seek to know whether the climate is changing, and if so, how dramatically, for what reasons, and to what consequences.

Environmental discourse arenas presume that complex relationships can and should empower communities' ability to address facts, values, policies and identifications in ways that are multi-dimensional (e.g., authenticity, power/control, advance/resistance, and power/knowledge distribution), multi-layered (e.g., layers of scientific investigation and analysis, transparency, aligned interests), multi-textual (e.g., scientific versus religious interpretation), and multi-vocal (e.g., relevant empowered voices). Such 'multi-level' participation should be capable of enlightening choices to solve problems in the public interest.

Environmental discourse centres on uncertainties, risk/reward distribution and power tensions. Risk management solutions are developed to prevent or mitigate disaster and make societies better places to live and work. Given that logic, Irwin (2009) wondered why communities either move forward or go in circles as they address environmental concerns, crises and potential disasters.

The problematic of public interest communication needs to appreciate and understand 'how "community" is rhetorically constituted to better understand the contested versions of reality that animate public discourses of risk assessment' (Spoel & Den Hoed 2014, p. 268).

Discourse arenas: public interest battlegrounds

The hydrocarbon industry cloaks itself in public interest texts: jobs, health, comfort, convenience, progress, lifestyle, and even national pride. Archetypal themes offer executives textual support for their strategic management plans, even by bending public interest to serve their interest. As Clegg, Courpasson and Phillips (2006, p. 2) mused, '[w]hat is organisation but the bending of individual wills to a common purpose?'. Strategic management seeks a favourable power distribution in discourse arenas. Language-based social constructions allow humans to bend reality, and thereby one another, to individual and collective wills, even as texts of climate change (Jaspal et al. 2014). Tensions arise from meeting, overcoming and managing resistance in all forms as the means and rationale for collective association.

Ideally, Sommerfeldt (2013, p. 280) reasoned,

> the normative role of public relations in democracy is best perceived as creating ... spheres of public discussions and policy formation as well as for maintaining networks among those organisations that check the power of the state and maintain social infrastructure.

But powerful organisations can AstroTurf issues (Lock et al. 2016) as well as empower hidden organisations to be more vocal and visible than their discourse role legitimatises.

This strategic option presumes that standards and incentives needed to dialectically enact legitimacy come from the community, not the organisation per se, especially if it is merely seeking its self-interest. Engagement can collaboratively foster mutual benefit, as ideas dialectically buffet one another. This process should improve the understanding of facts, values, policies and identifications but the process also can create discourse tangents and culs-de-sac. By how they engage, self-interested organisations can achieve the effect of a dog chasing its tail; powerful organisations using clandestine funding can bend discourse to serve their interests by convoluting strategies that respond to critics in ways that seemingly empower society's deliberative democracy but actually stalemate it and allow management to continue unabated.

As socially constructed, power includes the ability to resist resistance. Shaping that theme into contentious discourse, Hardy and Clegg (2006, p. 760) noted how 'instead of concerning itself with the use of power to prevent or constructively resolve conflict [critical approach], it focused almost exclusively on the use of power to defeat conflict [functionalist approach]'. As such, the strategic question is not whether industries or firms will resist those voices that obstruct their business plans, but how and when such strategies will be employed. Public relations/affairs personnel can challenge critics of business practices by putting information (including that which is highly scientific) into play that justifies and legitimatises management decisions (Kinsella 1999; Motion & Leitch 2007).

Within discourse arenas, 'hidden' organisations can be created and empowered to engage in communication practices while concealing their sponsors' and even members' identities (Scott 2013). Perplexed by such paradoxes, management scholars investigate hidden organisations as one way of discerning whether discourse arenas are tipped in favour of some and against the interests of others, and even the public interest (Askay & Gossett 2015; Jensen & Meisenbach 2015; Schoeneborn & Scherer 2012; Scott 2013, 2015; Stohl & Stohl 2011).

Discourse arenas consist of layered networks of interlocking relationships, interests, and dialectically voiced viewpoints. Scott (2015, p. 3) called to 'at least partially push back on the discourses that have favored transparency and openness over secrecy and concealment to better understand the complex role of hidden organisations in a global society'. Basic to such networks is the operational power to control and/or foster information dissemination (Maille & Saint-Charles 2014) and debate issues. Networks that seem to facilitate can actually frustrate the work of issue advocates. Resistance is a dialectical tactic to combat powerful organisational control, but counter-resistance moves can reshape the discourse arena to advance organisational self-interests (VanSlette & Boyd 2011), even by working (through hidden organisations) to craft and redefine alternative and hierarchically superior views of public interest.

Large organisations have become increasingly sensitive to the legitimacy expectations of their stakeholders' issue salience and capability to grant or withhold resources those organisations need or desire (Mitchell et al. 1997). Seeking orderly operations, organisations resist change – or work to control the change with a bias to serving the organisation's interest even at some disadvantage to stakeholders.

Advocacy and counter-advocacy: whether internal or external to an organisation or industry, competing voices raise issues that call for thoughtful, ethical response and, if justified, management changes. Companies that encounter scientific challenges can meet them head on by debating issues to achieve the best solutions for the largest number of interests. However, the battle over scientific conclusions can use spurious attacks that do not bring independently generated data under scientific scrutiny in ways that hone conclusions.

Collaborative decision making – deliberative democracy: rather than a zero-sum game, strategic reactions to critics' claims can opt for a win-win outcome through collaborative decision making. Critics can strategically motivate interested parties to transparently and authentically collaborate to solve complex scientific problems and increase community agency. To frustrate true collaboration, counter-resistance can shift issue positions in ways that confound efforts to achieve an agentic community.

Redefining issues as competing perspectives: to advance collective (public) interests, many voices come together in various discourse arenas (e.g., government agencies, competitors, customers, legislators, regulators and litigators). This can enrich discourse which in turn creates resistance against management's strategic planning preferences; colliding interests need to be collectively managed as self-governance (Heath & McComas 2015).

Resisting resistance: dialectics of individual/public interest

If power derives from knowledge, and if knowledge provides critics with power over the future of business plans, industry has substantial incentive to resist critics' attacks. Climate scientists use complex data gathering and analytical, probabilistic techniques to assert two straightforward claims: 1) rapidly increasing amounts of carbon are damaging the atmosphere; and 2) human actions (volition), including industrial processes, contribute to potentially cataclysmic damage. For obvious reasons, hydrocarbon-based companies have often taken a reactionary stance on climate change discussions. ExxonMobil has led such resistance (although it did oppose the 2017 decision by President Trump to withdraw from the Paris Accord).

Proclaiming its self-interest in 2014, the CEO of ExxonMobil assured shareholders, 'we are confident that none of our hydrocarbon reserves are now or will become "stranded"' (Rowell 2014; see also PR Newswire 2014). In the oil industry, the technical/financial term stranded refers to oil reserves being left underground, and not put into production and transformed into marketable products used to obtain profits. The company argued that because it was 'highly unlikely' that governments would successfully address climate change, it would continue drilling for oil and gas.

Scientific interpretation

How can public opinion that expresses public interest vastly differ from scientific evidence and reasoning? Some critics (People for the American Way n.d.; Michaelson 2012; Owen & Bignell 2010) indicted corporate influence for carrying out 'an orchestrated campaign … against climate change science to undermine public acceptance of man-made global warming' (Owen & Bignell 2010, para 1). Some supporters of climate science suggest:

> A complicated web of relationships revolves around a number of right-wing think-tanks around the world that dispute the threats of climate change. ExxonMobil is a key player behind the scenes, having donated hundreds of thousands of dollars in the past few years to climate change skeptics.
>
> (Owen & Bignell 2010, para 8)

Andrei (2011) detailed how nine out of ten groups denying climate change are linked to ExxonMobil.

Scientific discovery advances by noting patterns and reflecting varying degrees of probable certitude in the face of uncertainty (Douglas 2001). Deliberative democracy can foster dialogue based on expressions of public interest; organisations can remove their masks or shelter their interests (Boyd & Waymer 2011; Waymer 2013). As Krippendorff (1999) wondered, does dialogue actually help people experience and appreciate one another's ideas? Does it merely mask advocacy, the iron fist in the velvet glove? Rhetorical advantage goes to business interests when society fails to reach definite conclusions and when political economies do not obligate organisations to truly help resolve public policy issues (Heath 2011). Discord benefits enterprise and weakens the agency of society.

If the discourse of science is countered by voices that doubt scientific conclusions, those voices are expected to prove their claims as to the deficiency of such conclusions. They may, however, shift ground and offer competing interpretations, such as ones based on religious interpretation and faith. Consequently, the combat to define the public interest regarding climate change centres on three main issue positions: scientific argument, faith, or free enterprise.

Mathew (2015), a writer for the *International Business Times*, highlighted the email of a former climate expert for ExxonMobil that alleged the company spent millions to support deniers of climate change as long ago as the 1980s. In response to scientist James Hansen's testimony before a congressional committee in 1988 about fossil fuels' and greenhouse gases' effects on the earth, executives at Exxon decided to

> organise a disinformation campaign to raise doubts about global warming and hinder any efforts to contain it – efforts which Exxon feared would cut into its world-wide profits, which were almost entirely based on the sales of fossil fuels.
>
> (Mathew 2015, n.p.)

In that pursuit, as of 2015, critics believed that ExxonMobil had given front groups up to $27 million to research and comment on climate change (Masri 2015).

In 2015, the Union of Concerned Scientists (UCS) (2015) issued a series of documents, obtained through the US Freedom of Information Act, that reveal the extent to which ExxonMobil secretly funded, for more than a decade, a prominent, purportedly independent anti-global warming climate scientist, Wei-Hock ('Willie') Soon. The UCS found that Soon had received approximately $1.2 million in research funds between 2001 and 2012 from ExxonMobil, the American Petroleum Institute (API), the Charles Koch Foundation, and Southern Company, a large electric utility in Atlanta, Georgia. Soon's work was found to have overstated the role the sun plays in global warming, as demonstrated by his scientific peers (Union of Concerned Scientists 2015).

The UCS report (Union of Concerned Scientists 2015) highlighted the role the Smithsonian Institution played in funding individual critics of climate change. Organisations such as the Committee for a Constructive Tomorrow (CFACT) gave credence to Soon's claims. It is important to consider the mission statement of CFACT, which was founded in 1985 to provide 'a much-needed, positive alternative voice on issues of environment and development' (www.cfact.org/about/, downloaded 01/10/2017). Such corporate interests can assist but also confound scientific deliberation while ostensibly working to make it agentic.

God's will

Simply put, dialectic is a pressing of one proposition against another. Each statement can create interpretative frames for 'social reality because it helps shape the perspectives through which people see the world' (Hallahan 1999, pp. 206–207; see Bailey et al. 2014; Lakoff 2010). Sensitive to the framing that leads to and results from discourse processes, Pepermans and Maeseele (2014) wondered how reporters should discuss scientific wrangles without distorting them. Should they give 'balanced' coverage to both sides of an issue? Should the side with greatest scientific merit receive more media attention and should the contrast between it and alternative positions be highlighted? The paradox, Ihlen (2009, p. 244) found, is that of the four dominant corporate perspectives of climate change, ranging from concern to competitive opportunities, none called for 'the radical rethinking of systemic problems that the situation's gravity would seem to call for'.

The integrity of scientific discourse arenas can become convoluted when religious voices claim it is laughable that climate change advocates – those who contend that human-controlled climate change is occurring – would blame US citizens' decline in public opinion support for that hypothesis on ExxonMobil's funding of think tanks and religious right groups (DeWeese 2013). Rather than clarifying issues, multiple voices can create textual incoherence as self-contradictory frames. Emphasising that point, Lovell (2010) noted that both climate change advocates and critics use texts that emphasise apocalyptic visions. Those espousing religious interpretations do so with religious fervour whereas scientists do this with dire predictions of a total loss of a species or the collapse of ecosystems. Such collisions of faith (God's will) and sound science create a linguistic brew that distorts fruitful discourse.

Discourse arena watchdogs such as Coll (2012), staff writer at the *New Yorker* and author of *Private Empire: ExxonMobil and American Power*, detail how ExxonMobil works to reshape the climate debate by funding groups that directly challenge scientific claims and that use religion to counter science with claims of God's will. Coll claimed: 'the $26 million investment that Exxon made ... really created the infrastructure for what today is a very successful battle' being waged in society and for or against political candidates based on their stances on climate change.

In the United States, 'God's will' is not a trivial discourse struggling weakly in the face of science. For example, during a 2014 rally in Pittsburgh, an advocate who opposed restrictions on the coal industry prayed that the government be prevented from constraining the mining of coal that God had placed at humans' disposal. So too Public Service Commissioner elect Chip Beeker of Alabama prayed that since coal was created by God the federal government should not interfere in its mining and use as an energy source (Why evolution is true 2014). Brady (2014) reported that during a rally against US Environmental Protection Agency (EPA) standards, Joel Watts of the West Virginia Coal Forum referred to 'God-given coal fields' and prayed for resistance against the White House and the EPA. Such public statements by prominent officials give voice to the hopes of those who depend on hydrocarbons, supporting how their interpretation of climate change will defend them against lost jobs and an overly encumbered free enterprise.

Watchdogs of the discourse arena

If discourse arenas are expected to exhibit transparency and authenticity, they require discussion of competing issue positions and the sleuthing abilities of watchdogs such as investigative media. Starting with the leadership of John D. Rockefeller who founded Standard Oil in 1870, ExxonMobil's business was built on science and engineering. What is ironic about its support of religion-inspired climate change doubters/deniers is that company management does not tolerate faith as a means for discovering oil/gas reserves and producing them into finished products – and profits.

In addition to resistance to its business plan from most of the scientific community, the company's latest challenge, ironically, is coming from the values position expressed by the Rockefeller Foundation which has begun to divest itself of hydrocarbon stocks. The Rockefeller Foundation has asked religious organisations and pension funds to rely not only on financial gain, but also to support social gains of cleaner and more sustainable energy alternatives (Kaiser & Wasserman 2016).

Watchdogs look for discourse practices that empower weak arguments and divert attention from rigorous scientific conclusions. What today can be called the discourse arena, Burke (1969) called a wrangle in the marketplace of ideas. Such wrangles require cooperation (Heath 1986), deliberative democracy, but as Burke (1965) worried, '[l]et the system of cooperation become impaired, and the communicative equipment is correspondingly impaired, while this impairment of the communicative medium in turn threatens the structure of rationality itself' (p. 163).

Shifting the dominant frame from science to one of God's will creates incompatible logics to thereby stalemate a community's ability to engage in effective public interest communication. Using Burke's ideas on frames of acceptance, Hamilton (2003) explored the tensions between technical and cultural interpretations of risk. The historical/cultural frame for some members of each community is their means of understanding and assessing the technical elements of risk. If persons favour a religious orientation to climate change, scientific analysis is likely to be reframed, even denied as shown by the discussion above. But does that reframing lead to the best-case conclusions?

Discourse arenas should be improved by adding voices to enrich deliberation. The irony, however, is that additional voices can functionally cause deliberation to stalemate, to go in circles instead of moving toward enlightened choice. Hydrocarbon-based corporations can argue that until discourse advances, they are free (enterprise) to operate in their sense of public interest, but then they can work to prevent successful issue resolution.

The Center for Media and Democracy (n.d.) – a non-profit watchdog organisation founded in 1993, whose niche is investigating and exposing undue influence of corporations and front groups (AstroTurf and hidden organisations) on public policy – provided a detailed report on ExxonMobil's contributions to advocacy groups. ExxonSecrets.org lists more than 100 organisations, congresspersons' offices and interest groups that have received funding from ExxonMobil (and other petrochemical giants including Koch Industries). Among those religion-based groups that are or have been funded by ExxonMobil are Acton Institute for the Study of Religion and Liberty, Cornwall Alliance for the Stewardship of Creation, and the Heartland Institute.

What happens when both science and religion make their way into legislative chambers and the court of public opinion? Recent studies show that US citizens are more sceptical about 'human-caused climate change than they were ten years ago, despite virtually unanimous scientific consensus on the matter' (Michaelson 2012, para 1).

Conclusions

Burke's theory of language emphasises how meaning is imposed on reality through the naming, evaluating and attitudinising function of words. Thus, his theory of language helps explain and diagnose public interest communication. Even when positivistic aspirations are used to make scientific claims about the environment and climate change, those enactments simultaneously exist as a wrangle over public interest as faith and as free enterprise. Applying Burke's (1968) notion of terministic screens to public interest communication – in the context of environmental debates – gives scholars of public interest another, nuanced framework for exploring how understanding is produced – when collective, individual, and even masked collective and veiled individual interests collide.

In sum, the dialectics of discourse complexities press self-interest against other-interest (privilege versus obligation) (Hardy & Clegg 2006). Such critical attention shines light on how powerful organisations can engage dialectically to satisfy or frustrate the standards of scientific inquiry and thereby bend other interests (public and private) to their wills. Masked transparency can hide the wolf in lambskin (Smith & Ferguson 2013).

The climate change discourse arena is a place where issue positions clash, but its richness presumes fair and constructive dialogue. Discourse arenas can be self-correcting or suffer stalemate when one interest unduly controls the discourse for its self-interest rather than public interest. Public interest is dynamic, not static. Dialectics prevail to achieve lessons learned, or to spin as a dog chases its tail. By applying the dialectical tensions inherent to terministic screens, scholars can achieve nuanced explanations of the complexities of the public interest.

References

Andrei, M 2011 (May 10), '9 out of 10 top climate deniers are linked with ExxonMobil', *ZME Science.* www.zmescience.com/ecology/climate-change-papers-exxon-mobil/.

Askay, D A & Gossett, L 2015, 'Concealing communities within the crowd: Hiding organisational identities and brokering member identifications of the Yelp Elite Squad', *Management Communication Quarterly*, vol. 29, no. 4, pp. 616–641.

Bailey, A, Giangola, L & Boykoff, M T 2014, 'How grammatical choice shapes media representations of climate (un)certainty', *Environmental Communication: A Journal of Nature and Culture*, vol. 8, no. 2, pp. 197–215.

Boyd, J & Waymer, D 2011, 'Organisational rhetoric: A subject of interest(s)', *Management Communication Quarterly*, 25, pp. 474–493.

Brady, J 2014 (August 1), 'Tensions stir at EPA hearings on new emission rules', viewed August 1, 2014, www.npr.org/2014/08/01/336953717/tensions-stir-at-epa-hea rings-on-new-emission-rules?ft=1&f=3.

Brulle, R J 2010, 'From environmental campaigns to advancing the public dialog: Environmental communication for civic engagement', *Environmental Communication: A Journal of Nature and Culture*, vol. 4, no. 1, pp. 82–98.

Buber, M 1965, *Between Man and Man* (R G Smith, Trans.), Macmillan, New York.

Burke, K 1937/1968, *Counter-statement*, University of California Press, Berkeley, CA.

Burke, K 1939 (January 11), 'George Herbert Mead', *New Republic*, 97, pp. 292–293.

Burke, K 1950/1969, *A Rhetoric of Motives*, University of California Press, Berkeley, CA.

Burke, K 1965, *Permanence and Change* (2nd edn), Bobbs-Merrill, Indianapolis, IN.

Burke, K 1968, *Language as Symbolic Form*, University of California Press, Berkeley, CA.

Center for Media and Democracy n.d., 'Exxon Mobil SourceWatch', viewed August 26, 2014, www.sourcewatch.org/index.php/Exxon_Mobil.

Cheney, G 1992, 'The corporate person (re)presents itself'. In E L Toth & R L Heath (eds), *Rhetorical and Critical Approaches to Public Relations*, Lawrence Erlbaum Associates, Hillsdale, NJ, pp. 165–183.

Christensen, L T & Cornelissen, J P 2011. 'Bridging corporate and organisational communication', *Management Communication Quarterly*, vol. 25, no. 3, pp. 383–414.

Clegg, S R, Courpasson, D & Phillips, N 2006. *Power and Organisations*, Sage, Thousand Oaks, CA.

Coll, S 2012 (October 23), 'How Exxon shaped the climate debate', *PBS Frontline*, Retrieved from www.pbs.org/wgbh/pages/frontline/environment/climate-of-doubt/ste ve-coll-how-exxon-shaped-the-climate-debate/.

DeWeese, T 2013 (July 9), 'Exxon funding? Nope, never got the check!' *New American*, www.thenewamerican.com/reviews/opinion/item/15938-exxon-funding-nope-never-g ot-the-check.

Douglas, M 2001, 'Dealing with uncertainty', *Ethical Perspectives*, vol. 8, no. 3, pp. 145–155.

Fisher, W 1985, 'The narrative paradigm: An elaboration', *Communication Monographs*, vol. 52, no. 4, pp. 347–367.

Fisher, W R 1987, *Human Communication as Narration: Toward a Philosophy of Reason, Value, and Action*, University of South Carolina Press, Columbia.

Frandsen, F & Johansen, W 2013, 'Neo-institutional theory'. In R L Heath (ed.), *Encyclopedia of Public Relations*, 2nd edn, Sage, Thousand Oaks, CA, pp. 601–603,

Golant, B D & Sillince, J A A 2007, 'The constitution of organisational legitimacy: A narrative perspective', *Organisation Studies*, vol. 28, no. 8, pp. 1149–1167.

Hallahan, K 1999, 'Seven models of framing: Implications for public relations', *Journal of Public Relations Research*, vol. 11, no. 3, pp. 205–242.

Hamilton, J D 2003, 'Exploring technical and cultural appeals in strategic risk communication: The Fernald radium case', *Risk Analysis*, 23, pp. 291–302.

Hardy, C & Clegg, S R 2006, 'Some dare call it power'. In S R Clegg, C Hardy, T B Lawrence & W R Nord (eds), *The SAGE Handbook of Organisational Studies*, 2nd edn, Sage, London.

Harris, J D, Johnson, S C & Souder, D 2013. 'Model-theoretic knowledge accumulation: The case of agency theory and incentive alignment', *Academy of Management Review*, vol. 38, no. 3, pp. 442–454.

Heath, R L 1986, *Realism and Relativism: A Perspective of Kenneth Burke*, Mercer University Press, Macon, GA.

Heath, R L 1994, *Management of Corporate Communication: From Interpersonal Contexts to External Affairs*, Lawrence Erlbaum Associates, Hillsdale, NJ.

Heath, R L 2011. 'External organisational rhetoric: Bridging management and sociopolitical discourse', *Management Communication Quarterly*, vol. 25, no. 3, pp. 415–435.

Heath, R L & McComas, K 2015, 'Interest, interest, whose interest is at risk? Risk governance, issues management, and the fully functioning society'. In U F Paleo (ed.), *Risk Governance: The Articulation of Hazard, Politics, and Ecology*, Springer, Dordrecht, Netherlands, pp. 117–133.

Heath, R L, Palenchar, M J, McComas, K & Prouthau, S 2012, 'Risk management and communication: Pressures and conflicts of a stakeholder approach to corporate social responsibility'. In A Lindgreen, P Kotler, F Maon & J Vanhamme (eds), *A Stakeholder Approach to Corporate Social Responsibility: Pressures, Conflicts, Reconciliation*, Gower Publishing Limited, England, pp. 121–140.

Hill, J W 1958, *Corporate Public Relations: Arm of Modern Management*, Harper & Brothers Publishers, New York.

Hill, J W 1963, *The Making of a Public Relations Man*, David McKay Company, Inc., New York.

Ihlen, O 2009, 'Business and climate change: The climate response of the world's biggest corporations', *Environmental Communication: A Journal of Nature and Culture*, vol. 3, no. 2, pp. 244–262.

Irwin, A 2009, 'Moving forwards or moving in circles? Science communication and scientific governance in an age of innovation'. In R Holliman, E Whitelegg, E Scanlon, S Smidt, & J Thomas (eds), *Investigating Science Communication in the Information Age: Implications for Public Engagement and Popular Media*. Oxford University Press, Oxford, pp. 3–17,

Jaspal, R, Nerlich, B & Cinnirella, M 2014, 'Human responses to climate change: Social representation, identity and socio-psychological action', *Environmental Communication: A Journal of Nature and Culture*, vol. 8, no. 1, pp. 110–130.

Jensen, P R & Meisenbach, R J 2015, 'Alternative organising and (in)visibility: Managing tensions of transparency and autonomy in a nonprofit organisation', *Management Communication Quarterly*, vol. 29, no. 4, pp. 564–589.

Jian, G 2007, 'Unpacking unintended consequences in planned organisational change', *Management Communication Quarterly*, vol. 21, no. 1, pp. 5–28.

Kaiser, D & Wasserman, L. (2016, December 26), 'The Rockefeller Family Fund takes on ExxonMobil', *The New York Review of Books*, viewed 16 August 2017, www.nybooks.com/articles/2016/12/22/rockefeller-family-fund-takes-on-exxon-mobil/.

Kinsella, W J 1999, 'Discourse, power, and knowledge in the management of 'big science': The production of consensus in a nuclear fusion research laboratory', *Management Communication Quarterly*, vol. 13, no. 2, pp. 171–208.

Krippendorff, K 1999, 'Beyond coherence', *Management Communication Quarterly*, vol. 13, no. 1, pp. 135–145.

Lakoff, G 2010, 'Why it matters how we frame the environment', *Environmental Communication: A Journal of Nature and Culture*, vol. 4, no. 1, pp. 70–81.

Lock, I, Seele, P & Heath, R L 2016. 'Where grass has no roots: The concept of 'shared strategic communication' as an answer to unethical astroturf lobbying', *International Journal of Strategic Communication*, vol. 10, no. 2, pp. 87–100.

Lovell, B 2010, *Challenged by Carbon: The Oil Industry and Climate Change*, Cambridge University Press, Cambridge.

Maille, M-E & Saint-Charles, J 2014, 'Fuelling an environmental conflict through information diffusion strategies', *Environmental Communication: A Journal of Nature and Culture*, vol. 8, no. 3, pp. 305–325.

Masri, A 2015 (July 8), 'Newly leaked email reveals Exxon knowingly lied about climate change', *Reverb Press*, viewed 16 August 2017, http://reverbpress.com/business/newly-leaked-email-reveals-exxon-knowingly-lied-climate-change/.

Mathew, J 2015 (July 9), 'ExxonMobil funded naysayers for decades despite knowing about climate change', *International Business Times*, viewed 16 August 2017, www.ibtimes.co.uk/email-about-exxonmobil-reveals-how-energy-companies-disregard-climate-change-pursuit-profits-1510033.

Mead, G H 1934, *Mind, Self, and Society*, University of Chicago Press, Chicago, IL.

Michaelson, J 2012 (October 17), 'The vast right-wing conspiracy to lie about climate change has worked', *The Daily Beast*, www.thedailybeast.com/articles/2012/10/17/the-vast-right-wing-conspiracy-to-lie-about-climate-change-has-worked.html.

Mitchell, R K, Agle, B R & Wood, D J 1997, 'Toward a theory of stakeholder identification and salience: Defining the principle of who and what really counts', *Academy of Management Review*, vol. 22, no. 4, pp. 853–886.

Motion, J & Leitch, S 2007, 'A toolbox for public relations: The oeuvre of Michel Foucault', *Public Relations Review*, vol. 33, no. 3, pp. 263–268.

Mumby, D K 2005, 'Theorizing resistance in organisation studies: A dialectical approach', *Management Communication Quarterly*, vol. 19, no. 1, pp. 19–44.

Nyberg, D, Spicer, A & Wright, C 2013, 'Incorporating citizens: Corporate political engagement with climate change in Australia', *Organisation*, vol. 20, no. 3, pp. 433–453.

Owen, J & Bignell, P 2010 (February 7), 'Think-tanks take oil money and use it to fund climate deniers', *The Independent*, viewed 27 August 2014, www.independent.co.uk/environment/climate-change/thinktanks-take-oil-money-and-use-it-to-fund-climate-deniers-1891747.html.

People for the American Way n.d., 'The "green dragon" slayers: How the religious right and the corporate right are joining forces to fight environmental protection', viewed 25 August 2014, www.pfaw.org/rww-in-focus/the-green-dragon-slayers-how-the-religious-right-and-the-corporate-right-are-joining-fo.

Pepermans, Y & Maeseele, P 2014, 'Democratic debate and mediated discourse on climate change: From consensus to de/politicization', *Environmental Communication: A Journal of Nature and Culture*, vol. 8, no. 2, pp. 216–232.

Peterson, M N, Peterson, M J & Peterson, T R 2007, 'Environmental communication: Why this crisis discipline should facilitate environmental democracy', *Environmental Communication: A Journal of Nature and Culture*, vol. 1, no. 1, pp. 74–86.

PR Newswire 2014 (March 31), 'Shareholders: ExxonMobil takes crucial step of acknowledging carbon asset risk', viewed 25 August 2014, www.prnewswire.com/news-releases/shareholders-exxonmobil-takes-crucial-step-of-acknowledging-carbon-asset-risk–but-more-is-needed-253279031.html.

Rowell, A 2014, (April 14). 'Exxon's 25 year 'drop dead' denial campaign', *Oil Change International*, http://priceofoil.org/2014/04/14/exxons-25-year-drop-dead-denial-campaign/.

Schoeneborn, D & Scherer, A G 2012, 'Clandestine organisations, Al Qaeda, and the paradox of (in)visibility: A response to Stohl and Stohl', *Organisation Studies*, vol. 33, no. 7, pp. 963–971.

Scott, C R 2013, *Anonymous Agencies, Backstreet Businesses, and Covert Collectives: Rethinking Organisations in the 21st Century*, Stanford University Press, Stanford, CA.

Scott, C R 2015, 'Bringing hidden organisations out of the shadows: Introduction to the special issue', *Management Communication Quarterly*, vol. 29, no. 4, pp. 503–511.

Sillince, J A A & Mueller, F 2007, 'Switching strategic perspective: The reframing of accounts of responsibility', *Organisation Studies*, vol. 28, no. 2, pp. 155–176.

Simmons, M W 2007, *Participation and Power: Civic Discourse in Environmental Policy Decisions*, SUNY Press, Albany, NY.

Smith, M F & Ferguson, D P 2013, '"Fracking democracy": Issue management and locus of policy decision-making in the Marcellus Shale gas drilling debate', *Public Relations Review*, vol. 39, no. 4, pp. 377–386.

Sommerfeldt, E J 2013, 'The activity of social capital: Public relations in the public sphere, civil society, and democracy', *Public Relations Review*, vol. 39, no. 4, pp. 280–289.

Spoel, P & Den Hoed, R C 2014, 'Places and people: Rhetorical constructions of 'community' in a Canadian environmental risk assessment', *Environmental Communication: A Journal of Nature and Culture*, vol. 8, no. 2, pp. 267–285.

Stohl, C & Stohl, M 2011, 'Secret agencies: The communicative constitution of a clandestine organisation', *Organisation Studies*, vol. 32, no. 9, pp. 1197–1215.

Stone, D 2012, *Policy Paradox: The Art of Political Decision Making* 3rd edn, Norton, New York.

Suddaby, R & Greenwood, R. 2005, 'Rhetorical strategies of legitimacy', *Administrative Science Quarterly*, vol. 50, no. 1, pp. 35–67.

Union of Concerned Scientists 2015, 'The climate deception dossiers: Internal fossil fuel industry memos reveal decades of corporate disinformation'. Retrieved from www.ucsusa.org/sites/default/files/attach/2015/07/The-Climate-Deception-Dossiers.pdf.

VanSlette, S H & Boyd, J 2011, 'Lawbreaking jokers: Tricksters using outlaw discourse', *Communication Quarterly*, vol. 59, no. 5 pp. 591–602.

Walker, G B 2007, 'Public participation as participatory communication in environmental policy decision-making: From concepts to structured conversations', *Environmental Communication: A Journal of Nature and Culture*, vol. 1, no. 1, pp. 99–110.

Waymer, D 2013, 'Democracy and government public relations: Expanding the scope of 'relationship' in public relations research', *Public Relations Review*, vol. 39, no. 4, pp. 320–331.

'Why evolution is true' 2014, viewed 1 August, http://whyevolutionistrue.wordpress.com/2014/07/30/alabama-officials-god-created-coal.

Wittneben, B B, Okereke, C, Banerjee, S B & Levy, D L 2012, 'Climate change and the emergence of new organisational landscapes', *Organisation Studies*, vol. 33, no. 11, pp. 1431–1450.

Wright, C & Nyberg, D 2014, 'Creative self-destruction: Corporate responses to climate change as political myths', *Environmental Politics*, vol. 23, no. 2, pp. 205–223.

Wynne, B 2002, 'Risk and environment as legitimacy discourses of technology: Reflexivity inside out?' *Current Sociology*, vol. 50, no. 3, pp. 459–477.

3 Communicating public engagement, public interest and participation

Culturally centring community voices

Mohan J. Dutta

Introduction

In the backdrop of growing global distrust for the dominant structures of global organising that consolidate power and wealth in the hands of private transnational capital, public engagement, organisational listening, community dialogue and community participation have trended as pivots in *new* public relations theory and practice, positioned as strategic responses of the owners of private capital to public disenchantment with the deleterious effects of neoliberal[1] policies (Dutta 2015). These private sector-led initiatives of trust building are rhetorically positioned as avenues for democratic engagement and listening that serve the public interest (Johnston 2017) in academic and industry discussions of corporate social responsibility (CSR), strategic issues management, community relations, public engagement, organisational listening, and participatory crisis communication (Christensen et al. 2013; Johnston 2014; Heath & Palenchar 2009; Macnamara 2016; Valentini et al. 2012). Engagement, reflecting 'communication as a process of meaning-making between organisations and stakeholders' (Johnston 2014, p. 382), is positioned as an organisation-led framework for public participation, communicatively articulated as an avenue for building democracy and serving public interest (Macnamara 2016). This shift toward engagement, heralded as a paradigm shift for public relations in the 21st century (Men & Tsai 2013a, 2013b, 2014), I argue, is the new tool for reproducing neoliberal hegemony, serving the interests of private transnational corporations by co-opting public participation through the framing of such participation within the dominant logics of private capital and by securing the hegemony of private control over public interests (Dutta 2015). Through strategies of 'communicative inversion', the 'deployment of communication to circulate interpretations that are reversals of material manifestations' (Dutta 2015, p. 12), private capital increasingly co-opts public participation in the ambits of neoliberal hegemony, framing as public interest the agendas of private transnational capital. Against this backdrop, I draw on the tenets of the culture-centred approach (CCA) to extend Johnston's (2016, p. 104) articulation of 'public interest public relations' as anchored in listening to the voices of the margins produced by neoliberal capitalism.

As Pieczka (2018) outlines, public engagement is deployed both by private for-profit organisations as well as by public institutions such as governments or scientific institutions. The neoliberal transformation of global governmentality has, on one hand, increasingly privatised public spaces for engagement and, on the other hand, co-opted public institutions of engagement to serve private agendas (Dutta 2013). Private-led public engagement is a powerful instrument of control and manipulation that serves private interests communicatively inverted as public interests. These are seen to represent the common good, as beneficial to society, leveraging community resources and the interactivity of new media as tools for co-opting public participation to address the declining trends in public trust to serve organisational goals (the industry has been led here by the ongoing Edelman Trust Barometer and Edelman Engagement Reports that were initiated against the backdrop of the global financial crisis). By creating avenues for the public to participate within organisationally controlled, privately organised structures of participation, public engagement serves as a safety valve that protects organisational interests, potentially diffusing crises and minimising public resistance (Sashi 2012), promoting trust in private organisations, as well as minimising regulations directed at transnational corporations (TNCs) (Heath 2014). Community relations and CSR programmes, organisational dialogue sessions, and organisational listening exercises are presented as vehicles for public engagement, bringing the public into the folds of the organisation by turning them into stakeholders (Christensen et al. 2013; Roberts 2003; Sashi 2012). Of particular interest to organisations is public engagement with active and activist publics that threaten the organisational agenda (Dutta 2013; Heath & Palenchar 2009; Munshi & Kurian 2007) as well as customers who purchase the product or service being sold by the organisation (Men & Tsai 2013a, 2013b, 2014; Sashi 2012; Tsai & Men 2013). To the extent that these groups can be identified and defined as stakeholders, and be subsequently incorporated through programmes of public engagement, organisations are able to foster healthier climates of trust and public support for the organisation, further consolidating their privatised control over public lives.

In this chapter, I will critically examine the ways in which strategic tools of public engagement and public participation are co-opted into the agendas of private capitalist structures, serving private interests of profiteering. The language of serving public interest thus is deployed in such efforts of public relations as engagement toward serving the agendas of the status quo, consolidating power in the hands of elite local, national, regional and international actors in transnational networks of private profiteering. For instance, the narratives of serving democracy, development and public good are often paradoxically co-opted within efforts of community relations and CSR to strategically achieve goals of privatised organisational effectiveness. Increasingly, the role of the private sector has redefined public interest through the framework of public-private partnerships, communicatively inverting concepts such as democracy, participation, listening and voice within the architectures of neoliberal governmentality.

I will critically interrogate engagement, specifically exploring the ways in which communication is framed as public participation within top-down privatised systems, precisely to accomplish the strategic goals of mainstream private organisations. I will attend to the privatisation of engagement, co-optation of voice, consolidation of organisational reach, and erasure of opportunities of listening. Voices of subaltern communities and their public interests are systematically erased from the discursive space through the very performance of public engagement. Drawing then upon the CCA, I will articulate the role of infrastructures of listening, built outside and in resistance to capitalist organisational structures, as entry points for creating infrastructures of communication serving pluralistic public interests. Subaltern communities not represented in civil society represent a politics of resistance embedded in imaginations of radical democracies that hold states accountable to public interests as voiced by publics in local communities, and connected in national, regional and global networks of solidarity. Such ground-up participatory processes driving public interest advocacy, and rooted in logics of resistance to privatisation of public interests, offer an alternative imaginary for global networks that challenge public engagement as a neoliberal tool, grounded in alternative rationalities of community life.

Critically interrogating engagement

In this section, I will critically interrogate articulations of public engagement as a private resource (deployed predominantly by private organisations, but also increasingly by public organisations under public-private partnerships) (Hong & Yang 2011; Men & Tsai 2013a, 2013b; Tsai & Men 2013), attending to the interplays of power and control in shaping the discourses of public engagement (Munshi & Kurian 2007). Public engagement as a neoliberal tool incorporates public participation within the ambits of private organisations. Whose agendas are served by public engagement? Who initiates public engagement? Who establishes the terms of public engagement? In asking these three questions about the ownership, motives and processes of public engagement, I will argue that to the extent public engagement is situated within the ambits of private capital, initiated, conceptualised, designed, implemented and evaluated by private organisations, public engagement communicatively inverts the rhetoric of serving public interest to privatise these interests as profitable resources. More specifically, I will attend to the interplays of power and control, co-optation, co-branding and erasure constituted in the ambits of organisation-led public engagement.

Power, control, and communicative inversion

At the heart of theorising the 'public' in public relations is the framing of the public from the standpoint of private interests, defined as stakeholder (Pieczka 2018). Public engagement, interchangeably depicted as stakeholder engagement in the ambits of private organisations, reproduces this logic by seeing the public from the vantage of private organisational interest, and constructing public engagement as management of publics to drive organisational goals of profiteering. Tools of engagement, constituted within private logics, are driven by the profit-seeking goals of capital. For instance, in offering a framework of organisational listening, Macnamara (2016) points to the benefits of such listening to the organisational bottom line, in a section titled 'The bottom line of listening'. 'A number of management studies and independent academic studies show that two-way communication including listening leading to dialogue and engagement provides a number of bottom line outcomes for organisations' (Macnamara 2016, p. 308). He then goes on to list these outcomes, including improving employee performance, increasing productivity, reducing disputes, avoiding crises, improving customer satisfaction, and ultimately contributing to greater organisational profiteering and achieving sustainable growth. To the extent the agendas of public engagement are located within the ambits of private transnational capital, publics are constructed within the hegemonic framework of increasing organisational profits.

Through the technique of communicative inversion (see Dutta 2016), Macnamara's articulations of organisational listening as social equity and as counter to neoliberalism serve as instrumentalist tools of neoliberalism, ultimately constituted within the fabric of the organisational bottom line. Public engagement serves the functions of asserting the control of neoliberal hegemony while giving the performance of public participation for public good. The notion of engagement as an alternative to neoliberalism is the very conduit for reproducing neoliberal control by co-opting participation into the organisational bottom line, upholding the growth-driven logic of neoliberalism. Similarly, in practice-based discourses on engagement, such as the Edelman-led engagement initiatives that serve as exemplars of public engagement in public relations, public engagement is positioned as the solution to the trust deficit brought on by the financial crisis of 2008 and the rising global inequities in distribution of wealth. On the Edelman website that offers thought leadership on public engagement, the democratic and decentralisation function of public engagement is exemplified by the 'MyStarbucksIdea.Force.com site that solicits new product ideas from the crowd, reinforcing the company's relationship with its customers while the company listens and learns' (www.edelman.com/p/6-a-m/public-engagement/), depicting the theorisation of engagement within the private agendas of profiteering. Moreover, the decline in public trust is framed as a problem that necessitates private capital to deploy strategic tools of public engagement. Inherent in the notion of public engagement is the goal of increasing public trust in private organisations through strategic communication, thus implicitly contributing to the privatised bottom line of the organisation, reproducing the global control of neoliberal hegemony and co-opting both public resistance and support to the privatisation of public life. To the extent that public engagement is constituted within the hegemonic logics of private capital, such engagement colonises the possibilities of public participation, controlling democratic possibilities within the power structures and manipulative communication processes of transnational capitalism.

Similarly, in the academic literature responding to the emerging problems of public relations practice in a broader climate of trust deficit, engagement is tied to notions of interactivity, conceptualised, measured and implemented in web-based and social media-driven public relations practices, visualised as tools for improving organisational profit, growth and effectiveness (Men & Tsai 2014; Tsai & Men 2013). What drives engagement is the organisational logic of reproducing control amid large-scale public resistance to organisational processes of extending control. Organisational power and control dictate the nature of publics, the definition of publics, and the conceptualisation of public engagement, thus fundamentally threatening the possibilities for democratic public participation.

Public possibilities are framed within the narrow ambits of participation that serve organisational agendas in neoliberal capitalism (Dutta 2015; Munshi & Kurian 2007). Intrinsic then to the concept of engagement is the participation of stakeholders in organisational processes; the very framework of defining stakeholders co-opts publics into groups of strategic interest to the organisation (Dutta & Dutta 2013). Key stakeholders are identified and their needs are identified in order to serve the agendas of the organisation, participation being framed at this intersection of organisational needs and stakeholder needs. The overarching narrative of 'win-win' situations produced by participation obfuscates the materiality of participatory processes that are framed within the agendas of dominant organisations. The key element of public engagement as a strategic move is the deployment of communication to frame organisational needs as stakeholder needs, ultimately serving as a tool for reproducing the organisational agenda. To what extent is engagement an avenue for co-opting various public groups, and especially the activated and activist public groups that are likely to disrupt the strategic goals and functions of the organisation? Critical interrogation of public engagement programmes depict the ways in which processes and frameworks of public engagement are developed within the structures of dominant organisations. As a form of communicative inversion, public engagement positions itself as building democracy while it materially co-opts democratic participation within the organising structures of dominant state, civil society and private actors. Particularly salient here is the role of civil society as key players in consolidating participation into the structures of neoliberal hegemony (Dutta 2011, 2015).

Power is configured within dominant neoliberal organisations and within the pre-configured agendas of organisations, reflected in the community-directed activities that are deployed by these dominant organisations to achieve pre-configured strategic organisational goals. The community and its participation therefore get situated within the organisational logic and within the ambit of organisational agendas. The framing of the community within the organisational logic is intrinsically tied to the co-optation of the community to achieve organisational goals. Within the framework of globalisation processes, as TNCs work on projects that threaten to displace communities from their land and amid large-scale protests against displacement across communities globally, community engagement emerges as a strategy for carrying out the organisational agenda and for co-opting the possibilities of democratic resistance through a wide array of organisational activities framed under public engagement (Das & Padel 2010; Dutta 2014a, 2014b).

Similarly, in the realm of social media, public engagement is the tool for disseminating the organisational agenda among key stakeholders (Men & Tsai 2014). For instance, Men and Tsai (2014, p. 429) report that 'respondents who are more deeply engaged with corporate SNS [social networking site] pages tended to be more trusting of, more satisfied with, and more committed to the organisation'. Organisations referring to engagement often consider it as a form of participatory process where the goal of participation is to align the opinions and desires of target publics with the agendas and products of organisations. Trust with and commitment to the organisation thus are products of engagement. Measured in the form of items such as 'reading company posts, user comments or product reviews', 'engaging in conversations by commenting or asking and answering questions', and 'uploading product-related pictures' (Men & Tsai 2014, p. 424), engagement is constituted in the ambits of organisation-public relationships. Within social media scholars operationalise engagement from passive forms of message consumption to active forms of two-way conversation and participation (Men & Tsai 2013a, 2013b; Tsai & Men 2013). Engagement commoditises participation within the organisational agenda, seeking to tie in stakeholder responses to organisational goals. In the climate of negative public opinion and corresponding threats to trust, engagement can emerge as a strategy for co-opting alternative understandings within the organisational agenda. In this sense, participation framed within the lens of engagement continues to work toward serving organisational agendas, often providing alternative scripts in order to secure public trust in the organisation.

Consolidating organisational reach

To the extent that public engagement originates from within dominant social, cultural, political and economic organisations, the rules of engagement are designed to increase and consolidate the organisational reach. Public engagement is a tool that enhances the reach of the organisation within the community (Bruce & Brereton 2005; Brereton 2002). Through community engagement activities, the organisation discovers new markets and new strategies for penetrating these markets. The definition of stakeholder groups is constituted under organisational interests, and public interest is defined as the site for organisational intervention. For instance, in expanding its mining operations in Niyamgiri hills in Odisha that threaten to displace the indigenous community of the *Dongria Kondh*, the mining multinational Vedanta uses public engagement to consolidate its reach in the community (Das & Padel 2012). The framing of the community of the *Dongria Kondh* as backward and in need of development becomes the public rationality for pushing mining-as-development, thus consolidating the reach of Vedanta into the community and enabling its profitable business of mining extraction (Dutta 2015a, 2015b). The communicative inversion of mining as development, and hence in the public interest, obfuscates the life- and community-threatening nature of mining. Similarly, the poverty reduction strategy papers of the World Bank consolidate the reach of the neoliberal ideology of the Bank through the articulation of community participatory processes as avenues of decision making, pushing the top-down agendas of the Bank through tools of public participation (Dutta & Rastogi 2016). Along similar lines, the World Bank's citizen report cards use tools of public participation such as citizen reports (used as an example of organisational listening by Macnamara 2016, p. 287) to consolidate the reach of the Bank's neoliberal ideology into communities, and framing through communicative inversion the Bank's top-down mechanisms of neoliberal reforms as democratic.

Therefore, those sectors of the community get configured into the organisational mapping process as stakeholders that offer meaningful frames in relationship to organisational objectives. It is also through community engagement that organisations discover new sources of raw materials that may then feed into processes of extraction and production as well as smooth relationships with the community (Bruce & Brereton 2005; Brereton 2002; Das & Padel 2012). Consider, for instance, the following depiction of community engagement offered by Harvey and Brereton (2005, p. 3), capturing the experience of the Australian mining corporation Rio Tinto Australia:

> Within the minerals industry, a key driver for companies to improve their community engagement practices has been the desire to reduce the community risks associated with current and planned operations and smooth the path for obtaining access to new resources (Humphrey 2000, 2001; Brereton 2002).

They note how this is often expressed in terms that facilitate and protect the company, and industry more generally, and their social and legal 'licence to operate'. In recent years, the time taken to plan, finance, insure and regulate operations has increased substantially, 'particularly in the case of large-scale mines; in these circumstances, developing better community engagement processes has the potential to deliver real financial returns for a company' (Harvey & Brereton 2005, p. 3).

This illustrates how engagement is the gateway to new resources. Specifically articulated in the realm of mining here, the role of community engagement becomes one of extending and cultivating the reach of the extractive industry into target communities. In doing so, community engagement fosters positive relationships, minimises resistance from local community members, and secures the organisation's so-called licence to operate, thus ultimately contributing to profits for the mining corporation. For the minerals industry that specifically operates on the logic of profiting by displacement (of communities residing in areas where the extractive activities are carried out), community engagement is the mantra to securing access, communicatively inverted as serving the public interest.

Public engagement is a tool for discovering the community, for identifying the key facets of the community, and for bringing these facets into the fold of organisational knowledge and operations (Dutta 2014a, 2014b). Engagement activities provide the organisation with knowledge about the community and the best ways in which this knowledge can be exploited for organisational gains (see Humphreys 2000). In the realm of subaltern communities that are threatened by organisational operations such as in the cases of large-scale displacement caused by extractive activities, stakeholder engagement becomes a strategy for reaching the subaltern communities, for shifting local understandings in subaltern communities, and for minimising resistance to organisational operations (Das & Padel 2012; Dutta 2014a, 2014b). In such instances, engagement becomes a trope for the exploitation of subaltern communities, serving as an entryway into well-planned processes of community displacement. The knowledge gathered through engagement processes is critical to the development of organisational objectives and strategies, driving the strategic initiatives and tactical solutions that are devised by the organisation (see for instance Brereton 2002).

In other instances, organisations begin their initial exploration of community resources through processes of public engagement. Even as initial rounds of exploration are carried out in the community, engagement emerges as a strategy for generating community support, for reducing resistance to organisational operations, and for building a favourable climate of trust around the organisation (Bruce & Brereton 2005; Brereton 2002). Through the processes of early engagement, it is the organisational agendas that define the entry point into engagement. Engagement then also becomes a strategy for shifting attention away from the exploration activities and the gathering of knowledge that would then work toward serving organisational purposes. Even as such engagement activities with subaltern communities are defined in the language of win-win relationships, critical interrogations from activists depict that the terms of the win and what constitutes as winning are defined by the powerful organisation with resources and networks of influence (Das & Padel 2012).

Through the language of engagement, organisations deploy a variety of strategies that ultimately work toward displacing subaltern communities from their sources of livelihood (Dutta 2014a, 2014b, 2015). Engagement shaped in the form of community consultation processes often serves as an instrument for intelligence gathering in the community and for diffusing community resistance to organisational operations. Therefore, it is critical to interrogate who participates in the engagement processes and whose goals are served through these engagement processes.

Erasures in listening to the margins

Ironically, the framework of community engagement erases the voices of local communities through its performance of participation within neoliberal structures of profiteering (Das & Padel 2012; Dutta 2013). Participation is thus framed as a site for reproducing the agendas of powerful transnational capital. To the extent that organisations remain at the centre of listening processes framed as organisational listening, these processes perform communicative inversions, erasing the voices of the margins while giving the appearances of listening. At the same time, organisational listening gives voice to those positions at the margins that fit into its master rhetoric of free market-driven, growth-based development.

The forms of public participation configured within neoliberal structures require literacy, access to media, and spatial access to the sites of decision making located in the metropole, criteria that erase opportunities for recognition and representation of the subaltern (Dutta 2015). The literacy and language requirements of civil participation erase subaltern agency through their invitations to participation. Engagement itself, formulated within the ambits of the organisational agenda thus is a site of erasure, using its rules of participation to erase the opportunities for subaltern participation through lack of access to literacy, media and space. It is in this backdrop that culture-centred resistance is constituted on the very articulation of these inequities, attending to the erasures of opportunities for listening to the voices of subaltern communities. Listening to the voices of subaltern communities is conceptualised within the framework of structural transformation, interrogating the structures that constitute the very textures of marginalisation and marginalising processes.

Culture-centred approach to listening

Listening as an entry point to transformative change fosters community processes that examine opportunities for conversation, not simply in reformist initiatives that co-opt diverse voices in order to serve organisational agendas embedded within capitalist hegemony, but fundamentally in transformative communication processes that offer opportunities for transforming the overarching structures of neoliberalism as catalytic capitalism (Dutta 2004, 2013,

2014a, 2014b, 2015). Disrupting the very framework of organisational listening as the instrument of neoliberal reproduction, listening in the CCA seeks to build infrastructures for 'learning to learn from' the subaltern (Spivak 2004) that offer anchors for alternative rationalities that question the very organising logics of public relations and the capitalist organisations that public relations practices serve. Because organisational listening is the very tool for co-opting democratic possibilities, the CCA theorises listening as located outside the structures of neoliberal hegemony, instead offering a framework for crafting solidarities in partnership with subaltern communities.

Interrogating the location of listening exercises within organisational structures of capitalism, the CCA seeks to build infrastructures of listening in local communities, bypassing and inverting the platforms of global capitalism. Forms of public participation in community life emerge as sites of community collectivisation that challenge the mechanisms of exploitation written into the state-civil society-academe-market nexus. For instance, culturally centred participation of the *Dongria Kondh* in resisting the Vedanta mining in the Niyamgiri hills of Odisha in eastern India, fundamentally disrupt the public listening and engagement initiatives put forth by Vedanta and the state under the dominant structure of mining-as-development (Dutta 2015). Similarly, the participation of rural women farmers in Andhra Pradesh and Telengana in southern India under the collectives of the Deccan Development Society narrate an alternative rationality of development that inverts the neoliberal narrative of cash-based, commoditised, technology-driven, market-based agriculture as development (Thaker & Dutta 2016). Women farmers organise into cooperatives, or *Sanghams*, owning collectively an indigenous seed bank and a local community radio station that disrupt the hegemony of public-private-driven, Monsanto-owned Bt cotton, disseminated into the agricultural communities through private advertising and public engagement activities carried out by extension agents. Voicing agriculture as food-based agriculture embedded in indigenous knowledge systems, the women farmers offer an alternative to the neoliberal market-driven logic of agriculture. The participation of the women farmers from the margins in developing communicative processes is reflected in the performances, video narratives and community radio put together by the women farmers.

Structure therefore is explicitly theorised in the CCA, referring to forms of organising of resources and opportunities, with an emphasis on situating communicative processes in resistance to the hegemonic structures of capitalist organisations that extend the reach of neoliberalism. The rules, codes and processes of public participation thus emerge from within community life rather than from the ambits of dominant organisations. Listening, theorised at the interplays of culture, structure and agency, seeks to foster entry points for expressions of subaltern agency, drawing upon culturally circulated alternative rationalities, and challenging the organising logics of dominant structures (Dutta 2004, 2009). In fundamental opposition to the theorising of public participation, organisational listening and public engagement act as tools situated in the ambits of neoliberal hegemony, the conceptualising of community participation as radical democracy situated participation in resistance to the structures of neoliberalism (Thaker & Dutta 2016).

Listening, grounded in a commitment to subaltern and activist voices as anchors for inverting dominant structures, fosters openings for conversations that hold accountable transnational corporations, rendering transparent the financial and accounting practices of TNCs, and fostering opportunities for participation that closely examine the truth claims manufactured by neoliberal hegemony. The key element of listening is its anchoring in subaltern struggles for voice rather than in organisational co-optations of voice situated within the neoliberal commitments to effectiveness and efficiency. In this sense, rather than situating the agentic role of listening in the organisation as articulated in dominant frameworks of engagement and dialogue, listening radically situates agency in subaltern communities, situated in opposition to dominant structures of global organising (Dutta 2015). The recognition and representation of subaltern agency guides listening as 'solidarity with' communities that have been erased, bringing to national and global policy platforms co-constructed articulations in collaboration with subaltern communities. The theorisation of structure as an anchor to listening constructs listening as a process for imagining radical democracies in opposition to dominant structures of neoliberalism as opposed to organisational listening that serves neoliberal hegemony. Public interest communication, thus defined as direct public ownership of communicative structures and of sites of participation, emerges as a site for directly inverting the privatising logics of neoliberalism (Dutta 2013). Conceptualising capitalism as a mode of production as fundamentally unethical (Dutta 2011), listening in the CCA is conceptualised as activist politics that seeks to interrupt capitalist extraction (Dutta 2011; Ciszek 2015) and the oppressions perpetuated by dominant structures (Johnston 2015).

Listening and new ways of organising

Listening as an entry point to social change, fundamentally situated in resistance to neoliberal structures of organising as outside the structures of dominant state-private-civil society organisations, offers a framework for imagining new ways of organising and for conversing with new forms of creative organising processes that challenge the large-scale neoliberalisation of the globe (Dutta 2014a, 2014b). The academic work of listening is redefined outside and in resistance to the organisational structures of listening, framing the work of knowledge production as one of 'learning to learn from below' (Spivak 2004). Through acts of listening outside the mainstream sites of global-national-local organisations, spaces are fostered for 'rendering impure' the conceptual categories that constitute hegemonic organisational forms and the narratives of organisational and individual success that inundate these forms.

Take, for instance, the nature of organisational accounting practices in the context of the lessons learned in the financial crisis. Listening, as a strategy for engagement, fundamentally interrogates the nature of these practices, the location of power in the flow of organisational decision making, the information flows within and outside organisations, and the transparency of organisational information to the public. In this sense, listening is articulated in resistance to the status quo, outside the power configurations in dominant forms of organising and seeking actually to transform these configurations.

Through listening, the legitimacy of financial capital as a space for consolidating resources is closely interrogated. Given that the capital flows in financial structures operate on the basis of information inequities, listening works toward building information capacities and securing public access to information. The logics of the financial risk constructions, constructions of uncertainties in financialisation processes, and unequal information flows in communicative capitalism would be examined, suggesting alternative frameworks for understanding these flows and for constituting them through radical democratic participation. More fundamentally, listening would interrogate the very existence of the financial structures, the incentives built into these structures, and the meaningfulness of these structures within the contexts of economic growth and distribution of resources. In essence then, listening would foster the spaces for fundamentally examining the legitimacy of the structures under question. For instance, in the context of the anti-mining community resistance, community participation and solidarity with activist networks interrogate the financialisation of mining circulated through exchanges. Solidarity-based local-global partnerships such as the protests organised by Foil Vedanta in London at the annual shareholder meeting of Vedanta, or the campaign targeting financial investors such as the Norwegian Pension Fund, disrupt the global financial logics that feed mining development. Similarly, the occupation of homes by housing activists that collaborate in solidarity with vulnerable communities threatened to be displaced from their homes (because of exorbitant mortgage rates and instalments) disrupts the financial logics of the mortgage industry (Dutta 2013).

Similar to the information inequities in the financial sector, the profit flows in the extractive industries are driven by inequalities in opportunities for representation, recognition and participation. Listening in the context of engagement with subaltern communities threatened to be displaced by the extractive industries would fundamentally suggest that organisations in the extractive industries closely interrogate the very purposes they serve within these communities. The narrative of development would need to be closely examined, asking who really benefits from extractive projects that are couched under the façade of development. The rhetorical framework of public relations is interrogated by grounding the understandings of discourse in questions of materiality. Listening would also suggest the need for closely examining the profit motive as the defining parameter of modern extractive organisations. It would offer different entry points for conceptualising the role of communicators, shifting from one that serves organisational goals to one that serves the goals and interests of communities, and specifically of disenfranchised communities that are threatened by organisational practices. Solidarity reflects the partnership of communities with access to the structural frameworks of civil society and juridical formulations where the dominant market logics are reproduced with communities that are erased from these rationalities of the market through instruments of literacy and communication. For instance, the activist group Foil Vedanta is structured around the idea of listening to the voices of the *Dongria Kondh* who are threatened with displacement by the Bauxite mining operations in the Niyamgiri hills of Odisha. Here is how the organisation describes itself (www.foilvedanta.org): '*Foil Vedanta* targets the company in London where it is registered. It does this in solidarity and collaboration with people's movements fighting Vedanta at its various operations worldwide.' Note how in the framework of the organisation the sharing of solidarity as a strategy for connecting with people's movements against Vedanta across the globe is voiced. Solidarity with the erased margins of the neoliberal organising of development serves as a resource for fostering alternative ideas of development. Discourse constituted in relationship with materiality emerges in the voices of the grass roots. The structures of Foil Vedanta along with its location in London create strategic entry points to the dominant structures in London where Vedanta operates and secures its legitimacy. In August 2013, Foil Vedanta activists performed a carnival demonstration at the annual general meeting (AGM) of Vedanta in London, along with similar demonstrations in Johannesburg and New Delhi that interrogated the legitimacy of operations of Vedanta. Songs, street theatre and protest performances narrated the experiences of the *Dongria Kondh*. The voices of the *Dongria Kondh* were reflected in quotations painted on placards in the demonstrations outside the AGM site.

Listening and the role of the communicator

The established framework of communication management has envisioned the role of the communicator as serving the goals of the organisation. This narrowly restricts the role of communication within the dominant profit motive of the corporate organisation. However, as in the case of the extractive industries and in the domain of interrogating the environmental and human costs of these industries, a key role for communicators aligns with spaces of resistance in solidarity with disenfranchised communities, searching for and highlighting accurate information that is often covered up in dominant public relations practices situated within the organisational agenda. The shift in communicating with as opposed to communicating to is fundamental in envisioning an alternative role for communicators within the broader landscape of public relations. Here, the communicator, rather than working with the extractive industries or serving as a mouthpiece to whitewash the agendas of these extractive industries, fundamentally interrogates these practices of the extractive industries and seeks to resist them by working in solidarity with communities at the margins that are threatened by and displaced by organisational practices. Surma (2015, p. 401) proposes the concept of 'critical cosmopolitanism', as

> a reflexive endeavour ... to examine and disrupt the relationship between centre and periphery, privilege and vulnerability: to identify the relative social and temporal positions of interlocutors and those muted or silenced in the globalised context of individual, social and political interdependence.

Communication in the public interest therefore incorporates a commitment to a communicative practice of solidarity with subaltern communities, identifying communicative strategies so subaltern voices may be heard in spaces/sites of transnational capital.

The role of the communicator then shifts from working within the organisation to one that works in resistance to the organisation from outside, situated within the communities that are being disenfranchised, in gathering information grounded in experiences of the community and in listening to this information in national-global structures. The theorising of communication management moves beyond the taken-for-granted assumption about the organisation that is being served to actually working with communities that are being threatened or being displaced by organisational practices. Because transnational capitalism often secures its global reach by the very erasure of exploitative practices at the peripheries of global capital, it is salient to foreground the voices from these peripheries into the global centres of decision making, policy making and jurisdiction. For instance, Johnston (2015) discusses the role of public relations as communicative articulations of networks of activists, community groups, academics, media groups that challenge the government's communicative strategies of othering asylum seekers. The role of the communicator here is theorised in solidarity with subaltern communities, and in resistance to dominant organisational structures. Similarly, Munshi and Kurian (2015) redefine the role of public relations as representing the under-represented, drawing on the example of activist public relations of the Boycott, Divestment, and Sanctions (BDS) movement that draws attention to the neocolonial oppression of Israel in Gaza. Pal (2008) offers the example of public relations scholarship that seeks to co-create entry points for listening to subaltern communities of farmers who are threatened with displacement by state-led pro-capital initiatives of land acquisition for development. Kim (2008) offers the example of public relations as activism that works in solidarity with disenfranchised communities threatened by neoliberalism, and seeking to invert the dominant agendas of neoliberalism. In these examples, the role of the communicator is situated outside and in resistance to the structures of dominant organisations as opposed to the framework of organisational listening that takes for granted the hegemonic position of the organisation (Macnamara 2016).

Culturally centring listening decentres the knowledge claims circulated in and by dominant structures. Take, for instance, the large-scale environmental and human costs of extractive operations of Shell in Ogoniland, Nigeria (Dutta 2014a, 2014b). The dominant coalition of public relations works precisely within this structure to use the language of engagement as a whitewashing strategy, simultaneously working to erase the voices of local communities. Communication traditionally works to deflect attention from the environmental and human rights abuses and to manufacture interpretations that erase the environmental and human rights abuses (Dutta 2014a, 2014b). Engagement, originating from the status quo, is an attempt at folding in resistance to serve the agendas of the status quo. In contrast, listening grounds the act of communicating in the agency of the subaltern margins that have historically been erased precisely through violence and the simultaneous uses of forms of co-optation (Dutta 2014a, 2014b). Listening opens up the frame for communicators to work on issues of social justice in collaboration with local activists at the grass roots, bringing to the forefront the environmental and human rights abuses carried out by Shell, in opposing the whitewashing practices and dominant engagement practices of Shell that construct communication as a whitewashing strategy. Listening in this context foregrounds the role of Shell in militarising Ogoniland, in collaborating with the Nigerian government in applying force, and in documenting the large-scale depletion of the environment and local livelihoods through the operations of Shell. Listening opens up the possibilities for global circulation of stories of communities living in Ogoniland who have lost farmland, lost sources of food, and have to struggle every day with the impact of the environmental pollution. Everyday lived experiences of struggles with the livelihood and environmental impacts of community members in Ogoniland are synthesised with scientific data to offer entry points for structural transformation. In sum, a framework of listening grounded in the CCA foregrounds community voices, owned by community members, and in resistance to the dominant structures, thus putting a conceptualisation of public interest communication embedded in the struggles of the global margins.

Conclusion

In sum, in this chapter, I critically interrogate the role of engagement within the communication management literature as well as its location within the dominant agendas of communication management to serve organisational objectives, converting public sites into private opportunities. Public engagement, I argue, when situated in the realms of organisational goals, serve the agendas of neoliberal hegemony, turning communication into an instrument for public-private partnerships that serve the neocolonial agenda of transnational capital, creating new raw materials, sites of labour exploitation, and markets. Through strategies of communicative inversions, dominant structures in neoliberalism reinvent the concepts of participation, listening and voice precisely to perpetuate the agendas of the dominant status quo, serving and being served by state-capital-civil society-academe networks that constitute the neoliberal power structure. Publics are defined in the ambits of the organisational agenda, and are targeted to be managed through public engagement activities. Programmes of community dialogue and organisational listening perform the façade of dialogue and of resisting neoliberalism while fundamentally perpetuating the neoliberal status quo through individualisation, privatisation, and integration into the global free market.

To the extent, therefore, that public engagement is situated in the terrains of dominant public-private organisations, it serves to extend the reach of neoliberalism and co-opt democratic possibilities for participation within neoliberal agendas. Listening and voice transform community agency into marketing slogans, branding strategies and techniques of strategic management. The critical analysis offered in this chapter examines the co-optive purposes served by the narrative of bottom-up, grass-roots and participatory methods as conceived by TNCs, dominant nation-states, civil society, and dominant organisations such as the World Bank and International Monetary Fund. Drawing on the notion of public interest communication, the critique offers an opening for engaging with the CCA as a framework for listening to the voices of communities from the global margins and for centring the articulations of communities in the construction of radical democratic possibilities. As a method of public interest communication, listening in the ambits of the CCA is embedded in community ownership of the structures, forms and processes of participation and voice, organised collectively in resistance to the structures of state, civil society, market and academe that perpetuate neoliberal hegemony. Through listening, openings are fostered for alternative imaginations that are grounded in the participation of and collaboration among community members. The very definition of democracy is inverted, opening up discursive spaces to imaginations of radical democracies that co-create openings for other imaginations.

Note

1 Neoliberalism refers to a political economic framework of global organising, reflecting a complex web of political and economic thought that considers at its heart the principle of the free market as a driving mechanism for political, economic and social organising and, therefore, constructs governance in the image of the free market based on an individualist micro-economic model.

References

Amnesty International 2010, *Don't Mine Us Out of Existence: Bauxite Mine and Refinery Devastate Lives in India London*, Amnesty International.

Banerjee, S B 2008, 'Corporate social responsibility: The good, the bad, and the ugly', *Critical Sociology*, vol. 34, no. 1, pp. 51–79.

Basu, K & Palazo, G 2008, 'Corporate social responsibility: A process model of sense-making', *Academy of Management Review*, vol. 33, no. 1, pp. 122–136.

Brereton, D 2002, *Building the Business Case for Sustainable Development. Minerals Council of Australia 2002*, Sustainable Development Conference, Newcastle.

Bruce, H & Brereton, D 2005, *Emerging Models of Community Engagement in the Australian Minerals Industry*, Paper presented at the International Conference on Engaging Communities, August, Brisbane.

Campbell, J L 2007, 'Why should corporations behave in socially responsible ways? An institutional theory of corporate social responsibility', *Academy of Management Review*, vol. 32, no. 3, pp. 946–967.

Christensen, L, Morsing, M & Thyssen, O 2013, 'CSR as aspirational talk', *Organization*, vol. 20, no. 3, pp. 372–393.

Ciszek, E L 2015, 'Bridging the gap: Mapping the relationship between activism and public relations', *Public Relations Review*, vol. 41, no. 4, pp. 447–455.

Cloud, D 2007, 'Corporate social responsibility as oxymoron: Universalization and exploitation at Boeing', in S K May, G Cheney & J Roper (eds), *The Debate Over Corporate Social Responsibility*, Oxford University Press, New York, pp. 219–231.

Das, S & Padel, F 2010, 'Battles over bauxite in East India: The Khondalite mountains of Khondistan', viewed 20 March 2017, www.foilvedanta.org/articles/battles-o ver-bauxite-in-east-india-the-khondalite-mountains-of-khondistan/.

de Sousa Santos, B 2008, *Another Knowledge is Possible: Beyond Northern Epistemologies*, Verso, London.

Dutta, M J 2004, 'The unheard voices of Santalis: Communicating about health from the margins of India', *Communication Theory*, vol. 14, no. 3, pp. 237–263.

Dutta, M J 2005, 'Operation Iraqi Freedom: Mediated public sphere as a public relations tool', *Atlantic Journal of Communication*, vol. 13, no. 4, pp. 220–241.

Dutta, M 2009, 'Theorizing resistance: Applying Gayatri Chakravorty Spivak in public relations', in Ø Ihlen, B van Ruler & M Fredrikson, *Social Theory on Public Relations*, Routledge, New York, pp. 278–300.

Dutta, M 2011, *Communicating Social Change: Culture, Structure, Agency*, Routledge, New York.

Dutta, M 2013, *Voices of Resistance*, Purdue University Press, West Lafayette, IN.

Dutta, M J 2014a, 'A culture-centered approach to listening: Voices of social change', *International Journal of Listening*, vol. 28, no. 2, pp. 67–81.

Dutta, M J 2014b, 'Health activism as resistance: MOSOP as a site of culture-centered resistance in Niger Delta region of Nigeria', in D Kyun Kim, A Singhal & G L Kreps (eds), *Health Communication: Strategies for Developing Global Health Programs*, Peter Lang, New York, pp. 297–316.

Dutta, M J 2015, 'Decolonizing communication for social change: A culture-centered approach', *Communication Theory*, vol. 25, no. 2, pp. 123–143.

Dutta, M J 2016, *Neoliberal Health Organizing: Communication, Meaning, and Politics*, Routledge, New York.

Dutta, M J & Dutta, D 2013, 'Multinational going cultural: A postcolonial deconstruction of cultural intelligence', *Journal of International and Intercultural Communication*, vol. 6, no. 3, pp. 241–258.

Dutta, M J & Pal, M 2010, 'Dialog theory in marginalized settings: A subaltern studies approach', *Communication Theory*, vol. 20, no. 4, pp. 363–386.

Dutta, M & Pal, M 2011, 'Public relations in a global context: Postcolonial thoughts', in N Bardhan & K Weaver (eds), *Public Relations in Global Cultural Contexts*, Routledge, New York, pp. 195–225.

Dutta, M & Rastogi, R 2016, 'Deconstructing PRSP Measurement: Participation as Neoliberal Colonization', *Journal of Creative Communications*, vol. 11, no. 3, pp. 211–226.

Gershman, J & Irwin, A 2000, 'Getting a grip on the global economy', in J Y Kim, J V Millen, A Irwin & J Gershman (eds), *Dying for Growth: Global Inequality and the Health of the Poor*, Common Courage Press, Monroe, ME, pp. 11–43.

Godalof, I 1999, *Against Purity: Rethinking Identity with Indian and Western Feminisms*, Routledge, New York.

Harvey, D 2005, *A Brief History of Neoliberalism*, Oxford University Press, London.

Harvey, B & Brereton, D 2005, 'Emerging models of community engagement in the Australian minerals industry', in *International Conference on Engaging Communities*, Brisbane, August (Vol. 1).

Heath, R L & Palenchar, M J 2009, *Strategic Issues Management*, Sage, Thousand Oaks, CA.

Hong, S Y & Yang, S U 2011, 'Public engagement in supportive communication behaviors toward an organization: Effects of relational satisfaction and organizational reputation in public relations management', *Journal of Public Relations Research*, vol. 23, no. 2, pp. 191–217.

Hopwood, B, Mellor, M & O'Brian, G 2005, 'Sustainable development: Mapping different approaches', *Sustainable Development*, vol. 13, no. 1, pp. 38–52.

Humphreys, D 2000, 'A business case perspective on community relations in mining', *Resource Policy*, no. 26, pp. 127–131.

Johnston, J 2015, 'Public relations, the postcolonial other and the issue of asylum seekers', in D McKie, J L'Etang, N Snow & J Xiffra (eds), *The Routledge Handbook of Critical Public Relations*, Routledge, New York, pp. 130–141.

Johnston, J 2016, *Public Relations and the Public Interest*, Routledge, New York.

Johnston, J 2017, 'The public interest: A new way of thinking for public relations?' *Public Relations Inquiry*, vol. 6, no. 1, pp. 5–22.

Johnston, K A 2014, 'Public relations and engagement: theoretical imperatives of a multidimensional concept', *Journal of Public Relations Research*, vol. 26, no. 5, pp. 381–383.

Keck, M E & Sikkink, K 1998, *Activists Beyond Borders: Advocacy Networks in Transnational Politics*, Cornell University Press, Ithaca, NY.

Kemp, D 2004, *The Emerging Field of Community Relations: Profiling the Practitioner Perspective*', Paper presented at the Minerals Council of Australia Sustainable Development Conference 04, Melbourne.

Kim, I 2008, *Voices from the Margin: A Culture-centered Look at Public Relations of Resistance*, Unpublished doctoral dissertation, Purdue University, West Lafayette, IN.

Kruckeberg, D & Starck, K 1988, *Public Relations and Community: A Reconstructed Theory*, Prager, New York.

Lipari, L 2010, 'Listening, thinking, being', *Communication Theory*, vol. 20, no. 3, pp. 348–362.

Mackey, J & Sisodia, R 2014, *Conscious Capitalism, with a new preface by the authors: Liberating the heroic spirit of business*, Harvard Business Review Press, Cambridge, MA.

Macnamara, J 2016, *Organizational Listening: The Missing Essential in Public Communication*, Peter Lang, New York.

Mangold, W G & Faulds, D J 2009, 'Social media: The new hybrid element of the promotion mix', *Business Horizons*, vol. 52, no. 4, pp. 357–365.

Men, L R & Tsai, W H S 2013a, 'Beyond liking or following: Understanding public engagement on social networking sites in China', *Public Relations Review*, vol. 39, no. 1, pp. 13–22.

Men, L R & Tsai, W H S 2013b, 'Toward an integrated model of public engagement on corporate social networking sites: Antecedents, the process, and relational outcomes', *International Journal of Strategic Communication*, vol. 7, no. 4, pp. 257–273.

Men, L R & Tsai, W H S 2014, 'Perceptual, Attitudinal, and Behavioral Outcomes of Organization – Public Engagement on Corporate Social Networking Sites', *Journal of Public Relations Research*, vol. 26, no. 5, pp. 417–435.

Millen, J & Holtz, T 2000, 'Dying for growth, Part I: Transnational corporations and the health of the poor', in J Y Kim, J V Millen, A Irwin & J Gershman (eds), *Dying for Growth: Global Inequality and the Health of the Poor*, Common Courage Press, Monroe, ME, pp. 177–223.

Millen, J, Irwin, A & Kim, J 2000, 'Introduction: What is growing? Who is dying?', in J Y Kim, J V Millen, A Irwin & J Gershman (eds), *Dying for Growth: Global Inequality and the Health of the Poor*, Common Courage Press, Monroe, ME, pp. 3–10.

Minerals Council of Australia 2005, *Enduring Value: The Australian Minerals Industry Framework for Sustainable Development, Guidance for Implementation*, viewed 5 November 2017, www.minerals.org.au/file_upload/files/resources/enduring_value/EV_GuidanceForImplementation_July2005.pdf.

Ministerial Council on Mineral and Petroleum Resources 2004, *Draft Principles for Engagement with Communities and Stakeholders*.

Munshi, D & Kurian, P 2007, 'The case of the subaltern public: A postcolonial investigation of CSR's (o) missions', in S May, G Cheney & J Roper (eds), *The Debate Over Corporate Social Responsibility*, Oxford University Press, New York, pp. 438–447.

Munshi, D & Kurian, P 2015, 'Public relations and sustainable citizenship: Towards a goal of representing the unrepresented', in D McKie, J L'Etang, N Snow & J Xiffra (eds), *The Routledge Handbook of Critical Public Relations*, Routledge, New York, pp. 405–415.

Nish, S 2004, *Argyle Participation Agreement*. Unpublished correspondence November.

Padel, F & Das, S 2010. *Out of this Earth: East India Adivasis and the Aluminium Cartel*, Orient Blackswan, New Delhi.

Pal, M 2008, *Fighting from and for the Margin: Local Activism in the Realm of Global Politics*, Unpublished doctoral dissertation, Purdue University, West Lafayette, IN.

Pieczka, M 2018, 'Critical perspectives of engagement', in KA Johnston & M Taylor (eds), *Handbook of Communication Engagement*, Wiley, Chichester, pp. 549–568.

Pratt, C B 2008, 'Managing sustainable development in sub-Saharan Africa: A communication ethic for the global corporation', in K Sriramesh & D Vercic (eds), *The Global Public Relations Handbook: Theory, Research, and Practice*, Routledge, New York, pp. 843–860.

Rio Tinto, 'Communities policy', viewed 1 November 2017. www.riotinto.com/community/communities.aspx.

Rio Tinto, 'Communities standard 2004', Unpublished internal Rio Tinto document.

Roberts, J 2003, 'The manufacture of corporate social responsibility: Constructing corporate sensibility', *Organization*, vol. 10, no. 2, pp. 249–265.

Sashi, C M 2012, 'Customer engagement, buyer-seller relationships, and social media', *Management Decision*, vol. 50, no. 2, pp. 253–272.

Spivak, G C 2004, 'Righting Wrongs', *South Atlantic Quarterly*, vol. 103, nos. 2/3, pp. 523–581.

Surma, A 2015, 'Pushing boundaries: A critical cosmopolitan orientation to public relations', in *The Routledge Handbook of Critical Public Relations*, Routledge, New York, pp. 393–404.

Taylor, J 2004, *Aboriginal Population Profiles for Development Planning in the Northern East Kimberley*, CAEPR Monograph 23, Centre for Aboriginal Economic Policy Research, The Australian National University, Canberra.

Taylor, J & Bell, M 2001, *Implementing Regional Agreements Aboriginal Population Projections in Rio Tinto Mine Hinterlands: 1996–2016*, Unpublished CAEPR Report to Rio Tinto, Centre for Aboriginal Economic Policy Research, The Australian National University, Canberra.

Thaker, J & Dutta, M 2016, 'Millet in our own voices: A culturally-centred articulation of alternative development by DDS women farmers' sanghams', in *Globalisation and the Challenges of Development in Contemporary India*, Springer, Singapore, pp. 131–144.

Tsai, W H S & Men, L R 2013, 'Motivations and antecedents of consumer engagement with brand pages on social networking sites', *Journal of Interactive Advertising*, vol. 13, no. 2, pp. 76–87.

Valentini, C, Kruckeberg, D & Starck, K 2012, 'Public relations and community: A persistent covenant', *Public Relations Review*, vol. 38, no. 5, pp. 873–879.

Vedanta 2012, *The Lanjigarh Development Story: Vedanta Perspective*, Vedanta, London.

Wilce, R 2013, 'Corporate cash defeats GMO labeling in WA state preliminary results', *Public Relations Watch*, 6 November, viewed 20 March 2017, www.prwatch.org/news/2013/11/12295/corporate-cash-defeats-GMO-labeling-in-WA.

4 Climate change and the public interest
Science, legitimacy and diversity

Mhairi Aitken

Introduction

Climate change is a pervasive issue affecting almost all areas of policy either directly or indirectly. While the level and nature of response has been varied, around the world it is a major challenge affecting all nations. The global character and wide-reaching impacts of climate change have led to the establishment of a strong discourse presenting climate change as a global humanitarian crisis and one that must be addressed urgently as a matter of public interest. A climate politics has developed which, through science, media and policy institutions, has established climate change as the paramount environmental – and social – problem facing the world (Szerszynski & Urry 2010). However, as I will argue in this chapter, this discourse can have very negative and limiting effects on public engagement with climate change and the extent to which public interests are reflected and addressed in the ways that climate change is approached. Ultimately the dominant framing of climate change as an issue of universal public interest has had detrimental effects on the extent to which strategies for addressing climate change in fact reflect or serve public interests.

The chapter will begin by discussing the ways that climate change has been depoliticised and how a particular framing of climate change has come to dominate policy approaches and public discourses around climate change. While in some countries (notably the United States) climate change policy remains highly politicised, resulting in debate regarding the veracity of claims about the realities or causes of climate change, the concept itself is depoliticised as the nuances and complexities of what climate change means, how it is investigated and whose voices are heard in debates regarding approaches for addressing climate change are consistently overlooked.

It is therefore important to consider some of the political dimensions of climate change which are obscured by this restricted dominant framing. In particular, social or political factors influence scientific practices relating to climate change (as in all areas of science). The dominant framing of climate change tends to gloss over such dimensions presenting a positivist view of objectivity and neutrality in climate science. As the chapter will describe, this inaccurate and idealised vision of science is both unrealistic and harmful to public relationships with science. It also serves to close down debate and dissensus and marginalise non-expert voices. This has important implications for how mitigation and adaptation strategies are developed and implemented and leads to a dominance of modernist, technical policy responses while marginalising alternative approaches which challenge established systems and structures. This marginalisation of alternative voices and the preservation of an apparent consensus on what climate change means and how it should be approached is in fact detrimental for public interests. The chapter will illustrate this point through two examples. Firstly, it will discuss the ways that energy policies – particularly relating to the development of renewable energy – have been legitimised by reference to public interest arguments regarding climate change mitigation. This has been important for shaping how new energy technologies are developed and for restricting the ways that members of the public can engage in these processes. This is particularly evident in planning processes for proposed renewable energy developments where public interest justifications play an important role and limit the opportunities for expression of public opposition. The second example relates to the climate justice movement which has begun to receive increasing policy attention. Climate justice previously sat outside mainstream policy settings as a somewhat radical movement calling for 'System Change, Not Climate Change!'. The chapter will discuss its increasing influence and the greater policy attention it is receiving, and consider whether these are indicative of increased support for the transformational goals of the climate justice movement, or rather of the increased ambiguity in how climate justice is conceptualised and pursued. The increase in more pragmatic approaches to climate justice have resulted in greater influence but perhaps reduced the potential transformative impacts (Aitken et al. 2016a). Dominant approaches to climate change through maintaining a discourse based on public interest arguments have served to marginalise alternative approaches as well as alternative voices, and through doing so have restricted the range of policy responses considered for addressing climate change.

The chapter will then turn to consider how dialogic conceptions of the public interest might challenge dominant approaches to climate change and offer an alternative approach to understanding and addressing public interests relating to climate change.

The depoliticisation of climate change

Internationally there is growing consensus on the importance of taking action to mitigate climate change. Related policies are typically justified as being in 'the public interest'; however, this can conceal the range of interests and particular socio-political imaginaries shaping and restricting how climate change is framed and approached – or the ways in which the public interest is defined

(Aitken 2012; Swyngedouw 2010). This has implications for both the approaches and outcomes of climate change policies.

In a similar way to how sustainable development has previously been described as 'coloniz[ing] environmental policy by offering an objective from which one apparently could not wish to diverge' (Yearley 1996, p. 133), so the importance of mitigating climate change has become an aim which – in many countries around the world – policymakers cannot reasonably contest. The apparent consensus around climate change and the importance of reducing emissions combined with the ease by which dissenters can be discredited as climate sceptics, mean that policies consistently repeat the mantra of taking urgent action to address climate change. This mantra which (implicitly or explicitly) draws on notions of the public interest is used to justify a range of policies and actions in different areas. For example, in the United Kingdom climate change is connected to policies relating to transport, energy, health and business (Aitken 2012). Furthermore, it has been connected to controversial policy areas – such as nuclear energy (HM Government 2008) – and played a role in increasing support for previously unpopular policies. For example, Bickerstaff et al. (2008) have shown that framing nuclear energy in terms of emissions reduction and climate change mitigation (re-branding it as a 'low carbon technology') led to increased public support – or less public opposition – for the technology (although the result was described as a 'reluctant acceptance'). Thus, the public interest framing of climate change appears to hold considerable discursive power in giving legitimacy to a diverse range of policies.

Of course, this is not the same in all countries around the world. Indeed, the advent of the Trump administration in the United States has starkly exemplified the very political nature of climate change and considerable diversity of opinions regarding the reality, causes or significance of climate change. However, typically the debate in this regard relates to whether or not climate change is real, or whether or not the internationally agreed actions for addressing climate change are appropriate, rather than how climate change is framed and approached or how the public interest is defined. Climate change then remains depoliticised as a concept to be believed or denied with clear implications for policy and public responses. Questions regarding how climate change is understood, whose interests are influential in decision-making processes, or the many different ways that climate change does/will affect people around the world, remain unasked. Moreover, these questions remain just as unasked in countries where climate change mitigation is high on the agenda as they do in countries which are less clearly committed to this goal. Thus climate change as a concept is depoliticised even while internationally policies relating to this concept are highly politicised.

Despite a range of views expressed in relation to climate change and the inevitable uncertainties or ambiguities in climate science, a 'fragile consensus' has emerged both in relation to 'the "nature" of the problem and the arrays of managerial and institutional technologies to mitigate the most dramatic consequences' (Swyngedouw 2010, p. 215). This framing of climate change has inhibited public debate around the meanings of climate change. Where individuals challenge either climate science or policies relating to climate change they are often quickly branded a climate sceptic or denier, and individuals who are critical of technologies or policies justified in terms of climate change mitigation can receive hostile reactions (for example, see Nature 2010). This fragile consensus obscures the 'huge uncertainty as to the scale, impact and speed of future climate changes' (Szerszynski & Urry 2010, p. 2), and offers a much simplified representation of climate change and climate science. This

> produces a thoroughly depoliticized imaginary, one that does not revolve around choosing one trajectory rather than another, one that is not articulated with specific political programmes or socio-ecological project or revolutions.
>
> (Swyngedouw 2010, p. 219)

The hidden politics of climate change

Despite this depoliticised façade, climate change and climate science are highly political in a number of important respects. Firstly, political factors (as opposed to scientific breakthroughs) were influential in determining when climate change became a prioritised – and highly funded – topic of research (Hart & Victor 1993). Additionally, there is not simply one form of climate science providing unambiguous insights and understanding; rather there are multiple ways of investigating the climate or the role of greenhouse gases (GHG). Different scientific disciplines and methods compete for policy attention and funding, and political and social influences are inherent in decisions relating to which climate science gets funded, conducted and subsequently accorded policy attention (Hart & Victor 1993; Demeritt 2001). Additionally, the emergence of the Intergovernmental Panel on Climate Change (IPCC) as the key forum for mediating and assessing knowledge on climate change was itself a highly political occurrence (see Hulme & Mahoney 2010). Subsequently the IPCC has become a powerful body validating and prioritising certain knowledge claims over others (Hulme & Mahoney 2010).

Climate scientists do not operate in a vacuum, sealed off from social and political influences, but rather actively position and frame their work in particular ways so as to maximise its policy relevance (and/or secure funding). How research questions are framed and key concepts interpreted can reflect political, social or geographical positions and subsequently reinforce inequalities or policy biases (see Yearley 2005; Hulme 2009). The production of IPCC reports, for example, is not simply a process of reporting 'pure science' but rather is a political process prioritising particular forms and sources of knowledge claims (Hulme & Mahoney 2010).

Overlooking social and political factors within climate science presents an unrealistic picture of how the 'facts' have been constructed and simultaneously limits the extent to which non-experts can engage with the issue: 'The discourse on climate politics so far is an expert and elitist discourse in which peoples, societies, citizens, workers, voters and their interests, views and voices are very much neglected' (Beck 2010, pp. 254–255). This encourages members of the public to take a passive role, to

> sit back, and want to be told what they must do, rather than go out and learn as well as take their share of responsibility for what could have been presented as a more complex, multidimensional and inherently indeterminate set of human problems, which citizens and their representatives can and should help define.
>
> (Wynne 2010, p. 300)

Recognising the human and political nature of climate science should not be seen as a criticism of that enterprise or as a means of discrediting the scientific findings that are reported. Social, institutional and political factors enter into scientific practices and shape scientific understandings in all areas of science and at all stages of the research process (Irwin 2001). Latour and Woolgar (1979 [1986]) observed that whilst scientific practices are typically perceived to be well ordered and logical,

> [t]he elimination of alternative interpretations of scientific data and the rendering of these alternatives as less plausible is a central characteristic of scientific activity. Consequently, the practicing scientist is likely to be as much involved with the task of producing ordered and plausible accounts out of a mass of disordered observations as is the outside observer. [...] actual scientific practice entails the confrontation and negotiation of utter confusion.
>
> (Latour & Woolgar 1979 [1986], p. 36)

The traditional view of science suggests that science has authority because of its rigorous processes and methods; however, as Gieryn (1999, p. 27) contends, society cannot adequately understand what actually happens within science; instead: 'Epistemic authority is decided downstream from all that.' Gieryn (1999) argues that it is only after science leaves the laboratory and enters society in the form of claims to facts or knowledge or new innovations that it is given or denied credibility. It is not through the science itself, but rather the social or cultural positioning of science within society that science gains its authority and prominence. Thus, the achievements of science are social achievements – rather than direct results of 'objective' scientific practices. As Jasanoff (2003, p. 393) notes:

expertise is not merely something that is in the heads and hands of skilled persons, constituted through their deep familiarity with the problem in question, but rather [...] it is something acquired, and deployed, within particular historical, political, and cultural contexts. Expertise relevant to public decisions [...] responds to specific institutional imperatives that vary within and between nation states.

In 2009 the social dynamics of climate science were dramatically placed in the spotlight when emails from climate scientists working at the University of East Anglia were leaked. The resulting controversy was dubbed 'Climategate' and led to a brief period of intense public scrutiny and discussion of the human nature of scientific processes (see Hulme & Ravetz 2009). Much of this focused on a few emails which discussed 'a trick' to correct inaccurate data, and scientists' involvement in peer review of papers which contradicted their own findings or were critical of their work. This drew attention to the fallibility and imperfection of science and to the role of individual scientists in creating and presenting research findings. For individuals who were sceptical of climate science – or denied the existence of climate change – this scandal represented evidence of corruption in climate science and was said to demonstrate a conspiracy of scientists on climate change. However, the scandal can also be seen as an illustration of a widespread lack of understanding of the dynamics of scientific processes. The controversial behaviours illustrated through these emails reflected those previously described by Latour and Woolgar (1979 [1986]) and other scholars in the field of Science and Technology Studies (STS) as typical of scientific practice. Such factors are generally glossed over in policy and public discourses relating to climate change. As Stirling (2010, p. 1029) has noted, it is typically assumed that 'expert advice is [...] most useful to policy when it is presented as a single "definitive" interpretation'. Thus, expert committees are under pressure to reach consensus and to present unambiguous advice to policymakers. Policymakers, in turn, 'are encouraged to pursue (and claim) "science-based" decisions' (Stirling 2010, p. 1029) in such a way as to deny the existence of uncertainty, ambiguity or ignorance. Climate change is routinely presented as a scientific discovery – as something only comprehensible through scientific experimentation and analysis (Wynne 2010). This inaccurate representation of science and scientific processes can raise unrealistic expectations of the objectivity of science and of the definitiveness of scientific findings which can then leave science vulnerable to public outcries or disillusionment when inevitable imperfections or disagreements come to light (Salk 1979 [1986]). Additionally, placing science on a pedestal serves to limit the role of alternative knowledges in debates about scientific subject matter. If scientific knowledge is viewed as exceptional, other knowledges are positioned as less adequate or legitimate to engage in such debates. Therefore, non-experts are marginalised and the role of the public is restricted. Members of the public are thus largely excluded from debates around the meanings and implications of climate change and are instead positioned as passive observers or recipients – but not creators – of information about climate change.

Ecological modernisation: scientific construction of the public interest

Presenting a simplified picture of how science uncovers the apparent facts of climate change facilitates the fragile consensus on how to respond to these facts. The depoliticised discourse on climate change is suggestive of clearly defined mitigation strategies to address climate change and conceals the political nature of these strategies. The dominant policy approaches to addressing climate change reflect modernist and capitalist assumptions (Aitken 2012; Doyle & Chaturvedi 2010; Swyngedouw 2010; Szerszynski & Urry 2010). Whilst it can be contended that current levels of GHG emissions are a result of practices in highly industrialised countries and are connected to capitalist ways of life, 'the policy architecture around climate change insists that this "excessive" state is not inscribed in the functioning of the system itself, but is an aberration that can be "cured" by mobilizing the very inner dynamics and logic of the system (privatization of CO_2, commodification and market exchange via carbon and carbon-offset trading)' (Swyngedouw 2010, p. 223). As such the dominant policy framework around climate change stems from and perpetuates the cultural and economic position of highly industrialised countries (Doyle & Chaturvedi 2010). In doing so, it demonstrates a commitment to capitalism, economic growth and minimising disruption to industrialised economies (Aitken 2012). As Szerszynski and Urry (2010, p. 4) comment:

> Any description and prediction of climate change and its impacts is entangled with specific imaginaries of how society is, and how it ought to be; similarly even the most apparently technical of suggested responses will carry with it certain ideas of society.

This dominant approach to addressing climate change reflects the position of Ecological Modernisation (EM), which has been described as having come to dominate environmental policy debates since the 1980s (Barry & Paterson 2004; Hajer 1995; Mol & Spaargaren 2000). EM is, broadly speaking, a mechanism for challenging the premise underpinning more radical Green environmentalism that economic growth and environmental sustainability are conflicting goals (Barry & Paterson 2004; Mol & Spaargaren 2000). EM suggests that although modern institutions may need to adapt, they do not need to be radically transformed to address environmental challenges (Mol & Spaargaren 2000). From the perspective of industrialised economies EM offers an attractive approach. As noted by Sutton (2004, p. 150):

> ecological modernisation is a political programme, which promotes a particular way of dealing with environmental issues at the expense of

others. This political programme is especially attractive to northern governments as it is much less threatening than radical Green politics.

Within this context policies relating to climate change are formulated in ways which are non-threatening to industrialised states' economies and ways of life (Aitken 2012). This simultaneously limits the range of policy options to be considered and further restricts debate in this area. Where alternative approaches to addressing climate change are advanced they typically lack influence on policy and receive limited attention in mainstream policy or media.

The chapter will now discuss two examples from the UK, to illustrate the ways that this dominant framing of climate change has marginalised alternative perspectives.

Renewable energy

Since the turn of the century, the UK government has set out its vision for the 'energy future' in a series of white papers (DTI 2003; HM Government 2007; DECC 2009, 2011). These white papers have addressed a number of concerns, notably: energy security, economic interests and emissions reduction. Whilst they have emphasised the importance of low-carbon transitions, the challenges discussed and solutions identified highlight the centrality of modernist and economic rationales. Following the approach of EM, improvements in energy efficiency and reduction in energy demand, which may be crucial for tackling climate change, are largely sidelined in favour of pro-development solutions focused on building new infrastructure and creating new investment opportunities (for example, through investment in renewable energy technologies and new nuclear plant) (Aitken 2012). Accordingly, the UK government has set a target for 15 per cent of the UK's energy consumption to come from renewable sources by 2020. In Scotland the Scottish government aims for renewable sources to generate the equivalent of 100 per cent of Scotland's gross annual electricity consumption by 2020, and to provide the equivalent of 11 per cent of Scotland's heat demand by the same year (Scottish Government 2011).

Whilst there are clear economic rationales underpinning the drive for increased renewable energy capacity (e.g. creating new domestic industries, providing new sources of investment, diversifying UK energy supplies and reducing reliance on international imports), public interest arguments related to climate change mitigation are typically emphasised. This emphasis 'provides a worthy (depoliticised) cause which is mobilised to present a strong rationale for energy policies, and one which is very hard to credibly contest' (Aitken 2012, p. 220).

Prioritising policy approaches aimed at meeting current (and increasing) energy demand through new technologies and investment, rather than demand reduction which would require more fundamental changes to lifestyles and social structures, enables policymakers to vocalise strong commitments to addressing climate change whilst avoiding major disruption or challenges to the status quo. Out of this context renewable energy has been framed as a key component in the national strategy for addressing climate change through reducing emissions. Given that this entails the development of new energy infrastructure, it necessitates an important role for the planning system. Accordingly the government's commitments to developing renewable energy projects have been reflected in planning policies across the UK. Planning policies in England, Wales, Scotland and Northern Ireland assert commitments to sustainable development and addressing climate change (see, for example, Department for Communities and Local Government 2012; Scottish Government 2014). Climate change policy has been described as having an 'overarching' nature and it has been advised that 'it is important that proper weight is attached to climate change policy in relation to other planning considerations' (Arup & Partners 2010, p. 111). Planning policies emphasise both that planning has a central role to play in addressing climate change and also that climate change must be a central consideration in planning decisions (see Scottish Government 2014; Welsh Assembly Government 2016).

The strong policy commitments to developing renewable energy discussed above are reflected within planning policies across the UK. It is stated that the planning system should 'support the development of a diverse range of electricity generation from renewable energy technologies – including the expansion of renewable energy generation capacity – and the development of heat networks' (Scottish Government 2014, p. 154), and that:

> The Welsh Government is committed to using the planning system to optimise renewable energy generation [... and] recognise that the benefits of renewable energy are part of the overall commitment to tackle climate change by reducing greenhouse gas emissions as well as increasing energy security. Local planning authorities should facilitate the development of all forms of renewable and low carbon energy to move towards a low carbon economy to help to tackle the causes of climate change.
> (Welsh Assembly Government 2016, paras 12.8.8–12.8.9)

As such, in response to policies and targets emphasising the importance of developing renewable energy capacity, the planning system has developed an explicit bias in favour of renewable energy projects.

However, the planning system is simultaneously legitimated by claims to its democratic character and planning policies across the UK frequently reassert the importance of public participation in planning processes (e.g. Department for Communities and Local Government 2012; Scottish Government 2014); this includes the right of members of the public to make representations relating to particular planning applications. This situation can lead to an uncomfortable combination of commitments to development and public participation. At times the goals of developing renewable energy capacity and reflecting public views in planning processes and decisions may be in conflict with one another. How the public interest is conceptualised and mobilised becomes a key consideration when trade-offs are made between these goals.

Government energy policy emphasising public interest justifications for expanding renewable energy have been demonstrated to be highly influential in planning decisions (Aitken et al. 2008). Arup & Partners (2010) found that whilst local authority planning departments vary, planning inspectorates determining appeals increasingly rely on climate change considerations in justifying their decisions. Moreover, while public participation is an important component of planning processes, this participation is restricted to raising material considerations which set the boundaries as to what is and is not a legitimate issue. Material considerations are determined by the decision maker in relation to each planning application. Scottish planning policy lists a range of potential material considerations, including:

- Scottish Government policy, and UK Government policy on reserved matters
- The National Planning Framework
- Scottish planning policy, advice and circulars
- European policy
- the environmental impact of the proposal
- the design of the proposed development and its relationship to its surroundings
- views of statutory and other consultees
- legitimate public concern or support expressed on relevant planning matters

(Scottish Government 2009)

Considerable weight is attached to policy (Scottish, UK and European), technical assessments (including, for example, environmental impact assessments), and the views of experts (i.e. statutory consultees). Public concern/ support is, perhaps significantly, last on this list, and even then it is qualified as being *legitimate* public concern or support and only that expressed on *relevant* planning matters. Importantly, which aspects of public concern are considered legitimate and which planning matters are considered relevant are determined by decision makers. This is inevitably a subjective judgement, and previous research has demonstrated that in practice such judgements act to reinforce traditional hierarchies of knowledge prioritising expert and professional knowledge (Aitken 2009; Aitken et al. 2008). Furthermore, the emphasis on existing government policies as material planning considerations mean that these cannot be debated or challenged in planning fora, and that they therefore have an 'untouchable' status in planning processes (Aitken et al. 2008). In these ways defining material considerations and preventing critical discussion of underpinning policies can be used to close down debate and limit opportunities for public participation. In particular, it can uphold constructed boundaries between expert and public knowledge and serve to maintain the depoliticisation of climate change since it prohibits the opportunity to discuss or question the rationale underpinning the drive towards more renewable energy or the approach that has been taken to addressing climate change.

Clear boundaries exist as to what is acceptable and admissible within planning processes, and arguments that fall outside of these boundaries can be straightforwardly dismissed (Aitken et al. 2008). However, such boundaries do not exist naturally but rather are constructed and reinforced within each planning process (Wynne 1982). Furthermore, planning processes maintain legitimacy by creating the illusion of being objective fact-finding exercises; however, this illusion conceals a number of subjective value judgements which are necessary in order to reach a decisive outcome (O'Riordan et al. 1988; Wynne 1982). The unquestionable nature of policy within planning can also be seen as a means of restricting the range of possible arguments that participants can make and further as defining a set of 'rational' assumptions underpinning the decision-making process. Consequently, individuals (or types of evidence) that challenge or deviate from this set of assumptions can be easily disregarded.

More broadly, the depoliticisation of climate change and the related public interest justification for developing renewable energy capacity has had significant impacts on how public opposition to renewable energy developments has been conceptualised and approached. Much has been written about public opposition to renewable energy developments (particularly wind power) and it has frequently been asserted that this is responsible for slow rates of development (e.g. Barry et al. 2008; Bell et al. 2005; Breukers & Wolsink 2007). The literature on this subject – and policy responses – routinely frame public opposition as an obstacle or problem which needs to be overcome in order to achieve national targets for renewable energy capacity (Aitken 2010). Perhaps the clearest illustrations of this thinking are NIMBY (not in my back yard) explanations of opposition to renewable energy. Here it is presumed that individuals are supportive of renewable energy as a general concept but object to particular proposed developments in their area (Warren et al. 2005). Such explanations view objectors as purely rational, self-interested and individualistic actors; as such they overlook the range of complex contextual, social or personal factors shaping public responses (Devine-Wright 2005). NIMBY explanations are typically justified by reference to opinion polls which report that the majority of the public is supportive of renewable energy, so it is therefore assumed that local objectors would support the proposed development in other locations. However, this overlooks the limitations of opinion polls in engaging with the nuances of public preferences and also that public support is rarely unconditional. Thus, even in instances where individuals are in principle supportive of renewable energy development, public responses to particular developments are dependent on a range of conditions being met (for example, adequate public engagement, trust in the developer and plans being appropriate to the local geographical, social and economic context) (Aitken 2010). NIMBY explanations have been widely renounced in the academic literature due to their simplistic character-isation of public responses, yet remain widely mobilised – for example, actors within particular planning conflicts have been observed to refer to NIMBY explanations either to explain other people's opposition or to refute that they themselves are NIMBYs (Burningham 2000; van der Horst 2007). This is significant as it illustrates the extent to which the opposition expressed in (democratic) planning processes is framed as a problem through public inter-est justifications for renewable energy development. Thus opposition to poli-cies or projects justified in terms of climate change mitigation may be becoming socially unacceptable. Public participation in planning processes, or public engagement with renewable energy, is not then seen as a means of understanding and addressing public concerns or reflecting public preferences; rather, the planning system can be regarded as a bureaucratic system for legitimising and facilitating government policies (Aitken 2012).

Climate justice

The second example which illustrates the ways that the dominant EM fram-ing of climate change policy has marginalised alternative perspectives relates to climate justice. Climate justice captures the understanding that justice and climate change are inter-linked, and recognises that the impacts of climate change, and policies to mitigate or tackle climate change, will be experienced differently by different groups of people. This relates to the inequitable dis-tribution of the physical impacts of climate change and historic responsibility for the problem, as well as social justice implications of mitigation and adaptation responses (particularly how these are paid for and distributed) (Aitken et al. 2016a). Climate justice draws attention to disparities between those responsible for causing climate change, and those who are expected to be most impacted by it: 'the bitter effects of climate change will hit first and most powerfully the countries and people who did least to cause it' (Sachs & Santarius 2007, p. 53). Countries which industrialised earlier tend to have emitted a much larger share of the GHG currently in the atmosphere than less developed countries; and within industrialised nations there are disparities in GHG emissions, with poorer citizens of industrialised nations having far lower per capita emissions than their richer counterparts (Preston et al. 2013a). The climate justice movement has raised a number of dilemmas, not least regarding whether industrialised nations owe a 'climate debt' to the rest of the world and how we can (or whether we should) account for variations in responsibility within countries (Aitken et al. 2016a).

There are also justice issues associated with mitigation and adaptation strategies. For example, policies aimed at energy decarbonisation have raised energy bills and led to negative impacts on low-income households which tend to spend a higher proportion of their income on energy (Aitken et al.

2016a). This has meant that energy price increases tend to be socially regressive (Gough 2011). Low-income households that use electricity to heat their homes are likely to be hardest hit by the costs of energy policies in the future as the majority of these costs are placed on electricity to fund decarbonisation (Preston et al. 2013b).

Therefore, climate justice highlights the importance of climate change mitigation and adaptation strategies taking account of social justice considerations in order to address inequity in responsibilities, avoid disadvantaged groups being disproportionately affected by climate change impacts or climate change policies, and ensuring that the benefits of climate change policies are evenly distributed. Climate justice entails both distributive and procedural justice. To achieve distributive justice, policies to tackle climate change must ensure that vulnerable groups (such as elderly people, people on low incomes, or people with long-term health conditions) are not disproportionately affected by the negative impacts of climate change or by policies to address climate change. To achieve procedural justice, decisions regarding climate change policy must be made in a fair and inclusive way, so that diverse interests are considered and addressed and just outcomes are produced.

The climate justice movement has challenged capitalist systems of production and modernist structures calling for 'System Change, Not Climate Change!', and as such it is perhaps unsurprising that it has typically sat outside mainstream policy-making (Aitken 2012). Moreover, climate justice challenges dominant approaches to addressing climate change through raising questions relating to responsibilities for causing climate change and drawing attention to social justice implications of favoured mitigation and adaptation strategies. However, the movement has grown in momentum over the last decade (Aitken et al. 2016a; MRFCJ 2013), and there is evidence of its influence and impact having increased.

One notable example of the increasing impact of climate justice comes from Scotland where, in March 2012, the Scottish Parliament unanimously passed a motion 'strongly endors[ing] the opportunity for Scotland to champion climate justice' (Aitken et al. 2016a). This has been described as historic, with Scotland said to be the first country to debate such a motion (MRFCJ 2012), and reflects broader vocal commitments of the Scottish government for Scotland to be a world leader in addressing climate change (e.g. Scottish Government 2009). Given the policy context surrounding climate change and the ways that climate justice has challenged dominant approaches this may be considered a bold move. However, recent years have witnessed the emergence of many different forms or understandings of climate justice with varying implications for policy and action, and it may be this new ambiguity which has facilitated greater uptake of climate justice meaning 'the "boldness" of such a commitment may be less than first appears' (Aitken et al. 2016a, p. 227).

Approaches to climate justice can be conceptual, transformative or pragmatic, with significant implications for which actions or policies are pursued and/or prioritised (Aitken et al. 2016a). For some, climate justice calls for transformative change to renounce capitalist systems of production and requiring a move towards systems which prioritise equality and equity and respect environmental limits to growth (e.g. http://climatejusticecampaign. org). For others climate justice can be pursued through existing economic frameworks and policy mechanisms, such as emissions trading schemes (Posner & Weisbach 2010).

It is through taking more pragmatic approaches that the climate justice movement has received greater policy attention. These pragmatic approaches are largely uncritical of existing political and institutional structures or of EM-dominated approaches to climate change policy and bring the benefits of greater influence in mainstream policy-making. However, they might also be seen as using the rhetoric of climate justice to legitimate low-carbon business as usual rather than truly enacting the values and principles of the climate justice movement (Aitken et al. 2016a). The dominance of such approaches may mean that the transformative potential of climate justice is not realised. This illustrates that given the depoliticised discourse around climate change, approaches to addressing climate change may only impact on mainstream policy processes when they do not challenge existing systems and structures, meaning that approaches which challenge the status quo remain excluded or on the fringes of policy-making.

Modernist approaches to policy-making which prioritise expert and technical forms of knowledge over public or lay knowledge and technological solutions over social transformations dominate climate change policy and considerably restrict the opportunities for more human-centred approaches to achieve impact. Policy and media discourse on climate change typically obscures the range of alternative framings of climate change and alternative – potentially more transformative – approaches to mitigating and adapting to climate change. In this context technological solutions which create new industries supported by – and supporting – current social and economic structures are favoured over those which suggest the need for transformative change.

The importance of dissensus

Whilst the depoliticised discourse on climate change presents climate change mitigation as a global priority for protecting the *wider public interest*, in upholding the 'fragile consensus' it constrains public debate about the various meanings of climate change and the numerous ways it impacts on *diverse public interests*. In doing so, climate change is positioned as a scientific or technical issue and public knowledge and insights are marginalised. This discourse draws on positivist visions of science and traditional ideas of the relationship between scientific expertise and policy-making. Such a positivist approach is suggestive of a singular public interest which can be identified and served. This overlooks the heterogeneity of public interests and the level of uncertainty which exists around environmental, scientific or technological matters. It presumes that 'disinterested experts, working within the institutions of the modern nation-state, [can] objectively and rationally analyse a problem and arrive at a solution that is in "the public interest"' (Sandercock 1998, p. 197). It assumes that appropriate responses to environmental problems can be identified by 'a certain chosen, well-educated group' (Sandercock 1998, p. 197). However, the concept of the public interest is never invoked apolitically; any definition or interpretation of the concept is always a construction overlooking the multiplicity of public interests and loaded with subjective meaning and the values of those defining and interpreting it.

Given the widespread and diverse impacts of climate change – as well as climate change policies – there is no single or uncontested public interest but rather a range of conflicting, competing and diverse public interests, reflecting the pluralist nature of societies (Campbell & Marshall 2000, p. 306). Upholding a notion of the public interest inevitably marginalises the many diverse interests which are not represented or which challenge the singular conceptualisation. This singular view of the public interest focuses on the end goal of climate change mitigation and overlooks the public interests affected by the processes for reaching that (complex) goal. Turning attention to these processes and to the range of associated perspectives and interests offers an alternative way of conceptualising the public interest through dialogical approaches. Such conceptualisations are centrally concerned with processes (rather than outcomes) and the democratic rights of members of the public (Alexander 2002; Gross 2007).

This approach resonates with Habermas's (1976, 1989) calls to reclaim the public sphere through communicative action, whereby decisions should be reached 'through equal, open and constraint-free discussion' (Healey & Hillier 1996, p. 168). Habermas proposed the concept of 'ideal speech communities', where participation for all is possible, and undistorted communication can take place (Habermas 1976, p. 484). Rather than a focus on the achievement of rational, instrumental ends, communication can be based on mutual trust and comprehension, and attempts can therefore be made to harmonise different objectives through negotiation.

Such an approach resonates with literature relating to post-normal science which challenges positivist views of science. Post-normal science is described as being characterised by high levels of uncertainty, disputed values, high stakes and high levels of urgency for decision-making (Funtowicz & Ravetz 1993). This science is 'based on assumptions of unpredictability, incomplete control, and a plurality of legitimate perspectives' (Funtowicz & Ravetz 1993, p. 739). Under these conditions uncertainty is viewed as an inevitable part of science and hence 'is not banished but is managed' (Funtowicz & Ravetz 1993, p. 740). Moreover, whilst positivist approaches to science have sought to separate facts from values (prioritising facts), in post-normal science facts and values cannot be separated and values play an integral role. Funtowicz and Ravetz (1993, p. 742) contend that 'scientific expertise has led us into policy dilemmas which it is incapable of resolving itself'. Many areas of scientific research are characterised by uncertainties which can be inter alia practical, political or ethical. In these contexts science, whilst ever-more necessary, cannot provide definitive answers or policy recommendations (Luks 1999). The problem then becomes one not of discovering 'scientific facts' or universal truths but rather of understanding and managing complex realities. Therefore it is erroneous to maintain an illusion of objective science providing definitive answers, and policy-making should instead be more explicitly based on understandings and evaluations of uncertainties.

In the wake of the 'Climategate' scandal discussed above, Hulme and Ravetz (2009) urged climate scientists to 'show their working' and engage in a more open and transparent science: a science which reflects on its own processes of validation and mobilisation. Funtowicz and Ravetz (1993) have argued that given the complex and uncertain nature of post-normal science, a wider range of actors should be involved in its quality assurance processes. This should reach beyond narrow sets of scientists and professionals to the 'extended peer community', including members of the public. Opening up opportunities for wider involvement is seen to be beneficial not only for members of the public or for democratic institutions but also to science (Luks 1999).

An inclusive and transparent approach is needed at all levels. There is a role for extended peer communities in scientific processes (including in agenda-setting, funding, review and dissemination), policy-making (e.g. translating climate science and assessing and developing policy responses), and within decision-making at regional, national or local levels (for example, in planning processes related to particular developments). Questions around how climate science is framed and interpreted, what its implications are within particular geographical, social, political or cultural contexts, and how policymakers should respond to the challenges that it poses could all benefit from the inclusion of diverse voices and interests. Dialogical approaches to the public interest through focusing on processes rather than outcomes emphasise the need for meaningful and open public engagement at all stages and in relation to all decision-making processes, ensuring procedural and recognitional justice (Aitken et al. 2016a).

Conclusions

Climate change may be unique in the reach its relevance has over generations, continents and diverse policy areas. This global character and wide-reaching impacts have led to a strong discourse suggestive of a single global public interest in mitigating climate change. This universalising approach overlooks significant differences in responsibilities, likely impacts and potential responses, and simplifies discussions of climate change to binary arguments between climate change believers and deniers. Simultaneously, it has upheld traditional, positivist visions of science and scientific processes maintaining an unrealistic set of expectations regarding the role and certainty of scientific 'facts'.

Through this depoliticisation of climate change the role of the public has been reduced to that of a passive observer. This conceptualisation of climate change reflects the dominant approach to environmental policy-making in Northern states which is firmly underpinned by commitments to Ecological Modernisation. Decision-making is dominated by expert and technical knowledge, and alternative perspectives are typically discredited or dismissed. Moreover, potential strategies to address climate change do not receive policy attention if they do not fit within the existing dominant approach. Such dominant approaches are underpinned by (and reinforce) positivist views of science and modernist commitments to development and economic growth. Alternative voices are marginalised through restricted debate and the illusion of consensus on how climate change is understood and how it should be addressed.

The mobilisation of the public interest as a justification for climate change-related policies has led to a focus on outcomes overlooking the social and political factors influencing the processes leading to those outcomes. Taking a dialogic approach to the public interest and recognising the plurality of public interests affected by climate change and related policies provides an alternative view. This view highlights the potential value of dissensus and of embracing – rather than avoiding – disagreement. Whilst policymakers typically prefer to convey messages of certainty (Stirling 2010), it may be through recognition of uncertainty, ambiguity and plurality that climate change can be addressed in ways that reflect and serve the public interest(s).

References

Aitken, M 2009, 'Wind power planning controversies and the construction of "expert" and "lay" knowledges', *Science as Culture*, vol. 18, no. 1, pp. 47–64.

Aitken, M 2010, 'Why we still don't understand the social aspects of wind power: A critique of key assumptions within the literature', *Energy Policy*, vol. 38, no. 4, pp. 1834–1841.

Aitken, M 2012, 'Changing climate, changing democracy: A cautionary tale', *Environmental Politics*, vol. 21, no. 2, pp. 211–229.

Aitken, M, Christman, B, Bonaventura, M, Horst, DVD & Holbrook, J 2016a, 'Climate justice begins at home: Conceptual, pragmatic and transformative approaches to climate justice in Scotland', *Scottish Affairs*, vol. 25, no. 2, p. 225–252.

Aitken, M, Haggett, C & Rudolph, D 2016b, 'Practices and rationales of community engagement with wind farms: Awareness raising, consultation, empowerment', *Planning Theory & Practice*, vol. 17, no. 4, pp. 557–576.

Aitken, M, McDonald, S & Strachan, P 2008, 'Locating "power" in wind power planning processes: The (not so) influential role of local objectors', *Journal of Environmental Planning and Management*, vol. 51, no. 6, pp. 777–799.

Alexander, ER 2002, 'The Public Interest in Planning: From legitimation to substantive plan evaluation', *Planning Theory*, vol. 1, no. 3, pp. 226–249.

O. Arup & Partners 2010, *Take Up and Application of the Policies in the Planning Policy Statement on Planning and Climate Change*, Department for Communities and Local Government, London.

Barry, J, Ellis, G & Robinson, C 2008, 'Cool rationalities and hot air: A rhetorical approach to understanding debates on renewable energy', *Global Environmental Politics*, vol. 8, no. 2, pp. 67–98.

Barry, J & Paterson, M 2004, 'Globalisation, ecological modernisation and New Labour', *Political Studies*, vol. 52, no. 4, pp. 767–784.

Beck, U 2010, 'Climate for change, or how to create a green modernity', *Theory, Culture and Society*, vol. 27, nos. 2–3, pp. 254–266.

Bell, D, Gray, T & Haggett, C 2005, 'The "social gap" in wind farm siting decisions: Explanations and policy responses', *Environmental Politics*, vol. 14, no. 4, pp. 460–477.

Bickerstaff, K, Lorenzoni, I, Pidgeon, NF, Poortinga, W & Simmons, P 2008, 'Reframing nuclear power in the UK energy debate: Nuclear power, climate change mitigation and radioactive waste', *Public Understanding of Science*, vol. 17, no. 2, pp. 145–169.

Breukers, S & Wolsink, M 2007, 'Wind power implementation in changing institutional landscapes: An international comparison', *Energy Policy*, vol. 35, no. 5, pp. 2737–2750.

Burningham, K 2000, 'Using the language of NIMBY: A topic for research, not an activity for researchers', *Local Environment*, vol. 5, no. 1, pp. 55–67.

Campbell, H & Marshall, R 2002, 'Utilitarianism's Bad Breath? A Re-evaluation of the Public Interest Justification for Planning', *Planning Theory*, vol. 1, no. 2, pp. 163–187.

Demeritt, D 2001, 'The construction of global warming and the politics of science', *Annals of the Association of American Geographers*, vol. 91, no. 2, pp. 307–337.

Department for Communities and Local Government 2012, *National Planning Policy Framework*, viewed 11 March 2017, www.gov.uk/government/uploads/system/uploads/attachment_data/file/6077/2116950.pdf.

Department of Energy and Climate Change (DECC) 2009, *The UK Low Carbon Transition Plan: National Strategy for Climate Change and Energy*, viewed 11 March 2017, www.gov.uk/government/uploads/system/uploads/attachment_data/file/228752/9780108508394.pdf.

Department of Energy and Climate Change (DECC) 2011, *Planning Our Electric Future: A White Paper for Secure, Affordable and Low-Carbon Energy*, viewed 11 March 2017, www.gov.uk/government/publications/planning-our-electric-future-a-white-paper-for-secure-affordable-and-low-carbon-energy.

Department of Trade and Industry (DTI) 2003, *Energy White Paper: Our Energy Future – Creating a Low Carbon Economy*, viewed 11 March 2017, http://webarchive.nationalarchives.gov.uk/+/http:/www.berr.gov.uk/files/file10719.pdf.

Devine-Wright, P 2005, 'Beyond NIMBYism: Towards an integrated framework for understanding public perceptions of wind energy', *Wind Energy*, vol. 8, no. 2, pp. 125–139.

Doyle, T & Chaturvedi, S 2010, 'Climate territories: A global soul for the global south?' *Geopolitics*, vol. 15, no. 3, pp. 516–535.

Ellis, G, Cowell, R, Warren, C, Strachan, P & Szarka, J 2009, 'Expanding wind power: A problem of planning, or of perception?' *Planning Theory and Practice*, vol. 10, no. 4, pp. 523–532.

Funtowicz, SO & Ravetz, JR 1993, 'Science for the post-normal age', *Futures*, vol. 25, no. 7, pp. 739–755.

Gieryn, TF 1999, *Cultural Boundaries of Science: Credibility on the Line*, The University of Chicago Press, Chicago, IL & London.

Gough, I 2011, *Climate Change, Double Injustice and Social Policy: A Case Study of the United Kingdom*, UN Research Institute for Social Development, Geneva.

Gross, C 2007, 'Community perspectives of wind energy in Australia: The application of a justice and fairness framework to increase social acceptance', *Energy Policy*, vol. 5, no. 35, pp. 2727–2736.

Habermas, J 1976, *Communication and the Evolution of Society*, Polity Press, Cambridge.

Habermas, J 1989, *The Structural Transformation of the Public Sphere*, MIT Press, Cambridge, MA.

Hajer, MA 1995, *The Politics of Environmental Discourse: Ecological Modernization and the Policy Process*, Clarendon Press, Oxford.

Hart, DM & Victor, DG 1993, 'Scientific elites and the making of US policy for climate change research, 1957–1974', *Social Studies of Science*, vol. 23, no. 4, pp. 643–680.

Healey, P & Hillier, J 1996, 'Communicative micropolitics: A story of claims and discourses', *International Planning Studies*, vol. 1, no. 2, pp. 165–184.

HM Government 2007, *Meeting the Energy Challenge: A White Paper on Energy*, viewed 11 March 2017, www.gov.uk/government/publications/meeting-the-energy-challenge-a-white-paper-on-energy.

HM Government 2008, *Meeting the Energy Challenge: A White Paper on Nuclear Power*, viewed 11 March 2017, www.gov.uk/government/publications/meeting-the-energy-challenge-a-white-paper-on-nuclear-power.

Hulme, M 2009, *Why We Disagree about Climate Change: Understanding Controversy, Inaction and Opportunity*, Cambridge University Press, Cambridge.

Hulme, M & Mahoney, M 2010, 'Climate change: What do we know about the IPCC?' *Progress in Physical Geography*, vol. 34, no. 5, pp. 705–718.

Hulme, M & Ravetz, J 2009, 'Show your working: What "ClimateGate" means', *BBC News*, 1 December, viewed 11 March 2017, http://news.bbc.co.uk/1/hi/8388485.stm.

Irwin, A 2001, *Sociology and the Environment: A Critical Introduction to Society, Nature and Knowledge*, Polity Press, Cambridge.

Jasanoff, S 2003, 'Breaking the Waves in Science Studies: Comment on H.M. Collins and Robert Evans' "The Third Wave of Science Studies"', *Social Studies of Science*, vol. 33, no. 3, pp. 389–400.

Latour, B & Woolgar, S 1986, *Laboratory Life: The Construction of Scientific Facts*, 2nd edn. Princeton University Press, Princeton, NJ.

Luks, F 1999, 'Post-normal science and the rhetoric of inquiry: Deconstructing normal science?' *Futures*, vol. 31, no. 7, pp. 705–719.

Mary Robinson Foundation – Climate Justice (MRFCJ) 2012, *Scottish Parliament Passes Motion on Climate Justice*, viewed 24 November 2017, www.mrfcj.org/resources/scottish-parliament-passes-motion-on-climate-justice/.

Mary Robinson Foundation – Climate Justice (MRFCJ) 2013, *Climate Justice Baseline*, viewed 11 March 2017, www.mrfcj.org/media/pdf/ClimateJusticeBaseline.pdf.

Mol, APJ & Spaargaren, G 2000, 'Ecological modernisation theory in debate: A review', in APJ Mol & DA Sonnenfeld (eds), *Ecological Modernisation around the World: Perspectives and Critical Debates*, Frank Cass, London, pp. 17–49.

Nature 2010, Turbines and turbulence, *Nature*, 468, 1001.

O'Riordan, T, Kemp, R & Purdue, M 1988, *Sizewell B: An Anatomy of the Inquiry*, Macmillan Press, Basingstoke.

Posner, E & Weisbach, D 2010, *Climate Change Justice*, Princeton University Press, Princeton, NJ.

Preston, I, White, V, Thumim, J, Bridgeman, T & Brand, C 2013a, *Distribution of Carbon Emissions in the UK: Implications for Domestic Energy Policy*, Joseph Rowntree Foundation, York.

Preston, I, White, V, Croft, D & Sturtevant, E 2013b, *The Hardest Hit: Going Beyond the Mean*, Consumer Futures, London.

Sachs, W & Santarius, T 2007, *Fair Future: Resource Conflicts, Security, and Global Justice*, Zed Books, London.

Salk, J 1979 [2nd edition 1986], 'Introduction', in B Latour & S Woolgar, *Laboratory Life: The Construction of Scientific Facts*, Princeton University Press, Princeton, NJ, pp. 11–14.

Sandercock, L 1998, *Towards Cosmopolis: Planning for Multicultural Cities*, John Wiley and Sons, Chichester.

Scottish Government 2009, *Scottish Planning Series Circular 4 2009: Development Management Procedures*, viewed 24 November 2017, www.gov.scot/Publications/2009/07/03153034/0.

Scottish Government 2011, *2020 Routemap for Renewable Energy in Scotland*, www.gov.scot/Publications/2011/08/04110353/0.

Scottish Government 2014, *Scottish Planning Policy*, viewed 11 March 2017, https://beta.gov.scot/publications/scottish-planning-policy/pages/2/.

Stirling, A 2010, 'Keep it complex', *Nature*, vol. 468, pp. 1029–1031.

Sutton, PW 2004, *Nature, Environment and Society*, Palgrave Macmillan, Basingstoke.

Swyngedouw, E 2010, 'Apocalypse forever? Post-political populism and the spectre of climate change', *Theory, Culture and Society*, vol. 27, nos. 2–3, pp. 213–232.

Szerszynski, B & Urry, J 2010, 'Changing climate: Introduction', *Theory, Culture and Society*, vol. 27, no. 2–3, pp. 1–8.

van der Horst, D 2007, 'NIMBY or not? Exploring the relevance of location and the politics of voiced opinions in renewable energy siting controversies', *Energy Policy*, vol. 35, no. 5, pp. 2705–2714.

Warren, CR, Lumsden, C, O'Dowd, S & Birnie, RV 2005, '"Green on green": Public perceptions of wind power in Scotland and Ireland', *Journal of Environmental Planning and Management*, vol. 48, no. 6, pp. 853–875.

Welsh Assembly Government 2016, *Planning Policy Wales*, viewed 11 March 2017, http://gov.wales/docs/desh/publications/161117planning-policy-wales-edition-9-en.pdf.

Wynne, B 1982, *Rationality and Ritual: The Windscale Inquiry and Nuclear Decisions in Britain*, Society for the History of Science, London.

Wynne, B 2010, 'Strange weather, again: Climate science as political art', *Theory, Culture and Society*, vol. 27, nos. 2–3, pp. 289–305.

Yearley, S 1996, *Sociology, Environmentalism, Globalization: Reinventing the Globe*, Sage Publications, London.

Yearley, S 2005, 'Speaking truth to power: Science and policy', in S Yearley (ed.) *Making Sense of Science: Understanding the Social Study of Science*, Sage Publications, London, pp. 160–173.

5 Commercial media platforms and the challenges to public expression and scrutiny

Nicholas Carah

Introduction

Media companies are a critical part of the public culture of capitalist liberal democratic societies. They balance competing interests as private for-profit organisations expected to serve the public interest. For much of the 20th century the world's largest media companies – including Walt Disney, Comcast, Time Warner and News Corporation – operated a business model that involved investment in creating content. Accordingly, debates about the dialectical relationship between their commercial interests and responsibility to the public interest focused mostly on the qualities of the content they produced and social discourse they facilitated. The past decade has seen the rise to dominance of Google and Facebook as transformative media organisations. The 2016 *Top Thirty Global Media Owners* report ranked Google's parent company Alphabet as the world's largest media company with annual revenues of US$60 billion (O'Reilly 2016). Facebook, with annual revenues of over US$39 billion, is the world's fifth largest, and fastest growing, media company (Facebook 2018).

Google and Facebook are transformative because they invest in engineering a platform rather than producing content (van Dijck 2013). These companies build 'socio-technical infrastructure' that 'code[s] social activities into a computational infrastructure' (van Dijck 2013, p. 29). They do not employ writers, editors, journalists, producers, filmmakers or any other kind of human content producers. They employ computer engineers, technology designers, data analysts, marketers, and social researchers. If we are to understand the relationship between media and the public interest in the digital age, we need to develop ways of approaching media as much more than technologies of symbolic expression and discursive deliberation. Participation on media platforms generates data that is stored and processed by the platform, in addition to whatever symbolic content is conveyed from human to human. And that data is used to enhance the capacity of the platform to intervene in public culture: shaping the political news we read, predicting the books, music or films we might enjoy, determining who will see whom in public discussion. Following the terminology of computer engineers, we might argue that our engagement with media platforms – searching, streaming and expressing our views – trains the platform algorithms to make more finely tuned judgements about our public culture.

In this chapter I argue that media platforms are productively understood as media engineering companies (McStay 2013). Corporations like Facebook and Google build platforms that structure the expressions, rituals and logistics of public life. To learn what these companies might teach us about the changing nature of media, critical communication scholars must pay careful attention to their engineering projects, investments in new technologies and public announcements about their strategic plans. Their engineering activities illustrate an epochal shift in the role commercial media play as the infrastructure of public culture. I contribute to critical theories of public interest communication by considering how the engineering projects undertaken by media platforms like Google and Facebook challenge how we understand the public interest role of media organisations. I fully acknowledge that 'social media' raise many questions about media and the public interest that relate to the qualities of public discourse (Gillespie 2014; Papacharissi & de Fatima Oliveira 2012; Papacharissi 2015). For the most part, I sidestep questions about the responsibility of platforms to monitor and moderate the qualities of public speech or to provide open access to forums of public expression. I also deliberately focus on Google and Facebook because I argue they are the two transformative media corporations whose engineering projects are reconstructing what media are and how they intervene in public life. Facebook started out as a web-based social networking site, and Google as a search platform. Now both are more accurately understood as large-scale experiments in developing an historically significant infrastructure for data collection, storage and processing. They are making serious investments in artificial intelligence, augmented reality and logistics like automated transport and retail. In doing so, they are transforming what we understand media to be as institutions, technologies and infrastructure that undergird public life.

My aim is to argue for a critical account of media platforms and the public interest that follows the strategic investments and directions of the platforms themselves. This strategy of critical inquiry draws inspiration from Dallas Smythe (Smythe & Dinh 1983), who implored critical communication scholars to take the strategic plans and pronouncements of corporate media organisations as a useful record of how they act in the world. Following this impulse, we should pay attention to the fundamental process unfolding: the reengineering of media as a set of institutions and technologies whose data-processing capacity is at the heart of the interventions they are, and will, make in public life (Andrejevic 2007, 2013).

My beginning question then is: How can a critical account of public interest communication respond to the engineering projects and data-processing power of media companies? My proposition here is that public interest communication has been almost exclusively concerned with communication as symbolic expression. Johnston (2016, p. 18) illustrates that definitions of the public interest relating to media concern *disclosing* information judged to be of public importance because it enables citizens to make informed decisions and hold the powerful to account; and *preventing* the disclosure of false or misleading information. The public interest is framed entirely in terms of the role media play in creating and circulating symbolic information. As Johnston (2016) argues, the public interest is historically contingent, and as such, I argue that we are undergoing a period where a dramatic change in the role media play in public culture needs to be accompanied by a reconsideration of their relation to the public interest.

Public culture as an engineering problem

A new kind of public communication is emerging on media platforms that involve the interplay between human and machine judgement. Within established frameworks of the public interest, the role that media platforms' algorithmic machinery plays in judging, curating, optimising and shaping public expression deserves scrutiny. Present approaches to the public interest assume the primary actor to be humans working within institutional settings to decide what information will be disclosed to the public. This must be now augmented with accounts of the creation of computational machines that make decisions about who speaks and who is heard. Platforms tend to view the challenge of conceptualising and acting in the public interest as an engineering problem.

In a public relations video chat posted to Facebook in December 2016, the Chief Operating Officer Sheryl Sandberg and the Chief Executive Officer and Founder Mark Zuckerberg discussed key public affairs issues for the platform over the past year (Zuckerberg 2016). The chat with Sandberg followed several months of criticism regarding Facebook's role in influencing the 2016 US presidential election (Tufekci 2016). In a brief reference to the public debate about Facebook's role in amplifying the distribution of 'fake news' during the presidential election, Zuckerberg explained that:

> Facebook is a new kind of platform. It's not a traditional technology company. You know, we build technology and we feel responsible for how it is used. We don't write the news that people read on the platform. But at the same time we also do a lot more than just distribute news, and we're an important part of the public discourse.

Zuckerberg's admission that Facebook was more than just a distributor of news was taken by some commentators to be an admission that the company did recognise its *editorial* responsibilities (Gibbs 2016). An established view of commercial media and the public interest might assume that being 'an important part of the public discourse' involves institutionalising norms of human editorial judgement. For instance, newsroom studies illustrate how the professional values of journalists are embedded in the rules and routines of news organisations (Deuze 2005; Tuchman 1978). The culture of a newsroom is a site where commercial and public interests are negotiated and balanced. Norms about how reality is represented are institutionalised in ethical guidelines, style guides and editorial practices. Significantly, all of these processes have been undertaken by humans within media organisations throughout the 20th century.

Facebook's responses to issues regarding its responsibility to the public interest suggest that the platform does not intend to develop a human editorial culture. For instance, Facebook's response to controversy over bias in its 'trending topics' news stories was to remove the human editorial team allegedly causing the biased results and replace them with a 'more neutral' algorithm. In a Facebook post, the platform stated: 'making these changes to the product allows our team to make fewer individual decisions about topics' (Facebook 2016). In Facebook's response to its discovery of 3,000 advertisements produced by 'inauthentic' accounts during the US presidential election, it announced its plans to 'apply machine learning' to reduce these ads in the future (Stamos 2017). The implication here is that decisions made by humans are biased, and the more reliable and publicly responsible editorial practice involved engineering a better algorithm. In his chat with Sandberg, then, Zuckerberg wasn't signalling a move toward more human editorial judgement at Facebook, but rather acknowledging the platform had a new kind of engineering problem.

When Sandberg and Zuckerberg pointed to the key contributions the platform had made to public culture over the past year they didn't talk about content they produced or curated, or improvements they had made to processes of editorial judgement. Rather, they showcased logistical applications the platform had engineered, such as the Safety Check (Gleit et al. 2014). The Safety Check appears at the top of the Facebook News Feed of any users who are near to a natural disaster or crisis situation like a cyclone, earthquake or terrorist attack. The Check asks 'Are you safe?' If you click 'I'm safe', all your friends are notified via their News Feed. Facebook's public contribution here is infrastructural and logistical. At the intimate level the platform provides the infrastructure to tell loved ones you are safe. At the population level the data collected via the Safety Check has a logistical value. It can be provided to public authorities in real time to enable prioritisation of emergency resources.

The Safety Check offers one example of how media platforms like Facebook imagine their contribution to public culture and the broader public interest. They see their public value as media engineers, rather than facilitators of symbolic expression and public deliberation. By media engineering, I mean that the investment Facebook makes is not in the production of symbolic content but in the engineering of interfaces, algorithms, databases and protocols that shape the interplay between humans and increasingly calculative media platforms (Brodmerkel & Carah 2016; McStay 2013; van Dijck 2013). Of crucial importance, media corporations organised around *engineering* rather than *content production* view media first and foremost as infrastructure for collecting, storing and processing data (Packer 2013). Engineers do not focus on developing more compelling symbolic narratives; rather they work to expand the sensory capacity of media devices to collect information about lived experience, the logistics of storing data, and the computational work of processing that data (Andrejevic & Burdon 2015). These engineering activities change the way media intervene in public life and in doing so raise new questions about how media exercise power in public life. In this framework, media are not so much institutions that *narrate* public life; they instead become infrastructure for intervening in public life.

Media platforms and digital democracy

Thinking about digital media platforms primarily as engineering projects, presses back on accounts of the democratic affordances of digital media throughout the 1990s and early 2000s, which celebrated the emerging participatory culture of message boards, online chat, email lists and blogs. A 'surprisingly diverse array of political interests' (Dahlberg 2011, p. 855) from establishment institutions to radical activists took digital media to be inherently democratic because they enabled ordinary people to speak and be heard (Dahlberg 2011; Hindman 2008; Turner 2010). During this period, the capacity of ordinary people to create and distribute content on digital media seemed especially novel and democratic in contrast to the dominant mass media institutions, where the capacity to produce content was concentrated in the hands of elite owners and the professional meaning makers they employed. The emerging data-processing power of digital media was largely absent from these accounts, and even critical accounts mostly focused on issues such as the digital divide between who could and couldn't access platforms, or the emerging commercialisation of platforms with targeted advertising. Few accounts focused on the looming impact platforms' data-processing capacity would have on public speech itself. In the present moment, a rigorous account of media platforms and the public interest in the digital era must pay critical attention to the engineering culture, data-processing power, and interplay between human and machine judgements that now undergird our everyday public culture. Media institutions like Facebook and Google engineer platforms that are powerful non-human actors in public communication.

Dahlberg (2011) critically examines four influential discourses through the 1990s and 2000s that each articulated how democratic public culture could be extended through digital media technologies: liberal-individualist, deliberative, counter-publics, and autonomist Marxist. I turn to Dahlberg's framework here because of its significant historical value in carefully elaborating how the democratic potential of digital media was understood by establishment and activist political groups throughout the 1990s and 2000s.

In the liberal-individualist account digital media enable individuals to access information to make informed choices, express those choices, and for elites to aggregate those choices via automated data analysis of public opinion. In this position we see the expression of an establishment view about the value of linking participatory public expression with automated surveillance and data analysis. Digital media promise to make citizens more visible in terms of expression of views in pre-formatted modes, such as completing an online poll, sharing a news story, or commenting on a political issue. Each of these actions can be efficiently collected, analysed and aggregated by the computational machinery of digital media. In this sense, digital media enable the more efficient and organised management of public opinion. In the liberal-individualist account digital media enable individuals to access information to make informed choices, express those choices, and for elites to aggregate those voices via automated data analysis of public opinion. In this position we see the expression of an establishment view about the value of linking participatory public expression with automated surveillance and data analysis. This discourse is historically interesting, at least in the way Dahlberg critically documents it, for the way it emphasises the expressive affordances of digital media, but elides the logics of data processing that are central to 'aggregating preferences'. That is, exponents of this view do not attempt to make an emphatic account of surveillance and data processing as democratic, but rather shift emphasis to capacity for public expressions to be made and understood.

The deliberative position conceives digital media as an apparatus for reflexive, reciprocal and inclusive rational debate that generates consensus. The counter-public discourse emphasises the role digital media play in enabling activist and marginalised groups to form outside of dominant discourses. While both emphasise discursive engagement, in the counter-public discourse that deliberation can be agonistic, rather than deliberative, rational and consensus-building. In these discourses, digital media are celebrated for enabling previously excluded voices to give an account of their life and its conditions (Couldry 2010). The deliberative and counter-publics views each put the emphasis firmly on symbolic expression as the foundation of digital media's participatory culture and democratic affordances. For the most part, like the liberal-individualist position, deliberative and counter-publics discourses also ignore the data-processing power of digital media although they are more likely than the liberal-individualist to critically contend with how the political economy of media shapes public communication.

The autonomist Marxist position 'sees digital communication networks as enabling a radically democratic politics' that is self-organised, de-centralised and de-institutionalised (Dahlberg 2011, p. 861). This position goes beyond the norms of capitalist liberal democracy, to imagine radically new democratic formations based on a self-organising commons. The autonomist position is a radical critique of network capitalism. It is particularly valuable because, different to the liberal-individualist, deliberative and counter-publics discourses, autonomist Marxists understood the digital as a new mode of production. Digital media were always much more than platforms for symbolic expression; they were more primarily logistical infrastructure for organising the living capacities of humans to political, economic and cultural ends. Autonomists contributed dialectical accounts of how digital media were both products of capitalist production at the same time they produced forms of social organisation that threatened established power relationships.

These discourses are historically useful because they articulate early, and often utopian, visions of the democratic affordances of digital media. If we use the conventions of the digital democracy debates of the 1990s and 2000s as a reference point, then media institutions like Facebook, Google, Twitter, Instagram and so on seem remarkably different to broadcast media because of the presence of ordinary people creating, circulating and interacting with media content. It is their large-scale participatory culture that is most often the starting point for considerations of their role in public interest communication. With the exception of autonomist Marxism, they largely put the emphasis on forms of symbolic expression that constituted a new kind of participatory public culture. This was reasonable during the 1990s when the possibility of the internet as a public commons still seemed possible, if not likely, and the predominant online platforms were organised around symbolic expression mostly via written language. While these early views of digital media, at least as Dahlberg (2011) presents them, largely omit the data-processing power of media, it is possible to speculate how these positions could address the data economy of digital media. In the liberal-individualist account data is a useful part of the aggregation of preferences, whereas in the deliberative, counter-public and autonomist Marxist discourses the use of data to shape public communication would become a critical issue. As Dahlberg (2011) notes, the liberal-individualist position is concerned predominantly with individual rights, while the other positions are more inclined to address the systemic features of digital media platforms.

By the mid-2000s, especially with the emergence of major commercial platforms like Google and Facebook, strong critiques of the celebratory accounts of digital democracy began to emerge (Andrejevic 2007; Dean 2010; Hindman 2008). These critiques addressed a range of issues: questions of how access to digital media reflected larger divisions in society; the rapid commercialisation of the online commons and the appropriation of participation as free labour; the form and quality of online debate including its apparent polarisation into partisan bubbles and the emergence of 'snark' (snide comments), cynicism and 'trolling'; and importantly, the computational infrastructure of digital media, as a neglected element in early discourses about the democratic affordances of the internet.

Critical accounts of the democratic affordances of the internet began to argue that attention needed to be given to how participation acts as an alibi for submission to mass surveillance (Andrejevic 2007). In these critiques, a demand was made to address the interdependence between the participatory and data-processing affordances of digital media. For instance, in Dean's (2010) critique of communicative capitalism, digital media encourage individuals to express themselves, and construct that expression as empowering and enjoyable. Yet, they do not listen to the qualities of what is expressed. Rather, expression becomes part of a continuous flow of symbols and data within the networks of capitalist production. The continuous flow of symbols obfuscates the possibility for careful deliberation among humans, and the flow of data enhances the capacity of groups that control digital media platforms to monitor and shape public life (Andrejevic 2013). In a similar spirit, Clough (2008, p. 16) argued that the current moment is characterised by a shift where 'the function of media as a socializing/ideological mechanism has become secondary to its continuous modulation, variation and intensification of affective response in real time'. Significant here is the critical attention to changes in both the qualities *and* uses of public discourse. As Mark Andrejevic (2013) puts it, the invitation to engage in participatory mediated constructions of the self was accompanied by the rise of cynical distance to those representations. At the same time as those expressions lost their purchase as meaningful exchanges in a symbolic discussion between human participants, they acquired value as data within the commercial models of digital media industries. Drawing on this lineage of critical debate, in the following sections I consider how participation on digital media doubles as the labour of training the platform itself as an increasingly intelligent non-human actor in public life. This is historically significant. For all the uses humans have made of media technologies to facilitate public expression during the 20th century, that activity did not directly contribute to enhancing the calculative capacities of the medium itself. Public action and expression now *addresses and trains machines* in addition to influencing or persuading other humans (Striphas 2015).

Public communication is participation in training machines

Media platforms have a strategic interest in keeping users engaged with their feeds of content more frequently and for longer periods of time. The more user engagement platforms generate, the more attention and data are created for sale to advertisers. Platforms' content recommendation algorithms constantly 'train' on user data, refining their capacity to predict user preferences. Over time, customised feeds of content are filtered more precisely to match user preferences. For instance, when a user scrolls through their Facebook News Feed, each time they pause over, 'like', click or comment on a piece of content they generate data about their preferences, and the preferences of people like them. The News Feed gradually adapts to serve more content that matches their interests. This logic extends across platforms. For example, as we watch and rate films on Netflix, the platform learns what films we like. As we browse books on Amazon, it learns what books we like. As we click links and 'like' tweets on Twitter, it learns what political views we hold. I mean 'learns' here in terms of the capacity of a machine to accurately predict, rather than in the human sense of being able to make qualitative judgements about cultural objects based on schemas of taste, genre or political ideology.

Machines make judgements about culture that achieve the same ends as humans, but without using the same means and schemas.

The distinctive change here is not the development of procedures that regulate what ideas are created and circulated, but rather the creation of machines that make these judgements (Hallinan & Striphas 2016). Developing procedures that efficiently standardise the production of sustained audience attention has always been a feature of commercial media institutions. The institutional production of news, for instance, is defined by a bureaucratic culture that proceduralises decision-making and content production. Editors and journalists repeat a sequence of steps each day to produce a product – a newspaper or television news bulletin – that is similar in format. The format encodes knowledge, accumulated over time, about what kinds of news bulletins sustain the attention of the audience.

Consider the difference between reading a printed newspaper each morning and scrolling through a customised Facebook News Feed. The ordering of the stories in a newspaper is undertaken by a human editor. The editor makes judgements shaped by personal, institutional and professional factors: their sensibility about what is a good story, their personal values, their sense of responsibility to the public interest, the commercial imperatives of the institution, the implicit adoption of news values, and professional norms such as balance or objectivity. Every reader sees the same newspaper. In contrast, the ordering of stories in a Facebook News Feed is undertaken by a non-human algorithm. The important element here is not that a bureaucratic procedure once done by humans is now done by machines, it is rather the capacity of the algorithm to learn the preferences of individual readers and customise the feed of stories they see. The machine becomes an actor in shaping communication because it customises the news that each individual sees. The News Feed's capacity to make these judgements depends on users coding their social life into the computational architecture of the platform (van Dijck 2013). When the News Feed was introduced in 2006, the algorithmic decision-making was relatively simple. For instance, engineers programmed the feed to weight images higher than short text updates, based on the assumption that all users found images more engaging. Over time, however, the feed has been engineered to learn by training on the data generated by users as they interact with the platform.

On platforms like Facebook the ordering of public culture is increasingly delegated to machines (Hallinan & Striphas 2016). Human forms of public communication train machines to organise, curate and optimise their cultural experiences. Gillespie (2016) argues that platforms

> don't make content, but they make important choices about that content: what they will distribute to whom, how they will connect users and broker their interactions, and what they will refuse … we have to revisit difficult questions about how they structure the speech and social activity they host, and what rights and responsibilities should accompany that.

To this critical focus on the non-human decision-making power of platforms, we must also bring an understanding of the central role that participation in public life plays by coding lived experience into platform databases, enabling those platforms to more efficiently scrutinise, experiment with, and optimise their decision-making. Paying attention to how platforms structure social life means understanding public expression as not something that happens after the platform architecture is created, but as something that is always implicated in the construction of the material platform itself, and its capacity to intervene in public life. This is an important point. Think of a comparison between television and a social media platform. For all the time that the audiences spent watching television during the 20th century, that activity of watching contributed very little to the material form of the medium itself. In the case of a social media platform, however, the everyday act of watching and being watched continually transforms the platform and its capacity to be a non-human actor in public life.

Participation on media platforms, as much as it might constitute freely chosen forms of public communication, also always doubles as productive labour. The participatory labour characteristic of the digital economy was first theorised by autonomist Marxists as 'free' and 'immaterial' labour (Terranova 2000). Terranova (2000) examined the work undertaken by moderators in online chat forums of early commercial internet providers. She argued that this labour was free in the sense that it is both freely given as part of the conduct of everyday public culture, and that it is given *for free* in the sense that it was unpaid. These accounts elaborated how digital media were dependent on the freely given participation of users who organised, managed and produced the online networks of which they were a part. Andrejevic (2002) described this labour as the 'work of being watched'. The work of being watched has two facets: user-generated content and user-generated data. When users create and upload text, images and video to digital media platforms they produce the content that other users watch – they do the work of attracting the audience attention of peers that is then sold by platforms to advertisers. When users of all kinds interact with platforms they generate data that is used to target advertisements and refine platform algorithms, and is sold to third parties for market analytics. Surveillance of digital media users is not just used to target advertisements; it contributes directly to the development of the computational capacities of the platform itself. Public communication is now implicated in the generation of the computational capacity of media. The data our acts of public communication generate directly informs the creation of a media infrastructure more able to exert power over public life (Andrejevic 2013).

Public communication is participation in experiments

The development and training of an algorithmic media infrastructure depends on continuous experimentation with users. Public communication on social media routinely *doubles* as participation in experiments like A/B tests, which are part of the everyday experience of using platforms like Google and Facebook (Andrejevic 2013; Christian 2012; Crawford 2014). These tests, which are invisible to users, work like this: an A/B test involves creating alternative versions of a web page, set of search results, or feed of content. Group A is diverted to the test version, Group B is kept on the current version, and their behaviours are compared. A/B testing enables the continuous evolution of platform interfaces and algorithms. A/B testing is not unusual: *Wired* reported that in 2011 Google 'ran more than 7000 A/B tests on its search algorithm' (Christian 2012). The results of these tests informed the ongoing development of the algorithm's decision-making sequences. Two widely publicised experiments by Facebook – popularly known as the 'mood' and 'voting' experiments – illustrate how these A/B tests are woven into public culture, contribute to the design of platforms, and raise substantial questions about the impact the data-processing power of media has on public communication. Each experiment was reported in peer-reviewed scientific journals and generated extensive public debate (Bond et al. 2012; Jones et al. 2017; Kramer et al. 2014). In this section I consider the implications of these experiments for how we understand the relationship between media platforms' data-driven engineering and the public interest.

Facebook engineers and researchers published the 'voting' experiment in *Nature* in 2012 (Bond et al. 2012). The experiment was repeated, with similar results, during the 2012 presidential election (Jones et al. 2017). The experiment was conducted during the 2010 US congressional election and involved 61 million Facebook users. The researchers explained that on the day of the US congressional elections all US Facebook users who accessed the platform were randomly assigned to a 'social message', 'informational message' or 'control' group. The 60 million users assigned to the social message group were shown a button that read 'I Voted', together with a link to poll information, a counter of how many Facebook users had reported voting and photos of friends who had voted. The information group were shown the same information, except for photos of friends. The control group were not shown any message relating to voting. In total, 6.3 million Facebook users were then matched to public voting records, so that their activity on Facebook could be compared to their actual voting activity. The researchers found that users 'who received the social message were 39% more likely to vote' and on this basis estimated that the 'I Voted' button 'increased turnout directly by about 60,000 voters and indirectly through social contagion by another 280,000 voters, for a total of 340,000 additional votes' (Bond et al. 2012, p. 297).

The experiment, and Facebook's reporting on it, reveals how the platform understands itself as infrastructure for engineering public social action: in this case, voting in an election. Legal scholar and critic Jonathan Zittrain (2014) described the experiment as 'civic-engineering'. The ambivalence in this term is important: a positive understanding of civic engineering might present it as engineering *for* the public good because it mobilised democratic activity; a negative interpretation might see it as manipulative engineering of civic processes. Facebook certainly presented the experiment as a contribution to the democratic processes of civic society. They illustrated that their platform could contribute to participation in elections. The more profound lesson, however, is the power it illustrates digital media may be acquiring in shaping the electoral activity of citizens. Data-driven voter mobilisation methods have been used by the Barack Obama, Hillary Clinton and Donald Trump campaigns in recent presidential elections (Kreiss 2016). These data-driven models draw on a combination of market research, social media and public records data. While the creation of data-driven voter mobilisation within campaigns might be part of the strategic contest of politics, the Facebook experiment generates more profound questions. Zittrain, like many critics, raised questions about Facebook's capacity as an ostensibly politically neutral media institution to covertly influence elections. For example, the experiment could be run again, except without choosing participants at random; rather Facebook could potentially choose to mobilise some participants based on their political affiliations and preferences.

To draw a comparison with the journalism of the 20th century, no media proprietor in the past could automatically prevent a specified part of the public from reading information they published about an election. In contrast, Facebook's experiment demonstrates that the platform can do just this – exclude information from sectors of the community in order to manipulate an outcome.

This appears to be how some political operatives used Facebook during the 2016 US presidential campaign. Facebook announced in September 2017 that they had found 'approximately $100,000 in ad spending from June of 2015 to May of 2017 – associated with roughly 3000 ads ... [that] appeared to focus on amplifying divisive social and political messages across the ideological spectrum' (Stamos 2017). Although Facebook did not release specific details, these ads appear to be 'dark' posts, or in Facebook's terminology 'unpublished page posts'. These are promoted posts or ads that are only visible to the specific users targeted. They are commonly used in digital advertising, including by political campaigns, and they 'pose a serious transparency threat' to the mechanisms of accountability that govern political advertising and other kinds of public speech (Lapowsky 2017). The important point is this. The concerns raised about Facebook's 'get out the vote' experiments by Zittrain and others seem to be borne out. Kreiss and Mcgregor (2017) report that the major platforms embed consultants within Democrat and Republican political campaigns. These consultants help these campaigns to most effectively use the platform to engage with their targeted constituency. They are commercialising their capacity to influence the capacity of targeted groups to vote. Political operatives from election campaigns and foreign governments, just like advertisers more generally, use the Facebook platform to create 'dark' posts that are only seen by specific individuals, and not others. From a public interest perspective this is problematic because it undermines account-ability and scrutiny, it neuters the possibility of debate and deliberation, and it corrodes the process through which shared understandings of reality are produced.

Facebook's 'mood' experiment was reported in the *Proceedings of the National Academy of Science* in 2014 (Kramer et al. 2014). The mood experiment involved the manipulation of user News Feeds similar to the voting experiment. The purpose of this study was to test whether 'emotional states' could be transferred via the News Feed. The experiment involved 689,003 Facebook users. To this day, none of these users knows they were involved in the experiment. The researchers explained that the 'experiment manipulated the extent to which people were exposed to emotional expressions in their News Feed' (Kramer et al. 2014, p. 8788). For one week one group of users was shown a News Feed with reduced positive emotional content from friends, while another group was shown reduced negative emotional content. The researchers reported that 'when positive expressions were reduced, people produced fewer positive posts and more negative posts; when negative expressions were reduced, the opposite pattern occurred' (Kramer et al. 2014, p. 8788). In short, Facebook reported that they could, to an admittedly small degree, manipulate the emotions of users by tweaking the News Feed algorithm.

Much of the public debate about the mood experiment focused on the manipulation of the user experience, the question of informed consent to participate in A/B experiments, and the potential harm of manipulating the moods of vulnerable users. These concerns matter. But, as was rightly noted by Crawford (2014) and others, focus on this one experiment obscures the fact that the manipulation of the user News Feed is a daily occurrence – it is just that this experiment was publicly reported. And these experiments are legal. Users consent to being routinely involved in these experiments when they sign up to the platform (Crawford 2014). More importantly, the voting and mood experiments illustrate how public communication doubles as the creation of vast troves of data and participation in experiments with that data. In other words, when views are expressed on Facebook they not only persuade other humans, they contribute to the compilation of databases and the training of algorithms that can be used to shape our future participation in public culture.

The response of critics like Jonathan Zittrain (2014), Kate Crawford (2014) and Joseph Turow (2012) to the data-driven experiments described here, highlight some of the new public interest concerns the experiments generate. Crawford argues that all users should be able to choose to 'opt in' and 'opt out' of A/B experiments, and see the results of experiments they participated in. Zittrain proposes that platforms should be made 'information fiduciaries', in the way that other professions like doctors and lawyers are. Like Crawford, he envisions that this would require users to be notified of how data is used and for what purpose, and would proscribe certain uses of data. Turow (2012) proposes that all users have access to a dashboard where they can see how data is used to shape their experience, and choose to 'remove' or 'correct' any data in their profile. All these suggestions seem technically feasible, but would likely meet stiff resistance from the platforms. They are helpful suggestions because they help to articulate an emerging range of public interest communication concerns specifically related to public participation in the creation of data, and the use of that data to shape public thoughts, feelings and actions. None of these proposals, though, addresses directly the public interest in a collective sense; rather they are each formatted at the level of the individual consumer rights. In doing so, they replicate the values of the liberal-individualist discourse outlined by Dahlberg (2011) above.

Where critical public interest research and activism could make a necessary contribution is in articulating the collection and experimentation with public communication as data at the level of the public. We must address not just the choices offered to individual users, but the entanglement of media platforms with communication as a public act and interest and, importantly, the transparency with which this process takes place. The bigger question is that, as much as the algorithmic infrastructure of media platforms generates pressing questions about who speaks and who is heard, it also generates pressing questions about who gets to experiment with data and whether the public understands its role in the participatory process. Public communication is now a valuable resource used to experiment with public life. Mark Andrejevic (2014) describes this as the 'big data divide': the power relations of public communication now also include who has access to the infrastructure to *process* public culture as data and intervene in it on the basis of those experiments.

Media engineering and the public interest

To conclude, I suggest that there are two options for considering what media platforms as engineering projects mean for public interest communication.

The first is to retain an established account of public interest communication as only concerning discursive expression. To the extent that media have a public interest obligation this option extends only to the media's role in shaping public discussion, debate, dialogue and information sharing. Working within this public interest framework, critical accounts of media platforms would be confined to the role their algorithmic infrastructure plays in brokering speech acts.

The second option is to invite a more radical reworking of media and the public interest as going beyond discursive expression. This would involve reconceptualising media as fundamentally engineering enterprises that collect, store and process data. This option sees media organisations as engineering increasingly intelligent machines able to intervene in reality in a number of ways. If media are understood in this way then public communication must be understood as acts that not only address other humans but also address data-processing machines. Facebook and Google are each investing in augmented reality and artificial intelligence as the next generation of their platform architecture (Chafkin 2015; Recode 2016). So, as we 'attach' media devices to our bodies, in addition to whatever symbolic ideas we express, we also produce troves of data that train those machines and we make ourselves available as living participants in their ongoing experiments.

A critical account of public interest communication that contends with the engineering projects and data-processing power of media platforms has, I suggest, three starting points. Firstly, the politics of the user interface: How does everyday user engagement with a media platform generate data that trains the algorithms which increasingly broker who speaks and who is heard? Secondly, the politics of the database: How do media platforms broker which institutions and groups get access to the database? If the first concern attends to the perennial public interest question of who gets to speak, then this concern attends to the new public interest question of who gets to experiment. Thirdly, the politics of engineering hardware: How do we understand public interest communication in an historical moment when the capacity of media to intervene in reality goes beyond the symbolic? In particular, what will be the public interest questions generated by artificial intelligence and augmented reality? These technologies will take the dominant logic of media beyond the symbolic to the simulated. Media devices will automatically process data that overlays our lived experience with sensory simulations. Media become not so much a representation of the world, but an augmented lens on the world, customised to our preferences, mood, social status and location. A critical conceptual issue then for critical approaches to public interest communication is how to account for the presence and actions of media technologies as non-human actors in public culture.

While there is an emerging and important debate about the role platforms' algorithms and interfaces play as 'brokers' of symbolic expression (Clark et al. 2014; Crawford 2014; Hindman 2008), we should not frame this issue too narrowly. We need to consider what it means for the public interest when media institutions do not produce content, but instead are led by the effort to engineer a data-processing infrastructure that shapes everyday public life. The emerging investment of platforms in engineering projects like logistics, machine learning, artificial intelligence and virtual reality suggests that platforms are not creating more engaging forms of symbolic expression, but rather new kinds of media hardware and software. These investments ought to prompt us to reconsider what kinds of commercial and public institutions media companies are. If in the 20th century we understood media as flows of symbolic expression distributed via mass institutions, as we move forward media appear to be morphing into data-processing infrastructure that intervene in, experiment with and organise everyday life to challenge historical notions of what might have once been understood as public interest communication.

References

Andrejevic, M 2002, 'The work of being watched: Interactive media and the exploitation of self-disclosure', *Critical Studies in Media Communication*, vol. 19, no. 2, pp. 230–248.

Andrejevic, M 2007, *iSpy: Surveillance and Power in the Interactive Era*, University Press of Kansas, Lawrence.

Andrejevic, M 2009, 'Critical media studies 2.0: An interactive upgrade', *Interactions: Studies in Communication & Culture*, vol. 1, no. 1, pp. 35–51.

Andrejevic, M 2013, *Infoglut: How Too Much Information is Changing the Way we Think and Know*, Routledge, New York.

Andrejevic, M 2014, 'Big Data, Big Questions: The Big Data Divide', *International Journal of Communication*, vol. 8, pp. 1673–1689.

Andrejevic, M & Burdon, M 2015, 'Defining the sensor society', *Television & New Media*, vol. 16, no. 1, pp. 19–36.

Bond, R M, Fariss, C J, Jones, J J, Kramer, A D, Marlow, C, Settle, J E & Fowler, J H 2012, 'A 61-million-person experiment in social influence and political mobilization', *Nature*, vol. 489, no. 7415, pp. 295–298.

Brodmerkel, S & Carah, N 2016, *Brand Machines, Sensory Media and Calculative Culture*, Palgrave Macmillan, London.

Chafkin, M 2015, 'Why Facebook's $2 billion Bet on Oculus Rift Might One Day Connect Everyone on Earth', *Vanity Fair*, October, viewed 9 November 2017, www.vanityfair.com/news/2015/09/oculus-rift-mark-zuckerberg-cover-story-palmer-luckey.

Christian, B 2012, 'The A/B Test: Inside the technology that's changing the rules of business', *Wired*, 25 April, viewed 9 November 2017, www.wired.com/2012/04/ff_a btesting/.

Clark, J, Couldry, N, De Kosnik, A T, Gillespie, T, Jenkins, H, Kelty, C., ... & van Dijck, J 2014, 'Participations. Part 5: PLATFORMS', *International Journal of Communication*, vol. 8, pp. 1446–1473.

Clough, P T 2008, 'The affective turn: Political economy, biomedia and bodies', *Theory, Culture & Society*, vol. 25, no. 1, pp. 1–22.

Couldry, N 2010, *Why Voice Matters: Culture and Politics after Neoliberalism*, Sage, London.

Crawford, K 2014, 'The Test We Can – and Should – Run on Facebook: How to reclaim power in the era of perpetual experiment engines', *The Atlantic*, 2 July, viewed 9 November 2017, www.theatlantic.com/technology/archive/2014/07/the-test-we-canand-shouldrun-on-facebook/373819/.

Dahlberg, L 2011, 'Re-constructing digital democracy: An outline of four "positions"', *New Media & Society*, vol. 13, no. 6, pp. 855–872.

Dean, J 2010, *Blog Theory: Feedback and Capture in the Circuits of Drive*, Polity, Cambridge.

Deuze, M 2005, 'What is journalism? Professional identity and ideology of journalists reconsidered', *Journalism*, vol. 6, no. 4, pp. 442–464.

Facebook 2016, 'Search FYI: An Update to Trending', *Facebook Newsroom*, 26 August, viewed 9 November 2017, http://newsroom.fb.com/news/2016/08/sea rch-fyi-an-update-to-trending/.

Facebook 2017, 'Facebook Q4 2016 Earnings', *Facebook Investor Relations*, 1 February, viewed 9 November 2017, https://investor.fb.com/investor-events/event-deta ils/2017/Facebook-Q4-2016-Earnings/default.aspx.

Facebook 2018, 'Facebook Reports Fourth Quarter and Full Year 2017 results', *Facebook Investor Relations*, https://investor.fb.com/investor-news/press-release-deta ils/2018/Facebook-Reports-Fourth-Quarter-and-Full-Year-2017-Results/default.aspx.

Gibbs, S 2016, 'Mark Zuckerberg appears to finally admit Facebook is a media company', *The Guardian*, 22 December, viewed 9 November 2017, www.theguardian. com/technology/2016/dec/22/mark-zuckerberg-appears-to-finally-admit-facebook-is-a-media-company.

Gillespie, T 2014, 'The Relevance of Algorithms', in T Gillespie, P Boczkowski & K Foot (eds), *Media Technologies, Essays on Communication, Materiality and Society*, Cambridge, MIT Press, pp. 167–194.

Gillespie, T 2016, 'Governance of and by platforms', in J Burgess, T Poell & A Marwick, *The SAGE Handbook of Social Media*, viewed on 9 November 2017, http:// culturedigitally.org/wp-content/uploads/2016/06/Gillespie-Governance-ofby-Platfor ms-PREPRINT.pdf.

Gleit, N, Zeng, S & Cottle, P 2014, 'Introducing Safety Check', *Facebook Newsroom*, 15 October, viewed 9 November 2017, http://newsroom.fb.com/news/2014/10/intro ducing-safety-check/.

Hallinan, B & Striphas, T 2016, 'Recommended for you: The Netflix Prize and the production of algorithmic culture', *New Media & Society*, vol. 18, no. 1, pp. 117–137.

Hindman, M 2008, *The Myth of Digital Democracy*, Princeton University Press, Princeton, NJ.

Johnston, J 2016, *Public Relations and the Public Interest*, Routledge, New York.

Jones, J J, Bond, R M, Bakshy, E, Eckles, D & Fowler, J H 2017, 'Social influence and political mobilization: Further evidence from a randomized experiment in the 2012 US presidential election', *PloS One*, vol. 12, no. 4, e0173851.

Kramer, A D, Guillory, J E & Hancock, J T 2014, 'Experimental evidence of massive-scale emotional contagion through social networks', *Proceedings of the National Academy of Sciences*, vol. 111, no. 24, pp. 8788–8790.

Kreiss, D 2016, *Prototype Politics: Technology-intensive Campaigning and the Data of Democracy*, Oxford University Press, Oxford.

Kreiss, D & Mcgregor, S 2017, 'Technology Firms Shape Political Communication: The Work of Microsoft, Facebook, Twitter, and Google with Campaigns During the 2016 U.S. Presidential Cycle', *Political Communication*, Online first, pp. 1–23.

Lapowsky, I 2017, 'Facebook's election ad overhaul takes crucial first steps', *Wired*, 21 September, www.wired.com/story/facebook-election-ad-reform/amp.

McStay, A 2013, *Creativity and Advertising: Affect, Events and Process*, London, Routledge.

O'Reilly, L 2016, 'The 30 biggest media companies in the world', *Business Insider*, 31 May, viewed 6 November 2017, www.businessinsider.com/the-30-biggest-media -owners-in-the-world-2016-5///?r=AU&IR=T.

Packer, J 2013, 'Epistemology not ideology or why we need new Germans', *Communication and Critical/Cultural Studies*, vol. 10, nos. 2–3, pp. 295–300.

Papacharissi, Z 2015, 'Toward New Journalism (s) Affective news, hybridity, and liminal spaces', *Journalism Studies*, vol. 16, no. 1, pp. 27–40.

Papacharissi, Z & de Fatima Oliveira, M 2012, 'Affective news and networked publics: The rhythms of news storytelling on# Egypt', *Journal of Communication*, vol. 62, no. 2, pp. 266–282.

Recode 2016, 'Full video: Facebook COO Sheryl Sandberg and CTO Michael Scroepfer at Code 2016', *Recode*, 1 June, viewed 6 November 2017, www.recode.net/ 2016/6/1/11832608/sheryl-sandberg-michael-schroepfer-facebook-full-video-code.

Smythe, D W & Dinh, T 1983, 'On critical and administrative research: A new critical analysis', *Journal of Communication*, vol. 33, no. 3, pp. 117–127.

Stamos, A 2017, 'An Update on Information Operations on Facebook', *Facebook Newsroom*, 6 September, viewed 9 November 2017, https://newsroom.fb.com/news/2017/09/information-operations-update/.

Striphas, T 2015, 'Algorithmic culture', *European Journal of Cultural Studies*, vol. 18, no. 4–5, pp. 395–412.

Terranova, T 2000, 'Free labor: Producing culture for the digital economy', *Social Text*, vol. 18, no. 2, pp. 33–58.

Tuchman, G 1978, *Making News: A Study in the Social Construction of Reality*, Free Press, New York.

Tufekci, Z 2016, 'Mark Zuckerberg is in Denial', *The New York Times*, 15 November, viewed 9 November 2017, www.nytimes.com/2016/11/15/opinion/mark-zuckerberg-is-in-denial.html?_r=0.

Turner, G 2010, *Ordinary People and the Media: The Demotic Turn*, Sage, London.

Turow, J 2012, *The Daily You: How the New Advertising Industry is Defining Your Identity and Your Worth*, Yale University Press, New Haven, CT.

van Dijck, J 2013, *The Culture of Connectivity: A Critical History of Social Media*, Oxford University Press, Oxford.

Zittrain, J 2014, 'Facebook Could Decide an Election Without Anyone Ever Finding Out', *New Republic*, 2 June, viewed 9 November 2017, https://newrepublic.com/article/117878/information-fiduciary-solution-facebook-digital-gerrymandering.

Zuckerberg, M 2016, 'Live with Sheryl reflecting on 2016 and looking forward to the new year', *Facebook*, viewed 9 November 2017, www.facebook.com/zuck/videos/10103353645165001/.

Part II
Global contexts

6 Articulating national identity in postcolonial democracies

Defining relations and interests through competing publics

T. Kenn Gaither and Patricia A. Curtin

Introduction

Perhaps the most commonly used word in the West to describe African democracies is 'fragile.' Without long democratic traditions, Africa is a continent where normative Western notions of democracy are punctured by decades of colonialism, during which power was highly centralized and decidedly undemocratic. A 2016 *Economist* article suggested the rise of emerging democracies in Africa is tempered by worrisome signs the continent is regressing, particularly in central Africa, where 'incumbent leaders are changing or sidestepping constitutional term limits to extend their time in office, often provoking unrest' (*Economist* 2016, p. 23). Agulanna and Osimiri (2017 suggest modern Africa is plagued by 'pseudo democracies' where a flurry of problems exist, ranging from rigged elections and flawed voting systems to human rights abuses and blatant disregard for law. Such concerns aside, there are democratic success stories in Africa, and this chapter concentrates on two emerging democracies that are gaining international prominence for social reform, relative stability, and economic growth: Ghana and Mozambique (Thomas 2017; Lynn 2014). The two countries boast an emerging middle class that imbues the public interest in these nations with increasingly modern and progressive perspectives. The new middle class contrasts with rural dwellers, who often hold strong tribal roots, creating a dialectic that challenges the very notion of a unified 'public interest.'

Equally as fractious is the relationship between public relations and the public interest. Johnston (2016) points to the disagreement as to whether public relations works in the public interest or for the public interest. Regardless, the public interest in an emerging democracy is directly linked with national identity (Chandler 2004). The rhetoric of nationalism is maintained through the communicative practices of public relations, consistent with Curtin and Gaither's (2012, p. 33) contention that 'in postcolonial nations wracked by conflict, public relations practices are often government-sponsored efforts at nation-building.' In the West, the sine que non for effective public relations practice is democracy. How, then, to account for the tribal systems across emerging democracies in Ghana and Mozambique that are traditional and patrilineal, where there is no cultural adherence to democratic principles? What is the relationship between public relations and the public interest in such emerging democracies and how is the public interest conceptualized across scars of colonialism, through cultural traditions and within nascent nationalism?

This chapter suggests Africa has been both literally and figuratively constructed through the inherent asymmetry of colonialism, postcolonialism, and neocolonialism, all of which relate to who, specifically, speaks for and on behalf of the 'public interest.' The chapter uses critical/cultural and postcolonial theories to explicate the relationship between the public interest and communications practices by the state in emerging democracies, specifically in Ghana and Mozambique. It specifically asks how a postcolonial nation and emerging democracy is articulated by examining individual agency and the public interest in the lengthened shadow of colonialism. This treatment extrapolates the public from the public interest through the lens of Africa, where the legacy of colonialism has led some scholars to suggest there is a 'one-ness' or 'common Africanism' and shared 'African personality' (Boogaard 2017; Frenkel 1974; Nkrumah 1979). The chapter concludes by reconceiving the public interest in postcolonial nation-states as non-monolithic and heterogeneous, in part due to the tentacles of colonialism, which have indelibly shaped culture, governance, politics, and economics. As such, this approach privileges a shifting and fluid idea of *publics* over a more static notion of a *public*, and views colonialism as a constitutive force that elevates some publics and abrogates others.

Africa and the aftermath of colonialism

At the latter half of the 19th century, European powers eyed Africa for its natural resources, access to trade routes, and economic and human capital. To resolve territorial disputes on the continent, 14 European nations held the 1884–85 Berlin Conference, where Africa was carved up in an exercise of bureaucratic fiat, with Belgium, Britain, Portugal and Spain the primary beneficiaries (Lamb 1987). In the 1960s, many sub-Saharan countries gained independence and began nation building with the wounds of colonialism still fresh. Thomson (2016, p. 11) identified several elements that characterized these new African nations, including the previous imposition of artificial boundaries, the incorporation of Africa into the international modern-state structure, promotion of an African state elite, and absence of strong political institutions. Before democracy could take hold, Ghana and Mozambique both started with the tremendous challenges that many newly independent African nations faced:

> Djibouti had fewer than a hundred high school graduates at independence. The Congo had but a single senior African civil servant. Mozambique had an illiteracy rate of 90 percent. Zaire [now the Democratic

Republic of the Congo], a country as large as the United States west of the Mississippi, had only a dozen university graduates among its 25 million people. Several countries, such as Guinea-Bissau and Cape Verde, had not one African doctor, lawyer or accountant.

(Lamb 1987, p. 139)

Freedom from colonial overseers in postcolonial nations comes at a significant cost. Some scholars suggest the challenges facing African postcolonial nations are too great to overcome without reorganization (e.g., Amadiume 2001; Mann 2012), striking a tone far removed from the populace's great anticipation of African nationhood at independence, where scenes of jubilation and national celebrations played out across Africa. The shift from colonial to postcolonial required nations to completely reimagine their identities and rework the structures that had defined them. At stake was how a newly formed country defined itself – its essence, its identity, its culture and policies – to a global external audience and, perhaps more importantly, to its own citizens. Failure to promulgate a vision for nationhood left new countries in an amorphous state, with no structures to uphold their status as independent nations. Moreover, projecting a 'new' identity was seen as a precursory step toward reclaiming that which had been stolen during the colonial era, in which the machinery of imperialism controlled every aspect of African society (Herbst 2000).

Ghana and Mozambique are exemplars of the differences and similarities of the colonial legacy in Africa. Both are emerging democracies: that is, democracies but not fully democratic states, for reasons that might include a dominant political party, free but unfair elections, and a weak rule of law (African Elections Database 2004). Both countries are sub-Saharan, rich in natural resources and regional economic powers. Ghana's economic growth has slowed somewhat, but Mozambique is one of the continent's fastest growing economies, with both countries achieving double-digit investment growth from 2010 to 2015 (World Bank Global Economic Prospectus 2017). These economic indicators position the countries as part of the new 'vanguard of progressive reformist African states' (Newitt 2002, p. 185). Bhorat and Tarp (2016) cast Mozambique and Ghana as 'African Lions' for their economic dominance on the continent, and the rise of multi-party political systems has drawn further attention to them as potential models for the rest of Africa (Carbone 2003).

Postcolonial Ghana

Located on the west coast of Africa, Ghana was among the first African countries to gain independence from Britain in 1957. Fanon (1961) argued the first step for a postcolonial society is the reclamation of its past to find a voice and identity. For Ghana, part of its newfound identify was through its name. Under British rule, the country was known as the Gold Coast before adopting its current name after independence. The adoption of a native country name was a reclamation project, although there is debate over the meaning of the word Ghana. Some scholars argue it is named for an ancient empire that met its demise in the 12th century (Davidson 1995; Holl 1985), others that it was extrapolated from a native language in west Africa meaning 'Warrior King.' A third, and more humorous suggestion, relates to Ghana's first president, Kwame Nkrumah, whose swift rise to international acclaim was met with an equally dismal fall from power in 1966. According to this theory, Ghana is an acronym for 'God Has Appointed Nkrumah Already' (Owusu-Gyamfi 2012, para 3).

Nkrumah gained international stature in early Ghanaian nationhood for his bold vision of pan-Africanism, the ideology behind his vision of a 'United States of Africa' (Poe 2003, p. 46). In a broader sense, pan-Africanism is a belief 'that African peoples, both on the African continent and in the Diaspora, share not merely a common history but a common destiny' (Makalani 2011, para 1). Nkrumah's charisma and brash-talking idealism promised a great future for not only Ghana but all of Africa. He became a symbol of new Africa and favorite of the West because of his education in the United States and Britain. Early in his period in office, investment poured in and Nkrumah spent lavishly on building Ghana along the lines of his stated strategy of national unity. More than $16 million was spent on a conference hall to host a single meeting of the Organization of African Unity (OAU), while another $9 million was spent on a modern highway that was only a few miles long and often deserted (Lamb 1987). So revered was Nkrumah that Ghanaian schoolchildren began each day singing in chorus, 'Kwame Nkrumah is our messiah … Kwame Nkrumah does no wrong … Kwame Nkrumah will never die' (Sanders 1966, p. 138).

Walking an ideological tightrope, Nkrumah refused to outwardly align with either the Soviet Union or United States, although his professed ideology was Marxist (Boogaard 2017). While his Marxist leanings might suggest a predilection for tribalism where class is reasonably uniform, Nkrumah rejected tribalism as antithetical to his vision of African unity (Metz 1982). To Nkrumah, the Marxist position that class and class struggle and conflict are determinants of social structure clashed with a loosely defined ideology he called 'Nkrumaism' where he alone was the savior of Africa. This philosophy, in which Nkrumah bestowed quasi-supernatural abilities on his leadership, largely centered around what he called the 'African mind', where an authentic African identity existed, free from colonial power and external oppression (Mungazi 1996).

Of import is Nkrumah's insistence on an economic mode of production grounded not in neocolonialist structures but in a new socialist vision wherein production is for use and not profit, overseen by a state through a 'class conscious vanguard' (Metz 1982, p. 388). The Nkrumah future for Africa included the elimination of tribes and nationalism, which he believed was the only way for the continent to achieve its greatness. He saw the influence of neocolonialism as too great to break unilaterally and preached a utopian unity across the continent. The only way for Africa to emerge from colonialism, Nkrumah argued, was to free the African mind, where the unfettered cognitive abilities of African people could collectively shatter the burden of oppression. Unity began not at the tribal level, but at the state level, which fed Nkrumah's conception of pan-Africanism as being in the public interest.

Nkrumah used a battery of tactics to disseminate his vision of pan-Africanism, giving powerful addresses across the continent and financing initiatives such as 'unity conferences' and 'nationalist movements,' generating great interest from the global media (Sanders 1966, p. 139). In turn, Nkrumah wore Western suits to address international audiences, then switching from the *batakali* smock worn in northern Ghana to the colorful *kente* cloth for audiences in southern Ghana. Nkrumah's use of symbolism allowed him to project his own cult of personality while preaching a message of harmony and African pride. His picture appeared on stamps and on the national currency. His likeness blanketed the country on framed pictures hung in parlors and public buildings. A national newspaper cartoon serial was commissioned to tell his story. Poems were written about him. Keychains with his image were provided to all taxi drivers. Those who failed to use or display them could be imprisoned (Monfils 1977). Nkrumah was constructed as a godlike figure who could fix Ghana and Africa by appealing to the masses through a rhetoric of inclusion. The outward manifestations of Nkrumah's power centering on his status clashed with the very notion of pan-Africanism, which had an ontological foundation in unity through shared African values (Boogaard 2017). Chief among those values is collectivism and communalism: 'The African asks always not, "who am I?" but, "who are we?" and "my" problem is not mine alone, but "ours"' (Appiah 1992, p. 76). One could argue, over time, Nkrumah imposed restrictions on Ghanaians to enforce a pan-African philosophy that ultimately failed (Poe 2003).

Nkrumah's pan-Africanism is an arguable product of neocolonialism that raises noteworthy questions about notions of the public interest in Ghana. Because neocolonialism was a continental condition, Nkrumah sought a continental solution, but he found limited support from other African nations, which were either at various stages of postcolonialism or still colonized. Projecting a vision of unity within a nation and its different linguistic and cultural lines is a more realistic objective than trying to do so across nation-state lines, where difference is amplified by enormous differences. In Ghana alone, there are more than 100 linguistic and cultural groups (Obeng 1997). How to unify that which is disparate, or different, is an essential feature of nation building. Nkrumah's philosophy extended beyond the nation, however, toward continental building – a lofty aspiration that in time fizzled out as unachievable. Nkrumah's notion of the public interest was both Ghanaian and African, creating a tension between the local and global because he could not offer a cohesive vision of national identity without tying it to continental identity. While Nkrumah could essentially force a pan-African philosophy on his own people, the relative weight of his ideology weakened across nation-state lines, where his sway in political and cultural realms diminished, along with the very idea of pan-Africanism as viable and sustainable.

To narrow the broadness of African difference, Nkrumah envisaged a class-conscious oversight of production and believed the common man was ill-equipped to participate in a pure democracy. His concerns mirror those of Lippmann (1922), who viewed the ordinary public as too far removed from issues of governance to weigh in other than to assent or dissent. Nkrumah's ideology refuted colonialism and captured a perceived African authenticity while manufacturing his own greatness. These strategies allowed him to construct a national identity that was simultaneously united and divided, creating a façade that crumbled only when no amount of effective communication could hide economic collapse, stagnant growth, failed policies, widespread discontent, and confusion over internal narratives that were too inconsistent to offer a promising portrayal of the future of Ghana. As the country collapsed around him, Nkrumah made a dramatic shift toward authoritarianism:

> Newspapers and radio-TV were first gagged by a law which threatened two years' imprisonment for 'publishing news contrary to the public interest.' Editors either met every day ... or were telephoned by the party's 'media committee' to be told what was considered as 'significant news' and what was on the day's censorship list. To further discipline public opinion, Party sound trucks roamed the country playing martial music and blaring [Nkrumah's] praise. Printing presses as far away as Switzerland began turning out beautifully designed booklets and brochures, all praising his Messianic Dedication's holy name.
>
> (Sanders 1966, p. 142)

In 1966, Nkrumah's government was overthrown while he was on state visits to China and Vietnam. Nkrumah's avarice, coupled with draconian measures, including legalization of a lone political party and accusations of torturing dissidents, had drawn the ire of the United States, which he courted for aid. Ghana endured seven more governments into the new century after Nkrumah, contributing to an ongoing narrative of volatility and instability. Of those governments, four were military and three civilian, and five were overthrown by violence (Handley & Mills 2001). In 1981, J.J. Rawlings, a former flight lieutenant in the Ghanaian military, staged a military coup. Under Rawlings's leadership, Ghana introduced democratic reforms and a multi-party political system, an approach Adedeji (2001) called a 'bottom-up' strategy to spur citizen involvement in nation building as a matter of public interest. The Ghanaian economy flourished and he won the popular vote in elections in 1992 and 1996 (Herbst 1993). Since then, Ghana has had peaceful transitions of power and democratically elected governments. Coupled with its economic growth, the country has been called an 'African success story' by the World Bank (Opoku 2010).

The former Portuguese colony of Mozambique is another country where recent economic successes and democratic structures are still enveloped in a discourse of postcolonial fragility.

Postcolonial Mozambique

Located in southeast Africa north of South Africa is Mozambique, which gained its independence from Portugal in 1975. Known for its rich scenery and culture, the country is also rich in resources, including aluminum, oil, and tobacco (Workman 2016). While Mozambique is one of Africa's best performing economies, more than half its population remains under the poverty line (The World Factbook 2017). Any history of the country inevitably focuses on the country's lengthy civil war. A 1992 peace agreement between the country's single ruling party, Frelimo (Mozambique Liberation Front), and Renamo (Mozambican National Resistance Party), a rebel group turned political party, came on the heels of a decades-long war, resulting in more than 1 million deaths and 5 million displaced persons (Newitt 2002). Frelimo originated as a guerrilla movement for Mozambican independence from Portugal in the early 1960s. At independence, the movement morphed into a political party and installed Samora Machel as its president (Azevedo 1991).

Tensions in the country continue in 2017, with occasional skirmishes from Renamo insurgency groups in predominantly rural areas in Mozambique (Pearce 2017). The 1992 peace agreement introduced a multi-party democratic system, signaling the end of the country's Marxist orientation and single-party system. Gone were the colorful murals that canvassed the country's capital city of Mozambique with Marxist phrases. The country quietly changed from 'The People's Republic' to 'The Republic of Mozambique,' ushering in a new era of globalization and democratic reform (Fauvet 2013).

The economic performance of postcolonial Mozambique has fluctuated between extremes ranging from promising to abysmal; its economic growth has been marred by war, droughts, economic dependence on South Africa, drops in commodity prices, strict austerity measures, and mismanagement, leading some to liken its growth to a mirage (Castel-Branco 2014; Onyeiwu 2015). It defaulted on billions in loans in late 2016 into early 2017, and the International Monetary Fund (IMF) stopped emergency aid funds and demanded an external audit of the government's books in August 2016 (Furness 2016). The economy is one of the sparks that has reignited tensions between the feuding Frelimo and Renamo parties. When coal reserves and one of Africa's largest gas fields were discovered early in the 2000s, Renamo charged the wealth was lining the pockets of Frelimo elites and returned to guerrilla warfare (Hanlon 2016).

Mozambique emerged from a 'particularly burdensome legacy' of Portuguese colonization (Chabal 2002, p. 42). Portugal's colonial legacy was markedly bureaucratic and oppressive (Chabal 2002; Macamo 2005; Newitt 2002), even by colonial standards. The challenges of the newly independent country were clear at the outset: 'Mozambique was always going to have to struggle to bring together the various regions and peoples of this vast "geographically challenged" country' (Chabal 2002, p. 48). Similar to Ghana, the country's sheer sociocultural diversity presents complexities. More than 20 different languages are spoken, and society is organized around lineage-based chieftaincies (Newitt 2002).

Almost immediately after assuming power, President Samora Machel's government instituted a '24/20' order that mandated that many Portuguese had to leave the country within 24 hours with no more than 20 kilograms of luggage (Pitcher 2008). There is evidence Britain provided training and guidance to Ghana prior to independence (Montgomery 2004), a sharp contrast to the colonial model in which Portugal siphoned as many economic and human resources back to Portugal prior to independence of its colonies.

At the time of its independence, Mozambique was one of the world's poorest countries, with staggering illiteracy and one black doctor in the entire country. Of the country's estimated 4,000 university students, only 40 were African at independence (Lamb 1987). Not a single road or railroad connected north and south Mozambique (Wood & Dibben 2006). And unlike Ghanaian President Nkrumah, who pledged initial non-alignment to global powers, Mozambique took a sharp turn toward Marxism and alignment with the Soviet Union and Cuba. Under the new government, Machel leaned on his Frelimo party to give impetus to his vision of Mozambican identity:

> In the midst of political and administrative disarray, Frelimo asserted its own vision of national unity, swiftly consolidating one-party rule and implementing a range of other measures to limit opposition and establish control over the populace.
>
> (Rupiya 1998, para 9)

Renamo formed as an anti-communist opposition party and alternative to the single-party rule of Frelimo. South Africa (under apartheid) and the former Rhodesia (now Zimbabwe) backed Renamo in an effort to destabilize Mozambique to secure their own regional economic dominance. Renamo became synonymous with terror and a symbol of one of Africa's most ruthless counterinsurgencies (Wren 1989). A senior US diplomatic official called Renamo 'one of the most brutal holocausts against ordinary human beings since World War II,' referring to the group's record of rape, slavery, and countless other atrocities (Brooke 1988, para 2).

Mozambique abandoned its Marxist-Leninist economic policies when Machel died in a plane accident in 1986. Joaquim Chissano succeeded Machel and instituted democratic reforms, setting the country's trajectory toward an emerging democracy. In the country's shift from Marxism to democracy, one thread is Frelimo's continued assertion of the need for 'national unity,' sometimes by silencing opposition and curbing media free-doms (Darch 2016; Jentzsch 2016). Conversely, Renamo has threatened to leverage its regional strongholds and secede from Mozambique (Darch 2016). The case of Mozambique illustrates two contradictory narratives: one of Mozambique as a progressive pillar of economic growth; the other, a dueling political system bubbling beneath a democratic veneer. The case highlights the fragile nature of African democracy and the public interest, where often conflicting narratives collide in the liminal space between colonial and post-colonial, and the very idea of a 'nation' must be created and articulated. Who articulates the nation and how it is articulated are rooted in cultural con-structs artificially created and influenced by colonial powers. As these two national case studies demonstrate, the capricious drawing of national lines has left a complex legacy that casts shadows over governance:

> The problem is aggravated by the complex, multi-ethnic form of many African states, whose borders may have been created by colonial whim. Voting patterns often follow tribe or clan rather than class or ideology, so tend to lock in the advantage of one or other group.
>
> (*Economist* 2016, p. 240)

Articulation theory

Barker (2000) likened a nation to an articulation in that people in that nation can never meet in person and are different in terms of race, gender, class, age, among others, yet they are articulated as belonging to that nation. In Barker's terms, everyone can articulate, but only certain articulations will endure, often those that are consonant with – and part of – the dominant narrative of the nation. In this vein, a nation is a construct, or an imagined community (Anderson 1990). Boogaard (2017, p. 54) suggests pan-Africanism depends on the notion of an 'imagined community' that extends beyond territorial foun-dations and 'reflects a desire to build a nation, outside of the state, through a citizenry that extends beyond national boundaries.' Articulation, then, is a process of creating meaning around an identity, whether national, tribal, or continental. Owing its evolution to a range of theorists from Ernesto Laclau to Stuart Hall, to articulate is to suggest a 'joining of parts to make a unity' (Slack 1996, p. 116). If one meaning of articulation is to join together, its second meaning is 'to express,' giving it a dyadic connotation in which neither definition is more salient than the other. In Hall's terms, the theory is about the *process* of articulation:

> The so-called 'unity' of a discourse is really the articulation of different, distinct elements which can be rearticulated in different ways because they have no necessary 'belongingness.' The 'unity' which matters is a linkage between the articulated discourse and the social forces with which

it can, under certain historical conditions, but need not necessarily, be connected.

(in Grossberg 1986, p. 53)

Laclau prioritizes the hegemonic practices that take into account difference to provide some modicum of closure around that which is unstable or inchoate, calling into question issues of national identity: For example, what does it mean to be Ghanaian or Mozambican? Du Gay (1996, p. 48) extends the work of Laclau by suggesting that every identity is dislocated because it relies on an ill-defined 'other' to define itself: 'Every identity is always an ambiguous achievement because its emergence is dependent on its ability – power – to define difference.' Seen another way, an identity is partially defined by what it isn't, fundamentally fluid and stochastic. Both Hall and Laclau jointly resist the ensnarement of complete relativism by examining sites of struggle among discourses. Laclau views hegemonic practices as the structures that 'fix' difference to articulate identity. Hall's work extends beyond hegemony and power toward process and the overriding belief articulations are always contingent and variable, anchored relative to other forces, or 'one of many possible arrangements' (Weinstein n.d., p. 1).

Articulation theory provides an attempt to 'stabilize' that which is essentially immune to stasis (Barker 2000). What it means to be Ghanaian, for instance, is unfixed and bound by dominant discourses that form articulations, which themselves are always in flux through a dynamic system of cultural practices. An articulation, then, is not the only articulation, and an articulation is not a singular space as much as it is a site of contested and competing discourses. Much as Chapter 1 of this book highlights the saliency of Castells's network society, articulation theory views a network as a relational web, where relationships might be temporary or more enduring, forming *conjunctures* (Curtin 2015). At the heart of articulation theory are these relationships and the processes in which relationships form and are contextually articulated or broken apart through *disarticulation.*

Spaces that contextualize meaning are often presented in topographic terms by cultural theorists. Hall (1989, p. 42) calls them 'discursive fields' and Grossberg (1992, p. 398) 'mattering maps.' Articulation theory provides a structure for mapping the terrain of meaning making in multiple ways. First, it considers who, specifically, is the articulator. What is their stake in the articulation? What is written into existence and conversely written out of existence through this articulation? These questions might be transmogrified to the public interest by asking, what is the role of communication in fracturing or unifying the public interest in a postcolonial emerging democracy? What is the role of individual agency vis-à-vis public interest in a nation whose history has been irrevocably altered by a colonial power? How is the public interest constituted in nations where there are dozens of languages, varied cultures, and dramatically uneven socioeconomic development? In critical/cultural theory, such questions are inexorably tilted toward who has the power to define and decide dominant articulations. The possibilities are far-reaching, from heads of state and politicians to village chiefs to political systems and cultural mores; identifying how and where power resides in people, systems and structures is the key to understanding why some articulations last and others do not. Second is the nature of the articulation itself. A case can be made that Africa is commonly articulated in the West as a monolith, when in fact it comprises 54 independent countries, more than 2,000 different languages, and dramatic cultural, economic and sociopolitical differences (Brenzinger et al. 1991). Laclau suggests that a nebulous hegemonic class

> imposes a uniform conception of the world on the rest of society, but to the extent that it can articulate different visions of the world in such a way that their potential antagonism is neutralized.
>
> (Laclau 1977, p. 161)

Seen another way, articulation writes realities in and out of existence. Articulation theory seeks to dislocate dominance by revealing strands of discourses that have been unified, closely analyzing the resultant and constitutive notions of identity as sediments of multiple – not only Western – discourses. It validates that which might have been written out of consideration, uncovering hidden differences and the role of relative power in shaping worldviews. Chakrabarty (2000) picks up on the relationship between knowledge, discourse, and power by describing non-Western histories as subaltern, conceived within a 'master narrative' that could be called 'the history of Europe.' Chakrabarty's 'master narrative' of Africa is articulated through and by European power structures that seek to reinforce dominance, often ignoring the rich African history that existed long before colonialism. It is not unreasonable to conclude the public interest in Africa must be carefully scrutinized to examine how it is articulated and by whom, followed by the voices that are not privileged in the articulation, a move that could decenter colonial influence and permit multiple perspectives to arise – those of the 'other.'

Identity crisis: public relations and the public interest

The first aspect of articulation – to express – links with the communicative processes at the core of the public interest. A nation is expressed through narratives that accumulate around it. For postcolonial African nations, the colonized had no agency to challenge dominant narratives imposed by colonial rule, which viewed Africans as uncivilized and incapable of self-governance. The dominant discourse was one that was in the language of the colonial power and favored those Africans who spoke the dominant language, adopted its cultural characteristics and its interests. To Portugal, only those Africans who learned Portuguese, adopted Portuguese cultural norms, converted to Catholicism, and worked in respectable jobs could become *assimilados* (Kaiser 2017). The irony of the few who became *assimilados* is that they were neither fully embraced as Portuguese nor accepted by the population at large for shunning their African roots. The displacement of identity is a common characteristic of the colonial experience, and articulation theory suggests displacement is at least partially related to cultural practices and social norms that are not set in a vacuum; they are located at a complex intersection of narratives that can connote who is a public in the public interest. In the cases of Mozambique and Ghana, scholarly literature identifies some cultural similarities among African nations south of the Sahara, often pointing to the communal aspects of cultural identity. Pratt (2003) believes it is pointless to separate the self from the whole:

> For the African, the very notion of the self is counterproductive to his or her penchant for communitarianism, which, in turn, explains the African penchant for tribal institutions and her or his strong loyalty to the tribe in preference to the nation.
>
> (p. 450)

Julius Nyere, the first president of Tanzania, launched an entire economic policy around the communal African practices called *ujamaa* (familyhood). The plan ultimately failed but shows the attention accorded to this cultural value.

The communitarianism of Africa is embedded in the bantu word *Ubuntu*, an idiomatic expression that Archbishop Desmond Tutu (2013, on YouTube) of South Africa defines as a state of humanity in which 'a person is a person through other persons.' Tutu's definition ties in to a common cultural thread of collectivism manifest in much of sub-Saharan Africa (Rensburg 2003; Wu & Baah-Boakye 2009). While it is dangerous to overgeneralize, there is evidence that the idea of the collective – tribe, clan, kin, family, and community – are 'traditional' African values (Poe 2003, p. 157). These values position the community in Africa within several spaces; there is the 'self' – the community itself; the nationalist frame as 'part of'; and thirdly, the pan-African, where the community is subsumed by many.

Identity in postcolonialism is caught between the top-down, forced identity of colonizer, and the identity that is created from the bottom up, where human agency is captured through counter-narratives that challenge dominant systems. Some narratives are advanced through public relations and its many forms that can help educate citizens on matters of the public interest. As Rensburg (2003, p. 148) notes, '[c]ertain public relations techniques originated at the dawn of African civilization … The concept of public relations was practiced in Africa long before the era of colonialism.' Far from a historical artifact, public relations shares a common link with public interest through valorization of publics. In Africa, those publics are constructed through the communal and collective more than the individual, making the public interest inextricably linked to cultural values including family, kin, and tribe.

How communication is used to build a nation and bring people together to forge a shared identity are public relations concerns that must take into account the postcolonial experience and cultural characteristics that might require practitioners to use tactics foreign to many Western public relations practitioners. Pratt (2009) notes that folk media, such as dance, song, and storytelling, might be effective public communication measures in Ghana. In sub-Saharan Africa in general, Pratt (1986, p. 529) cites the 'known effectiveness of plays, puppetry, story-telling, songs, and folklore in the rapid dissemination of information.' In the same study, Pratt argues that face-to-face communication is highly valued and that Africans are more likely to listen to local opinion leaders than radio programs for important information. These insights extend the lens for understanding public relations as a truly global concern by demonstrating its robust practice within and outside of highly developed economies. Other issues that bleed into development are regulatory environments for growth, such as type of government, economic policy, and population growth, among many other factors. According to the 2013 World Population Data Sheet, sub-Saharan Africa will more than double in population by 2050, from today's 1.1 billion to 2.4 billion. Unprecedented population growth in Africa is one factor that led Macamo (2005) to question whether it was even meaningful to refer to the world as a global village.

Articulating a national identity: public relations and public interest

Articulation theory illuminates power by foregrounding it in the nation building of postcolonial nations, where the transfer of power from colonialist to a formal state is also a shift in locus from the external to the internal. In the cases of Mozambique and Ghana, the early articulations of nationhood were quilted into nationalism. In both cases, the discursive emphasis on 'national unity' was more public relations strategy than tactic. The articulation, or pulling together of the disparate, was a necessary condition of governance through power. Nkrumah's pan-Africanism helped construct Ghana as an independent nation to internal publics who knew only of British oversight and a nation known as the Gold Coast. In Mozambique, Machel emphasized unity to suture warring political parties into the concept of a modern nation-state disentangled from Portuguese oversight. 'Unity' was at once aspirational and inspirational; the challenge to Ghana and Mozambique was how to translate the articulation of unity into national identity at the micro-level, where political affiliation and tribal allegiance meant more than nationalism. The fault lines of those articulations persist today through single-party political systems and ethnic favoritism, problems mentioned in a 2012 BBC News report on politics in Africa:

> The challenge to democracy in Africa is not the prevalence of ethnic diversity, but the use of identity politics to promote narrow tribal interests. It is tribalism ... But in the absence of efforts to build genuine

political parties that compete on the basis of ideas, many African countries have reverted to tribal identities as foundations for political competition … In essence, tribal practices are occupying a vacuum created by lack of strong democratic institutions.

(Juma 2012, para 9)

Ghana and Mozambique demonstrate how a rallying cry of national unity can serve as a discursive hammer under oppressive regimes, pounding patriotic messages into powerless publics that might have very little in common other than geographic proximity. Articulating identity is a necessity because it provides structure for governance; but holding that structure in place against a combustible dynamic of cultural difference is the enduring challenge. In Mozambique, early public interest was defined by Marxism: the public interest is what the state says it is. The state interest did not parallel the public interest defined by Renamo, the major opposition party. The public interest was as fragile as the notion of nationhood, and Renamo offered a competing discourse to challenge state power and dislocate the public interest from culture and communication to ideology. The controlling features and centralized mechanisms of the state seeped into every realm of the public sphere, providing boundaries around any otherwise organic notion of a public interest. The ethnic communities that constitute the whole were exhorted to embrace the whole and shed existing identities.

Articulation theory would suggest a more effective strategy is both/and rather than either/or to address Laclau's question of what, exactly, constitutes national identity. Seen another way, to be 'Ghanaian' is to not be something else. The something else, or 'other' is part of what articulates what it means to be Ghanaian. A Ghanaian is not a product of the colonial forebear, the Gold Coast. A Ghanaian is not British, nor *Ashanti*, Ghana's largest ethnic group (Semple 2012). A Ghanaian is not Christian. A Ghanaian does not speak English. A Ghanaian embodies a permutation of some of these or all of these into a cultural space that constitutes a meaning as 'Ghanaian.' That meaning vacillates as culture changes and publics morph. Heterogeneity of publics amplifies the unfixed nature of national identity, where a 'community' is under constant encroachment from external forces both real and imagined. Globalization and urbanization are two forces that constantly swirl around notions of culture and affect the public interest. The complete unevenness from which postcolonial emerging democracies were born – colonizer/colony, black/white, ruling/mass, democracy/autocracy – are but some of the conditions that call for the public interest to be researched outside of political systems and ideologies that are not democratic and in contexts of difference where inequality persists.

Despite Ghana's reputation as a model emerging democracy, pockets of conflict exist, often along regional and tribal lines. According to Brechenmacher (2016, para 14), Ghana's reputation as vaunted democracy is under stress: 'In northern Ghana, for example, election-related conflict is closely intertwined with chieftaincy disputes, with local tribal divides mirroring national partisan lines.' In Mozambique, certain ethnicities have dominated the political system, prompting calls for greater representation of marginalized ethnic groups in the democratic process (Manning 2016). The continued inclusion of ethnicity in the voting process is a stark reminder that the public interest is fragmented through difference along tribal lines, which raises questions about whether that interest is more influenced by local concerns (tribe, ethnic status, class) or national concerns, including democracy and fair and legitimate elections. How the nation-state is articulated and by whom become matters of the public interest. A strong but democratic central government can arguably 'manage' the public interest, but culture is equally as formidable in shaping that interest.

How emerging democracies are born is also germane. Both Ghana and Mozambique have instituted structural adjustment programs at the behest of the IMF, resulting in civil unrest. Virtanen (2016) suggested the public interest for democracy in Mozambique is not support for economic liberalism, but resistance to the structural adjustment policies adopted by the government in the 1990s. In Mozambique, riots protesting structural adjustment prescribed measures have occurred, and Ghana has seen labor strikes for its adoption of structural adjustment programs (Kraus 1991). The adoption of such aid programs illustrates the inherent asymmetry that comes with foreign aid packages, where self-determination is sacrificed for an infusion of cash resources and agenda-driven global aid organizations. The public interest in such cases is understood in relation to economic considerations and government policy, providing important context for understanding the shape of the public interest and the struggle for controlling articulations entrenched in communicative practices.

At a *prima facie* level, the public interest cannot exist as a monolithic structure unless difference is recognized and accounted for through competing narratives. Failure to account for competing narratives is failure to recognize the same resistance that fractures a universal public interest. In Ghana, Nkrumaism resisted colonial power and imposed autocratic rule; in Mozambique, the Frelimo party formed to oppose Portuguese rule. Resistance is at the bleeding edge of postcolonialism, where Seth (2013, p. 9) describes the postcolonial nation as a 'serrated – not smooth – place, led and represented by middle classes but not inclusive of vast numbers of society who are strangers to what one might call "the culture of imperialism."' The absence of democratic history and recency of colonialism are factors that limit spaces for some notions of 'public interest' and provide yet another context for viewing the elusive nature of the public interest. A germane question in Africa is perhaps not what the public interest is, but who articulates its meaning. The cases of Ghana and Mozambique illustrate the variance of publics and shifting notions of identity, where tribal and ethnic ties are still articulated through a power struggle in which political decision making might not be in the public interest, but slant toward those of shared lineage to power structures. For public relations to realize its full global capacity, ongoing attention is needed to unpack the narratives that form around the public interest with attention toward the power structures that dominate at cultural, political, and micro-levels. How the public interest is understood is an exercise that requires the uncovering of multiple meanings and identities, recognizing the fallacy of a unified public, and accounting for the fluid interplay between historical, cultural, and communicative practices that provide a context to challenge both dominant narratives and normative concepts of public relations.

References

Adedeji, JL 2001, The legacy of J.J. Rawlings in Ghanaian politics, 1979–2000, *African Studies Quarterly*, vol. 5, no. 2, pp. 1–27.

African Elections Database 2004, viewed 3 January 2017, at http://africanelections.trip od.com/terms.html.

Agulanna, CO & Osimiri, P 2017, African Worldview and the Question of Democratic Substance in IE Ukpokolo (ed.), *Themes, Issues and Problems in African Philosophy*, Palgrave Macmillan, New York, pp. 333–349.

Amadiume, I 2001, *Re-inventing Africa: Matriarchy, Religion and Culture*, St. Martin's Press, New York.

Anderson, B 1990, *Imagined Communities: Reflections on the Origin and Spread of Nationalism*, Verso, New York.

Appiah, KA 1992, *In My Father's House: Africa in the Philosophy of Culture*, Oxford University Press, New York.

Azevedo, M 1991, 'Mozambique and the West: The Search for Common Ground, 1975–1991', *Conflict Quarterly*, spring, pp. 30–50.

Barker, C 2000, *Cultural studies theory and practice*, Sage Publications, Thousand Oaks, CA.

Bhorat, H & Tarp, F 2016, The pursuit of long-term economic growth in Africa, in H Borat & F Tarp (eds), *Africa's Lions: Growth Traps and Opportunities for Six African Economies*, Brookings Institution Press, Washington, DC, pp. 1–36.

Bivins, TH 1993, Public relations, professionalism and the public interest, *Journal of Business Ethics*, vol. 12, no. 2, pp. 117–126.

Boogaard, VVD 2017, Modern post-colonial approaches to citizenship: Kwame Nkrumah's political thought on pan-Africanism, *Citizenship Studies*, vol. 21, no. 1, pp. 44–67.

Brechenmacher, S 2016, *Ghana's Vaunted Electoral Process Under Stress*, Carnegie Endowment for International Peace Research Paper, 1 December, viewed 13 June 2017, http://carnegieendowment.org/2016/12/01/ghana-s-vaunted-electoral-proces s-under-stress-pub-66307.

Brenzinger, M, Heine, B & Sommer, G 1991, Language death in Africa, *Diogenes*, vol. 39, no. 153, pp. 19–44.

Brooke, J 1988, Visiting State Department Official Condemns Mozambique's Rebels, *The New York Times*, 27 April, viewed 23 January 2017, www.nytimes.com/1988/04/ 27/world/ visiting-state-department-official-condemns-mozambique-s-rebels.html.

Carbone, GM 2003, *Developing Multi-party Politics: Stability and Change in Ghana and Mozambique*, Crisis States Research Centre working papers series, vol. 1, no. 36,

Crisis States Research Centre, London School of Economics and Political Science, London.

Castel-Branco, CN 2014, Growth, capital accumulation and economic porosity in Mozambique: Social losses, private gains, *Review of African Political Economy*, vol. 41, no. 1, pp. 26–48.

Chabal, P 2002, The construction of the nation-state, in P Chabal, D Birmingham, J Forrest, M Newitt, G Seibert & ES Andrade (eds), *A History of Postcolonial Lusophone Africa*, Indiana University Press, Bloomington, IN, pp. 29–88.

Chakrabarty, D 2000, *Provincializing Europe: Postcolonial Thought and Historical Difference*, Princeton University Press, Princeton, NJ.

Chandler, D 2004, *National Interests, National Identity and 'Ethical Foreign Policy'*, paper presented at the International Sociology Association Conference, London, 'Racisms, Sexisms and Contemporary Politics of Belonging/s,' London, August.

Curtin, PA 2015, Exploring articulation in internal activism and public relations theory: A case study, *Journal of Public Relations Research*, vol. 28, no. 1, pp. 19–34.

Curtin, PA & Gaither, TK 2007, *International Public Relations: Negotiating Culture, Identity and Power*, Sage, Thousand Oaks, CA.

Curtin, PA & Gaither, TK 2012, *Globalization and Public Relations in Postcolonial Nations: Challenges and Opportunities*, Cambria Press, Amherst, NY.

Darch, C 2016, 'Separatist tensions and violence in the 'model post-conflict state': Mozambique since the 1990s', *Review of African Political Economy*, vol. 43, no. 148, pp. 320–327, http://dx.doi.org/10.1080/03056244.2015.1084915.

Davidson, B 1995, *Africa in History*, Touchstone, New York.

Du Gay, P 1996, *Consumption and identity at work*, Sage Publications, London.

The Economist 2016, Africa's Fragile Democracies, 20 August, viewed 20 June 2017, at www.economist.com/news/leaders/21705319-end-cold-war-multi-party-democracy-has-flourished-many-countries-it-now.

Fanon, F 1961, *The Wretched of the Earth*, Penguin Books, London.

Fauvet, P 2013, Mozambique: From Marxism to market, *BBC News*, viewed 25 January 2017, www.bbc.com/news/world-africa-21655680.

Frenkel, MY 1974, 'Edward Blyden and the Concept of African Personality', *African Affairs*, vol. 73, no. 292, pp. 277–289.

Furness, V 2016, 'Mozambique on the brink despite IMF agreement', *Global Capital*, viewed 23 January 2017, www.globalcapital.com/article/zvnrmg8cqy95/mozambique-on-the-brink-despite-imf-agreement.

Grossberg, L (ed.) 1986, On postmodernism and articulation: An interview with Stuart Hall, *Journal of Communication Inquiry*, vol. 10, no. 2, pp. 45–60.

Grossberg, L 1992, *We Gotta Get Out of This Place: Popular Conservatism and Postmodern Culture*, Routledge, New York & London, pp. 384–410.

Hall, S 1989, 'Ideology and Communication Theory', in B Dervin, L Grossberg, BJ O'Keefe & E Wartella (eds.), *Rethinking Communication, Vol. 1: Paradigm Issues*, Sage, Newbury Park, CA, pp. 40–52.

Handley, A & Mills, G 2001, *From military coups to multiparty elections: The Ghanaian military-civil transition*, Working paper series, 42, Conflict research unit, Netherlands Institute of International Relations, The Hague.

Hanlon, J 2016, Mozambique: Nyusi grapples with Guebuza's toxic legacy one year on, *African Arguments*, viewed 20 January 2017, http://africanarguments.org/2016/02/15/mozambique-nyusi-grapples-with-guebuzas-toxic-legacy-one-year-on/.

Herbst, J 1993, *The Politics of Reform in Ghana, 1982–1991*, University of California Press, Berkeley, CA.

Herbst, J 2000, *States and Power in Africa*, Princeton University Press, Princeton, NJ.

Holl, A 1985, Background to the Ghana empire, *Journal of Anthropological Archaeology*, vol. 4, no. 2, pp. 73–115.

Jentzsch, C 2016, Here are 4 reasons why Mozambique isn't a post-war success story, *The Washington Post*, 2 February, viewed 20 January 2017, www.washingtonpost. com/ news/monkey-cage/wp/2016/02/02/here-are-four-reasons-why-we-should-ques tion-mozambiques-post-conflict-success-story-narrative/?utm_term=.863c9f73971c.

Johnston, J 2016, *Public Relations and the Public Interest*, Routledge, New York.

Johnston, J 2017, The public interest: A new way of thinking for public relations? *Public Relations Inquiry*, vol. 6, no. 5, pp. 5–22.

Juma, C 2012, Viewpoint: How tribalism stunts African democracy, *BBC News*, 27 November, viewed 6 February 2017, www.bbc.com/news/world-africa-20465752.

Kaiser, D 2017, 'Makers of bonds and ties': Transnational socialisation and national liberation in Mozambique, *Journal of Southern African Studies*, vol. 43, no. 1, pp. 29–48.

Kraus, J 1991, The struggle over structural adjustment in Ghana, *Africa Today*, vol. 38, no. 4, pp. 19–37.

Laclau, E 1977, *Politics and Ideology in Marxist Theory*, New Left Books, London.

Laclau, E & Moffe, C 1985, *Hegemony and Socialist Strategy: Toward a Radical Democratic Politics*, Verso, London.

Lamb, D 1987, *The Africans*, Vintage Books, New York.

Lippmann, W 1922, *Public Opinion*, Simon & Schuster, New York.

Lynn, M 2014, Africa's rapid growth is down to industry and free markets, *The Telegraph*, 16 September, viewed 7 June 2017, www.telegraph.co.uk/finance/economics/ 11100698/Africas-rapid-growth-is-down-to-industry-and-free-markets.html.

Macamo, ES 2005, *Negotiating modernity: Africa's ambivalent experience*, St. Martin's Press, New York.

Makalani, M 2011, Pan-Africanism, *Africana Age*, viewed 30 January 2017, http:// exhibitions. nypl.org/africanaage/essay-pan-africanism.html

Mann, M 2012, Postcolonial development in Africa, *Foreign Policy Journal*, viewed 30 January 2017, www.foreignpolicyjournal.com/2012/06/03/post-colonial-developm ent-in-africa/.

Manning, C 2016, Political Tensions Threaten Mozambique's Tenuous Peace, *World Politics Review*, 21 January, viewed 13 June 2017, www.worldpoliticsreview.com/a rticles/ 17725/political-tensions-threaten-mozambique-s-tenuous-peace.

Metz, S 1982, In lieu of orthodoxy: The socialist theories of Nkrumah and Nyerere, *The Journal of Modern African Studies*, vol. 20, no. 3, pp. 377–392.

Monfils, BS 1977, A Multifaceted Image: Kwame Nkrumah's extrinsic rhetorical strategies, *Journal of Black Studies*, vol. 7, no. 3, pp. 313–330.

Montgomery, ME 2004, *The Eyes of the World were Watching: Ghana, Great Britain, and the United States, 1957–1966*, viewed 3 February 2017, http://drum.lib.umd. edu/bitstream/handle /1903/155/dissertation.pdf?sequence=1&isAllowed=y.

Mungazi, DA 1996, *The Mind of Black Africa*, Praeger, Westport, CT.

Newitt, M 2002, Mozambique, in P Chabal, D Birmingham, J Forrest, M Newitt, G Seibert, ES Andrade (eds.), *A History of Postcolonial Lusophone Africa*, Indiana University Press, Bloomington, IN, pp. 185–236.

The New York Times, 25 February 1966, pp. 12, 'U.S. officials show no regret over removal of Nkrumah', viewed 22 January 2017, https://timesmachine.nytimes.com/timesmachine /1966/02/25/79315479.html?pageNumber=12.

Nkrumah, K 1979, *Selected Speeches of Kwame Nkrumah*, vol. 1, J Obeng (ed.), Afram, Accra.

Obeng, SG 1997, 'An analysis of the linguistic situation in Ghana', *African Languages and Cultures*, vol. 10, no. 1, pp. 63–81.

Onyeiwu, S 2015, *Emerging Issues in Contemporary African Economies*, Palgrave Macmillan, New York.

Opoku, DK 2010, 'From a 'success' story to a highly indebted poor country: Ghana and neoliberal reforms', *Journal of Contemporary African Studies*, vol. 28, no. 2, pp. 155–175.

Owusu-Gyamfi, C 2012, *What is the Meaning of Ghana and Where Did We Come From?*, viewed 4 January 2017, www.modernghana.com/news/377043/1/what-is-the-meaning-of-ghana-and-where-did-we-come-from.html.

Pearce, J 2017, 'Mozambique: Unexpected truce still hangs in the balance', *The Conversation*, viewed 23 January 2017, http://allafrica.com/stories/201701180046.html.

Pitcher, MA 2008, *Transforming Mozambique: The Politics of Privatization, 1975–2000*, Cambridge University Press, New York.

Poe, DZ 2003, *Kwame Nkrumah's Contribution to Pan-African Agency: An Afrocentric Analysis*, Routledge, New York.

Pratt, CB 1986, 'Communication policies for population control: Nigeria in the African context', *The Journal of Modern African Studies*, vol. 24, no. 3, pp. 529–537.

Pratt, CB 2003, 'Managing sustainable development in sub-Saharan Africa: A communication ethic for the global corporation', in K Sriramesh & D Verĉiĉ (eds), *The Global Public Relations Handbook: Theory, Research, and Practice*, Lawrence Erlbaum Associates, Mahwah, NJ, pp. 441–458.

Pratt, CB 2009, 'Using the personal influence model to guide theory building for participatory communication in Africa', *Communicatio*, vol. 35, no. 1, pp. 30–49.

Rensburg, R 2003, 'Public relations in South Africa: From rhetoric to reality', in K Sriramesh & D Verĉiĉ (eds), *The Global Public Relations Handbook: Theory, Research, and Practice*, Lawrence Erlbaum Associates, Mahwah, NJ, pp. 145–178.

Rupiya, M 1998, 'The Mozambican peace process in perspective', *Conciliation Resources*, viewed 11 January 2017, www.c-r.org/accord-article/historical-context%C2%A0war-and-peace-mozambique.

Said, EW 1979, *Orientalism*, Vintage, New York.

Sanders, LS 1966, 'Kwame Nkrumah: The fall of a messiah', *Ebony Magazine*, viewed 23 January 2017, https://books.google.com/books?id=71nrBoK-ilEC&printsec=frontcover&source=gbs _ge_summary_r&cad=0#v=onepage&q&f=false.

Semple, K 2012, 'With fanfare, Ashanti people from Ghana install their New York chief', *The New York Times*, 3 June, viewed 12 June 2017, www.nytimes.com/2012/06/04/nyregion/ ashanti-group-from-ghana-installs-its-new-york-chief.html.

Seth, S 2013, 'Introduction', in S Seth (ed.), *Postcolonial theory and international relations: A critical introduction*, Routledge, New York, pp. 1–12.

Slack, JD 1996, 'The theory and method of articulation in cultural studies', in D Morley & KH Chen (eds), *Stuart Hall: Critical Dialogues in Cultural Studies*, pp. 112–127, Routledge, London and New York.

Thomas, A 2017, 'The inclusiveness of Africa's recent high-growth episode: Evidence from several countries', in S Kayizzi-Mugerwa, A Shimeles, A Lusigi & A Moummi (eds), *Inclusive Growth in Africa: Policies, Practice, and Lessons Learnt*, Routledge, New York, pp. 3–22.

Thomson, A 2016, *African Politics*, Routledge, New York.

Tutu, A 2013, *Who We Are: Human Uniqueness and the African Spirit of Ubuntu*, Desmond Tutu, Templeton Prize 2013, retrieved 12 January 2017, www.youtube. com/watch?v=0wZtfqZ271w#t=162.

Virtanen, P 2016, 'Pacted transition to democracy: The case of Mozambique', *Modern Africa*, vol. 4, no. 2, pp. 23–48.

Weinstein, M n.d., 'Articulation theory for beginners', viewed 25 January 2017, www. personal.kent.edu/~mweinste/CI67095/Articulation.PDF.

Wood, G & Dibben, P 2006, 'Ports and shipping in Mozambique: Current concerns and policy options', *Maritime Policy & Management*, vol. 32, no. 2, pp. 139–157.

Workman, D 2016, 'Mozambique's top 10 exports', *WTEx: World's Top Exports*, viewed 23 January 2017, www.worldstopexports.com/mozambiques-top-10-exports/.

World Bank Global Economic Prospectus 2017, viewed 18 January 2017, http://p ubdocs. worldbank.org/en/831651481727540580/Global-Economic-Prospects-Janua ry-2017-Sub-Saharan-Africa-analysis.pdf.

The World Factbook 2017, viewed 16 January 2017, www.cia.gov/library/publications/ the-world-factbook/.

World Population Data Sheet 2013, viewed 24 January 2017, www.prb.org/Publica tions/ Datasheets/2013/2013-world-population-data-sheet/data-sheet.aspx.

Wren, C 1989, 'Finally, Mozambique Sees a Way to Halt its Own Devastation', *The New York Times*, 6 August, viewed 23 January 2017,www.nytimes.com/1989/08/06/ weekinreview/   the-world-finally-mozambique-sees-a-way-to-halt-its-own-devasta tion.html.

Wu, MY & Baah-Boakye, K 2009, 'Public relations in Ghana: Work-related cultural values and public relations models', *Public Relations Review*, vol. 35, no. 1, pp. 83–85.

7   In whose interests?

Media, political communication and First Nations Australians

Jane Johnston, Susan Forde and Boni Robertson

Compared with the experience in similar developed settler countries, Indigenous engagement in Australia is not based on a comprehensive legal framework or treaty that enshrines certain rights for First People, or gives First People significant levels of control ...

(Hunt, *Closing the Gap*, 2013)

Introduction

This chapter examines the interlocking fields of media and political representation, public policy and perception, and the public interest as it relates to First Nations Australians. We begin by expanding on several key questions raised in the *Closing the Gap* issues paper, cited above, which argues that Australia lags behind other similarly developed settler countries – notably New Zealand, the United States and Canada – in implementing sustainable governance policies, mutually determined between governments and its Indigenous peoples. The issues paper proposes that: 'Key considerations for Aboriginal people and organisations when engaging with governments are: "On whose terms? About what? How?" These are critical issues' (Hunt 2013, p. 7). We add to these two equally probing and critical questions: In whose interests? and How are they communicated?

In attending to these questions, we examine how the interests of Australian Indigenous peoples fare in terms of media and political representation, communication management, public policy, and social perception. We explore key themes of participation, accountability, understanding and agency, and look at how these line up with acceptable expectations of the public interest. Our most urgent concern is to explore the apparent disconnect between what is in the interests of Indigenous peoples, and popularised notions of the national public interest. The latter appears to refer to the interest of the broader population which, by implication, either excludes Indigenous peoples or, alternatively, makes interest decisions on their behalf. Specifically, we are examining the public interest as it is represented in political communication and media in Australia, asking: What is the public interest in the context of

Indigenous affairs and politics in Australia? What institutional discourses contribute to the establishment of a national public interest which appears to exclude core interests of Indigenous peoples?

Media and managing perceptions

According to Sullivan, Indigenous affairs are driven by the management of public perception more than any other area of public policy in Australia (Sullivan 2011, p. 71). Public perception is, in turn, dependent on media representations in an increasingly mediatised society in which politics is repeatedly beholden to media logics[1] and norms. Following scholars such as Dewey (1927) and Habermas (1984, 1987), we argue that the inseparable nature of politics and communication, often channelled through the news media, provides a controlling and managed environment for determining what is in the public interest. What evolves is a perception of a public interest that is not necessarily driven by the people in question – in this case Australia's Indigenous peoples – but a public interest as determined by and serving the expectations of decision-makers, often white Australians, and very often the political interests of politicians, rather than those who are most affected. As Sullivan elaborates:

> The wishes of white Australia, the context in which those wishes are formed largely through mass media images and reporting, and the ability of government to convince white Australia of adequate funding, appropriate programs and commensurate performance are significantly more influential than the voices of Aboriginal citizens.
>
> (Sullivan 2011, p. 76)

The significance of the media in this context cannot be overstated or underestimated. With Aboriginal and Torres Strait Islanders representing about 3 per cent of Australians according to the most recent census data available (Australian Bureau of Statistics 2011, 2016), many non-Indigenous people do not have direct contact with Indigenous people. Instead, they gain their knowledge and understanding from external representations, including news stories, often incorporating an 'exchange of partisan views that are not well grounded in reality' (Australian Bureau of Statistics 2011, p. 7). In turn, 'this allows the media a critical role in influencing policy by representing Aboriginal people to the population at large and thereby controlling the political imperatives for the government of the day' (Sullivan 2011, p. 7). At the same time, mediatisation theory suggests that political imperatives align with the needs of the media, underpinning what evolves as policy and legislation. So, the media have a double role in representing Aboriginal and Torres Strait Islanders: firstly, through their inextricable connections with politicians, their media minders and the discourses that emerge out of political communication; and secondly, in their de facto role of representing Indigenous people, life and issues, to those who are disconnected with this sector of society. The public interest is thus seen through the prism of dominant narratives that evolve within this wide-open, yet paradoxically media-centric environment. One major outcome is that, in terms of accountability and management, '[t]he media forms its own constituency, blending its own interests with those of "the public" that it constructs, effacing itself from the record of political influence' (Sullivan 2011, p. 72).

The media's role here is therefore crucial, and has form. Reporting 25 years ago, the Royal Commission in to Aboriginal Deaths in Custody pinpointed the critical and negative role of the Australian media in constructing ideas of Aboriginal Australia and the direct impact these constructions had had on community esteem and sense of worth. The Royal Commission found that media portrayals of Indigenous people had marginalised this group to a significant extent, impacting upon their ability to take part in mainstream society, to be educated, to gain employment, and so on (Johnston 1991). Media reports about Indigenous issues which included very little Indigenous voice were also identified as a key reason why Aboriginal and Torres Strait Islander people felt excluded from the main conversations occurring about their communities and their lives (Johnston 1991). A quarter of a century after this report, Aboriginal people remain well behind the broader Australian population on all key markers of health, education, and income (Australian Bureau of Statistics 2016a). Particularly concerning is the statistic that while Aboriginal people make up less than 3 per cent of the Australian population, they comprise 27 per cent of the prison population (Australian Bureau of Statistics 2013).

Fundamentally, in privileging a top-down approach to determining Indigenous public policy, power relations are central. Mansell points out that attempts to reform injustices against Indigenous people have been carried out at the behest of non-Indigenous Australians. 'It is they who have stated what is in the best interests of Aboriginal people in the future' (Mansell 1992, p. 1). In particular, in a communication context, we argue that power is unevenly meted out in the relationship management between government and Indigenous people through demands of accountability imposed on Indigenous people but not on government (Sullivan 2011; Commonwealth of Australia 2012). Additionally, there is disproportionate resourcing in the capacity to access the media, harness public relations, and contribute to public policy (as indicated above, all social and economic markers bear this out; see Australian Bureau of Statistics 2016a). With this in mind, we are drawn to the field of critical theory which directs attention to power, and we couple it with mediatisation theory which examines the way media norms and cultures saturate understandings of society and thereby potentially drive public policy. We use these theories to situate our interrogation of how the 'interests' of First Nations Australians are managed, incorporating threads of public interest theory, particularly as it pertains to process and participation. We draw on the case study of the Northern Territory Emergency Response (NTER, also known as 'the intervention') to illustrate our argument. Our chapter deals with a complex and dense field of inquiry and while we focus our examination on communication and media issues in order to examine these through a public interest lens, we must also provide context. Accordingly, our chapter incorporates issues of governance, political representation, and media management in its analysis of public interest communication. Most important is our examination of these factors on public perceptions of First Nations people, and the development of policy that delivers culturally apt and targeted services.

Whiteness and critical theory

Our understanding of critical public interest theory calls for parallel considerations of context and power. Within the context of Australian society, the media play a key role in the broader public understanding of indigeneity. While around 3 per cent of Australians are Indigenous, this population is not equally distributed, with the mostly remote regions of the Northern Territory comprising 29 per cent Indigenous people, and other parts of the country including less than the 3 per cent average. Notably, the Australian Capital Territory (ACT) – the centre of the Commonwealth government – is home to just 1.7 per cent of Indigenous citizens (Australian Bureau of Statistics 2011). According to the 2012 Australian Reconciliation Barometer (ARB)[2] the limited personal contact that many in the general community have with Aboriginal and Torres Strait Islander people is paralleled by secondary sources, like the media 'that may not present a balanced perspective' (ARB 2012, p. 5). In turn, this results in high levels of prejudice and low levels of understanding about one another (ARB 2012, p. 5). The 2010 ARB found that nearly 40 per cent of non-Indigenous Australians nominated the media as their main source of information about Indigenous Australians, further noting:

> The importance of the media as a source of information on Indigenous Australia is concerning given that only 16% of general community respondents agree that the media presents a balanced view of Indigenous Australia
>
> (ARB 2010, p. 12)[3]

As Proudfoot and Habibis (2015) rightly point out, this makes the media a powerful influence on public opinion and policy direction, highlighting the need for critical interrogation.

In light of the lack of contact across cultures, it is notable that scholars have used the idea of critical whiteness theory to examine the treatment of Indigenous Australians (Moreton-Robinson 2000, 2009, 2015; Proudfoot & Habibis 2015; Weedon 2004). Bourdieu's concept of habitus provides a building block here by positing the idea of a 'matrix of perceptions, appreciations, and actions' which, in turn, integrates experiences, and causes individuals to view the world in a particular way (Bourdieu 1977, p. 83, cited in Proudfoot

& Habibis 2015). In proposing 'whiteness' as a strategic rhetorical strategy, Nakayama and Krizek (1995) argue that 'communication scholars have often overlooked the importance of whiteness as an influence in their research', and suggest its use as a rhetorical construction. This strategy is used in the examination of Indigenous Australia by Proudfoot and Habibis, who explain that: 'By focusing on the dominance of white social constructs, whiteness theory shifts attention from marginalised disadvantaged groups to the investigation of the behaviours and experiences of those that are dominant' (Proudfoot & Habibis 2015, p. 173). And so, the normative cultural nature of Euro-Australian ideologies, values and perceptions, including those of the mainstream media, form an 'invisible standard against which all other values and behaviours are judged ... in a taken-for-granted, everyday reality' (Proudfoot & Habibis 2015, p. 173; see also Pease 2010, p. 112).

Moreton-Robinson clarifies:

> Race matters in the lives of all peoples; for some people it confers unearned privileges, and for others it is the mark of inferiority. Daily newspapers, radio, television, and social media usually portray Indigenous peoples as a deficit model of humanity. We are overrepresented as always lacking, dysfunctional, alcoholic, violent, needy, and lazy ...
> (Moreton-Robinson 2015, p. xiii)

Indeed, she posits that Australian national identity – overwhelmingly based on 'white possession' as expressed through the characterisation of surf lifesavers, 'diggers',[4] surfers, farmers, mates and so on as 'real Australians' – is based on the dispossession of Indigenous peoples. It plays out in the marginalisation of 'nonwhite migrants and Indigenous people' who do not embody the same principles as the digger, the heroic surf lifesaver, and so on (Moreton-Robinson 2015, p. 21). She notes white Anglo, heterosexual and middle-class males are overrepresented in government, the legal profession, the judiciary, bureaucracies – all the major institutions of society – and continue to shape society in their own image (Moreton-Robinson 2015, pp. 81–82). A disparity exists in the level of Indigenous representation in government, which for many years was non-existent, and remains extremely low. While in 2017 there were three Indigenous parliamentarians in the Australian Parliament, Indigenous people nevertheless remain underrepresented; until the 1970s there was no Indigenous representation at all. This lack of representation was reflected in the *Recognising Aboriginal and Torres Strait Islander Peoples in the Constitution Report* that found Australia was out of step with some countries – New Zealand was cited as an example – in having no dedicated Indigenous seats in Parliament (Commonwealth of Australia 2012, p. 177). Moreover, critics argue that ministers and their political staff have

> little or no experience outside the narrow world of politics ... There is a real need to improve the inherent lack of diversity and ensure our

policymakers better reflect the background, cultures, gender and experiences of the communities on which our policies impact.

(Colvin 2014)

This is evidenced institutionally by governments and media in the development of initiatives and policies relevant to Indigenous peoples, as illustrated in the NTER discussed in this chapter. Critical whiteness theory, then, provides a basis to understand the broad and pervasive way Indigenous peoples are constructed within settler societies, and the impact this has not only had on their status within society, but on the enactment of policy. We now take this consideration back to a discussion of media and examine how the notion of mediatisation further illuminates considerations of the public interest and First Nations Australians.

Mediatisation, public perceptions and Indigenous Australians

The dominant or mainstream media play a key role in managing public perceptions, interfacing with governing bodies (including media minders and politicians), and, ultimately, influencing the adoption of policies that frame the lives of Indigenous individuals and communities. Each of these functions can be considered through the lens of mediatisation.

Mediatisation is understood as the 'processes whereby the logic and institutionalized norms of the media affect the behavior of actors and institutions belonging to other societal subsystems' (Laursen & Valentini 2014, p. 28; see also Asp & Esaiasson 1996; Esser & Strömbäck 2014; Koch-Baumgarten & Voltmer 2010; Strömbäck 2008). While relevant for any aspect of society, the interface between politics and political communicators with the media is most notable (Asp 1986; Johnston & Forde 2017). Asp notes how

political actors have, to a great extent, adapted to the requirements which the mass media place on their coverage of the political world. This tendency to adaptation is called 'the mediatization of politics'.

(Asp 1986, p. 380)

And so, while essentially a media theory, mediatisation is also a way of understanding and analysing the broader socio-political environment (Johnston & Forde 2017). The adaptation by political actors includes acceptance of the norms or logics of the media. This includes news values (Galtung & Ruge 1965) and, in particular, the news value of conflict, commonly found to be an essential ingredient for news coverage (Johnston 2013; Tiffen 1989).

While McCausland (2004, p. 85) warns that it is difficult to isolate the interaction between media coverage of current events, political leadership and rhetoric, and community attitudes – with no clear linear causality between the creation of negative stereotypes of Indigenous communities – qualitative research has found close links between these variables (see, for example,

Australian Reconciliation Barometer 2010, 2012; McCallum et al. 2012). One journalist, in giving evidence to the 1991 Royal Commission into Aboriginal Deaths in Custody, outlined how media norms operated in this environment:

Racial stereotyping and racism in the media is institutional, not individual. That is, it results from news values, editorial policies, from routines of news gathering that are not in themselves racist or consciously prejudicial. It results from the fact that most news stories are already written before an individual journalist is assigned to them, even before the event takes place. A story featuring Aboriginals [sic] is simply more likely to be covered, or more likely to survive sub-editorial revision or spiking, if it fits existing definitions of the situation.

(cited in Plater 1992)

This statement – now widely cited across the post-Royal Commission literature – finds much common ground with international scholarship into how media generally treat the representation of minorities (see, for example, Cottle 2000; Couldry & Curran 2003; Dutta 2011; Dutta & Pal 2011; Forde 2011; Johnston & Forde 2017; Meadows 2000; Weedon 2004). Cottle (2000) highlighted the need to recognise how discourses, narratives and media representations are produced within and through state, institutional and everyday practices and discourses. McCallum, Meadows, Waller, Dunne Breen and Reid examined connections between media and Indigenous policymaking in Australia, finding 'the way Indigenous issues are portrayed in mainstream news media does impact on the way Indigenous affairs policies are developed, communicated and implemented' (McCallum et al. 2012, p. vii).

McCallum et al. (2012) used mediatisation theory to examine the embedded nature of media within the political framework, in policymaking and Indigenous representations (see also Johnston & Forde 2017). They cite one 'extreme example of mediatized policymaking' as illustrated in the announcement of the Australian NTER (or 'the Intervention') in June 2007, 'whereby Australia's Prime Minister announced a military-led incursion into Northern Territory (NT) Indigenous communities to instigate a suite of policies that fundamentally changed the direction of Indigenous affairs policy' (McCallum et al. 2012). This political action and policy initiative – the Intervention – comfortably fits with historical media representations of Australian Indigenous peoples and, to this end, was a publicly acceptable response to perceived Aboriginal 'problems'. However, the media's coverage of this event has been widely criticised as contributing to a moral panic about violence and child abuse in Aboriginal communities, compounding the already stereotyped, negative and over-simplistic portrayal of Aboriginal communities, and identifying problems as a threat to social order (Proudfoot & Habibis 2015). This reinforces and extends the social discrimination against Indigenous Australia. In their critical discourse study of this event, Proudfoot and Habibis found mainstream news supported the government, presenting the argument that 'white governance was needed to restore civility and moral order to remote Aboriginal communities in the NT' (Proudfoot & Habibis 2015, p. 178). They further found that the news media emphasised bipartisan non-Indigenous and Aboriginal support that constructed a sense of national unity about what was perceived as a national emergency.

Media representations which reflected the political rhetoric of the time centred on the perceived public interests being served via the 'national interest' with a focus on the 'little children' and 'little victims' in the communities (Proudfoot & Habibis 2015, p. 174). In short, the media both *perceive* and *assert* that various public interests are well served by the Intervention. Proudfoot and Habibis conclude by noting that in attaching its investment to discriminatory policies, coupled with an absence of meaningful consultation, the government of the day confirmed 'the institutional and cultural power of white Australia over its First Nations peoples ... potentially adding to earlier damaging narratives of their engagement with the Australian state' (Proudfoot & Habibis 2015, p. 184).

In their research, McCallum et al. (2012) found policymaking in this instance was *media-driven*; that is, the NTER policies were framed for the benefit of the media. Their interviews with policymakers found that although the policymakers rarely had any direct contact with journalists, they were media experts who understood and monitored news, could anticipate how an issue might play out in the news media, adapt their practices to pre-empt public responses to their policies, react to negative and positive news stories, and use the news media strategically to develop publicly successful policies (McCallum et al. 2012). Importantly, they found close relations between policymaking, communication and media, with senior managers and communication staff working together in the implementation of new policies; indeed, 'the media was seen as absolutely hand in glove with successful policy implementation' (McCallum et al. 2012, pp. 17–18).

The findings confirm the importance of the communication roles in government and the impact this has on policy areas. Ultimately, they found that '[p]olicymakers identified the 2007 NT Intervention as a "template" for media-driven policymaking in Indigenous affairs' (McCallum et al. 2012, p. 18), adding:

> our study has found that media-related practices are intimately woven into the fabric of policymaking. Media logic operated at all levels of the policy process, from development, through announcement, to implementation.
>
> (McCallum et al. 2012, p. 21)

McCallum, Waller and Meadows found Indigenous leaders had identified the need for their own spokespeople to become 'media savvy' – to influence policymaking they had to learn and then adjust to media agendas and routines in order to have their messages about Indigenous health and education initiatives heard. It was only when Aboriginal people began adapting to these logics that they started to feel an impact. Still, they felt the more conservative Aboriginal voices were more likely to gain traction with mainstream media outlets and that these voices were the most likely to be amplified (McCallum et al. 2012a, pp. 105–108). These tendencies are compounded with further consideration of the resourcing of and access to media, and to the political and policy processes. We therefore now turn to issues of both accountability and resourcing to foreground a focused consideration of First Nations people and the public interest in Australia.

Accountability and resourcing

Sullivan (2011) and Tiernan (2014) point to flashpoints in history and changes in the administration of the Australian public sector in the 1970s and 1980s which led to significant shifts in Indigenous affairs and relationships between government and Aboriginal and Torres Strait Islander people. A new managerial regime (New Public Management, NPM) was said to lead to 'a democratic deficit' that disadvantaged Aboriginal people more than most others. It reduced the accountability of government 'while demanding oppressive accountability from its Aboriginal population' (Sullivan 2011, p. 68). The new system shifted public accountability more towards ministers 'thus requiring greater attention to controlling the perception of achievement' (Sullivan 2011, p. 69). With this emerged the increased adoption of media management to ensure that the public, via the media, were apprised of the minister's achievements and the perception of ministerial performance. This is easily read as a move to mediatised politics, with government public relations controlling what Sullivan describes as 'mediated accountability, which requires careful management' (Sullivan 2011, p. 72).

A central element in this was inequitable resourcing. Moloney (2006) proposes resource subsidies for those who are otherwise disadvantaged as a way of redressing imbalance, based on 'the need to regulate the quality and quantity of public knowledge … in the interests of equal participation' (Moloney 2006, p. 170). His argument supports the process model of the public interest, which suggests the public interest is not outcome-based; rather it is based on making sure the process is fair and equitable (Moloney 2006, p. 80). The paradox is that without access to resourcing, minority groups such as Indigenous Australians cannot contribute to public interest discourse in the same way as other actors, such as politicians, and are often excluded and silenced because of this. Alternatively, Indigenous voices that *are* heard are often the same spokespeople over and over again; sources that are easily accessed by the media and who deliver established media angles on particular issues. Indigenous media are the best and most representative source for the Aboriginal public interest, or more clearly, for the voices of Indigenous Australia (Meadows 2000; Forde et al. 2009), but again, resource inequity is a defining characteristic. Most Indigenous media exist through the

Australian community broadcasting network – a valued but under-resourced sector – with little capacity for widespread audiences due to limitations on community media marketing, and public relations. The introduction of National Indigenous Television (NITV) in 2007 improved resourcing to government-supported Indigenous media and identified an Indigenous-only station as the nation's third public broadcaster. Resourcing, however, was limited. According to Rennie (2014), NITV was originally funded for AU $48.5 million over four years (equating to just over AU$12 million annually), which compared poorly to the budget for Canada's Aboriginal Peoples' Television Network at the equivalent of AU$36 million *per year*, and Maori Television in New Zealand which was similarly funded to AU$32 million per year. Other forms of Indigenous media – national newspapers, online news sites, and social media blogs – exist and serve an essential purpose for community (Meadows 2015), but their resourcing and reach cannot compare to nationally funded public broadcasters (the Australian Broadcasting Corporation, for example, receives close to AU$1 billion per year in public funding to operate television, radio and online services; see McNair & Swift 2014) or commercial news organisations.

In both the media and political spheres, then, resource inequities impact on the capacity of Indigenous interests to be advanced and to have equal voice and purchase. Parliamentarians, for example, are well served by resources and their staffers contribute significantly to the dominant discourses of Indigenous affairs. Australia has been found to have a higher ratio of ministerial advisers per minister than most comparable countries, at a ratio of more than eight to one (Sullivan 2011; see also Podger 2006, p. 12). Political staffing is described as 'large, active [and] interventionist' (Tiernan 2007, p. 150) and, further, 'the gatekeepers for today's governments. Armed with formidable weapons, including modern communication technology and taxpayers' funds, they are well placed in the battle to control the information' (Grattan 2007, p. vii).

We argue that when placed within the context of equity with Indigenous human resourcing, which brings with it access to communication and public opinion, there is a significant imbalance with a concomitant public interest imperative at stake. In an earlier article, two of the chapter authors (Johnston & Forde 2017) identified how the government has, on occasion, facilitated access to media training for Indigenous people – for example, in the context of the widely publicised public apology to the Stolen Generation – where Indigenous people were included in the government's media agenda in this highly mediatised event.[5] Indeed, 'in preparing and accommodating members of the Stolen Generation', Prime Minister Kevin Rudd 'gave participants "ownership" of the event and also undoubtedly assisted in managing the way it was represented', which ultimately reflected on the new government (Johnston & Forde 2017, p. 13). Where Indigenous peoples' views *suit* the government's agenda, then they are brought in to the media discussion and indeed trained to maximise their agency with the media. In other circumstances, when the Indigenous perspective – perhaps, the Indigenous public interest – is at odds with the policymakers' agenda, then the lack of Indigenous voice and agency is not a priority to be addressed or facilitated.

First Nations peoples and the public interest

While there is a buoyant literature that relates to public interest in Australian law and public administration (see, for example, Meyerson 2007; Wheeler 2006), scant attention has been paid to the public interest as it relates to specific socio-political issues in contemporary Australia. The public interest had rarely, if ever, been invoked in relation to Australian Indigenous issues – that is, until the publication of a series of essays, *Who Speaks for and Protects the Public Interest in Australia?* in 2015. Following others who have examined the public interest internationally, and in difference contexts (see, for example, Dewey 1927; Flathman 1966; Goodin 1996; Johnston 2016), its 39 short essays on topics including the environment, mental health, education and Indigenous futures recognise the abstract and complex nature of the public interest. Indigenous leader Pat Dodson's essay argues for a pragmatic approach to the public interest, reflective of others who have argued for a similarly practical response (see, for example, Dewey 1927; Johnston 2016):

> We seem to spend a lot of negative energy caught up in false binaries around white guilt and black victimhood, white blindfolds and black armbands, collective rights versus individual responsibility, symbolic reconciliation versus practical reconciliation, the Left versus the Right, and so on. The outcome of this dissonance is policy that responds to ideology and ingrained prejudice rather than the needs or aspirations of those to whom it is directed.
>
> (Dodson 2015, p. 37)

Dodson's essay is reflective of the idea that policy development is conducted from within normative white frameworks of the 'settler state and its institutions' with 'conquest and domination' remaining the philosophical foundation of the relationship (Dodson 2015, p. 37; see also Moreton-Robinson 2015). Moreover, he points to the small numbers of Indigenous Australians as lacking the power or capacity to exert significant influence over policy matters, particularly where rights, interests and aspirations are seen to conflict with the mainstream. Robertson et al. argue that in order for governments to achieve policies which can overcome Indigenous disadvantage, future research is needed to investigate non-Indigenous attitudes towards, and knowledge of, First Nations peoples. 'This is essential … particularly where the development of policies pertaining to Indigenous peoples requires cooperative action and the support of the broader Australian population' (Robertson et al. 2005, p. 1).

Dodson calls for a new approach which moves beyond consultation and ideology, and gives serious consideration to incorporating the idea of free, prior and informed consent in policy and practice. This, he argues, must be based on a series of premises including constitutional recognition of Indigenous Australians, accompanied by 'meaningful dialogue and substantive reform' (Dodson 2015, p. 37). His argument is consistent with many of the fundamental assumptions of the public interest (see, for example, Dewey 1927; Sorauf 1957), that those with less political or social representation, or weaker, subaltern publics, should be treated equally within representative democracies. Accordingly, invoking the public interest reminds those in decision-making positions that they must recognise and consult interests of the 'unorganized, unrepresented or underrepresented' (Sorauf 1957, p. 639). 'The public interest then becomes a symbol for the attempt to recognize and consult interests that might be forgotten or overlooked in the pressure of political combat' (Sorauf 1957, p. 639). However, even where minority interests are consulted, such as in the case of Indigenous land rights, 'whitewashes' in interest outcomes have occurred. Banerjee highlights this in her examination of colonial discourses and the national interest:

> granting of Native Title did not always mean control of the land and its resources, especially when the clarion call of 'national interest' was sounded. Tourism, the creation of national parks and mining interests were all enclosed under the rubric of national interest and in almost every case, Aboriginal interests were put last.
>
> (Banerjee 2003, pp. 255–256)

For Indigenous health leader Kerry Arabena, the public interest is tied to not only the future of Indigenous people, but the future of the environment and living ecosystems. Her essay (2015) points to the common threat of environmental degradation shared by both Indigenous and non-Indigenous people, which must be managed for collective public interest outcomes. to be achieved:

> why is 'care for country' only for Aboriginal and Torres Strait Islander people? Why can't all people care for country? In order to ensure our country is available for future generations we have to reconcile older knowledge traditions with modern ones, then act on how to live within the structure and functioning of the planet. Our new public interest processes need to reconcile human and ecosystem health, and find a language for new discourses that allow this to happen.
>
> (Arabena 2015, p. 39)

She argues for a relational focus in building public interest capacity (between peoples and across institutions); situational (concerned with place); and integrated (between and across diverse knowledge systems and ecosystems) (Arabena 2015).

Arabena's words are echoed by public intellectual Bob Douglas, who sees a binary between the public interest and special interests, arguing that pressure on governments to maintain a 'business-as-usual' approach and neglect reforms of long-term public interest 'are enormous' (Arabena 2015, p. 70). Douglas's argument speaks to the public interest in Indigenous affairs, of resourcing, and of universal issues such as the environment. He notes: 'The entrenched special interests of those who stand to lose by reform are well resourced and well organised and easily have the ear of government and the media' (Douglas 2015, p. 90). He supports economist Ross Garnaut's (2013) argument for the introduction of a new, independent, non-government body to coordinate debate on issues relating to the public interest – an independent centre of public interest, a Public Interest Council (see below). This would find representation in multiple organisations and institutions to serve as a balance to other peak bodies that stand for business and the economy, such as the Committee for Economic Development Australia (CEDA) and the Business Council of Australia (Douglas 2015, p. 70; see also Garnaut 2013).

As an internationally recognised authority, Garnaut's ideas around a Public Interest Council add weight to the normative approach presented by critical theorists and social justice thinkers like Dewey (1927), Rawls (1971), Habermas (1996) and Sandel (1996). He presents a social-contract model not centred on social stability, norms and justice, but economics and, as such, these provide a compelling layer of argument for a public interest watchdog of sorts. At the same time, the economic arguments are bound tightly with social justice issues. 'Modern economic life everywhere is testing how far private interests can set the rules for a market economy … making reform in the public interest more and more difficult' (Garnaut 2013, p. 18). Garnaut admits:

> The public interest is the much harder choice, but it has better consequences … [however,] the public interest approach will not be chosen unless many Australians are prepared to support policies that sometimes go against their immediate interest.
>
> (Garnaut 2013, p. 4)

The binary exists between long- and short-term approaches to the public interest – the latter consistent with what Garnaut calls 'the Great Australian Complacency of the early twenty-first century' (Garnaut 2013, p. 5). But, he suggests, 'let us consider alternatives to sleepwalking into a deeply troubled future as if we had no choice at all' (Garnaut 2013, p. 5). The choice for the public interest is to manage and adjust living standards to accommodate the post-boom economy – or expect this will come from externally driven factors – with the country's disadvantaged being the worst hit. The 'unhappy reality that policy change in the public interest seems to have become more difficult over time' (Garnaut 2013, p. 17), is attributable to two things: first, a social shift whereby private interests set the rules for the market, where 'everyone pushes ... to the limit for their own advantage' (Garnaut 2013, p. 18); second, the range of instruments available to influence policy including the 'modern media' which have 'transformed the way that the old media presents public policy choices' (Garnaut 2013, p. 17). As such, this second element centres firmly on an environment of mediatisation where private interests and self-interest become intractably embedded, driven by the powerful, the rich and the well-resourced.

Garnaut does not specifically address issues of Indigenous inequality in his proposal, though it is implicit that his public interest approach is intended to address the disadvantaged. Others, such as the Chairman of the Productivity Commission Gary Banks (2005), however, cite inequality of Indigenous Australians as a 'reform challenge' for the future. Delivering addresses to the International Monetary Fund, World Bank and Organisation for Economic Co-operation and Development in 2005, he proposed that

> while many Australians have benefited from the strong growth in household incomes over the past dozen years ... it would be difficult to argue that current disparities between Indigenous and other Australians were satisfactory.
>
> (Banks 2005, p. 24)

Meanwhile, commentators are not optimistic of public interest outcomes. Tiernan (2014, p. 31) proposes that while Garnaut has outlined 'a reform blueprint for Australia after the boom ... [the] political culture – the inability or unwillingness of entrenched interests to make concessions to the "public interest" – now represents the greatest impediment to reform'.

Conclusion

Australia, like many other countries, has grappled with the public interest as a way to inform debate, policy and reform. And, like other countries, it returns to the idea that a public interest criterion is intrinsically useful because it requires decision-makers to consider many factors that might otherwise be ignored (Garnaut 2013; Rice 2015; Wheeler 2006). So, too, we argue that the public interest can speak to the interests of those who might otherwise get lost in the maelstrom of modern politics – the Indigenous Australians who represent less than 3 per cent of the country's population but who surely occupy a heightened place in the nation's history and culture.

If government is serious about considering Indigenous interests as part of the wider public interest agenda, Sullivan suggests consideration should be made of the following:

> Aboriginal development cannot continue to be directed from the centre in Canberra and state capital cities. Planning, implementation and accountability should occur at the local and regional levels, and intrusive

financial regulation should give way to processes of continual reciprocal accountability in narrative, as well as statistical, form.

(Sullivan 2011, p. 70)

Following this, consideration should be made of developing a Public Interest Centre (or Council) that includes a diverse range of voices on Indigenous issues to mitigate the current marginalisation of Indigenous voice in policy development, debate and implementation on issues concerning their communities. In his proposal for an Independent Public Interest Centre, Garnaut's views align with elements of classic conceptualisations from Dewey (1927), but more so Lippmann (1927), that it should be initiated by government and constituted of agencies, departments, universities and the 'best of the media' (Garnaut 2013, p. 16). However, this line-up would be no simple task. As we have seen, the demarcation between political views and positions is not a simple one – as political logics have moved to adapt to media logics.

Certainly, giving Indigenous peoples greater voice would be essential for a greater public interest communication agenda. This would assist to bring the narrative about the Indigenous public interest in to discussions about the broader, mainstream public interest. This might set media and political agendas on a path of highlighting commonalities rather than binaries in relations between Indigenous peoples and the more recent settler society. So, too, the 'best of the media', as Garnaut describes it, should not preclude Indigenous media – indeed, quite the reverse. A balance must be struck, with diversity of voices at all levels. Earlier considerations identify the resource inequities evident in the media landscape, significantly limiting Indigenous opportunity and potential to impact on debates surrounding community issues and subsequent policy initiatives (see, for example, Rennie 2014; Forde et al. 2009). Molnar and Meadows cited Indigenous media practitioners' views that (in the case of Indigenous media policy), policy decisions are taken 'behind' Indigenous people and their communities, and that attempts to establish Indigenous media voices were only gained through struggle and opposition from both dominant media groups and a government reluctant to resource it (Molnar & Meadows 2001, pp. 5–6). This historical context sets up an inequity that continues through to the present day.

Alternative models to Garnaut's centre, such as Ireland's Constitutional Convention, which saw government ministers working alongside citizens to identify big social issues including gay marriage, are indicative of the potential of an independent centre of national polity (O'Mohoney 2014). Likewise, other countries' moves to implement constitutional changes that mandate Indigenous representation in parliament, such as in New Zealand, can provide for public interest communication fora. In whatever forms and models that might arise, however, equitable and fair communication opportunities must be ensured if public interest communication is the goal. A deeper understanding of the impact of whiteness and more recent mediatised policy practices must be reached if this goal is to be realised.

Notes

1 Media logics are a central component of mediatisation theory, explained as the ways in which the media organise, process and transmit information, including presentation, focus and emphasis (see Altheide & Snow 1979; Johnston & Forde 2017).
2 This is described as a biennial national research study that measures the progress of reconciliation between Aboriginal and Torres Strait Islander and non-Indigenous Australians.
3 These are the most recent references to media in this biennial report which, despite noting the re-launch of the National Indigenous Television station (NITV) as part of Australia's Special Broadcasting Service in 2012, does not follow up on media in the 2014 report. Notably, the 2010 statistics on media bias or representation were not followed up in either subsequent Barometer Report.
4 The term 'digger' is a familiar and commonly used Australian word to refer to an Australian soldier. The word was in original use in World War I, when national myths and stories about the bravery of the Australian 'diggers' at Gallipoli and on other battlefields began (see Nicoll 2001).
5 In 2008 Prime Minister Kevin Rudd apologised to the country's 'Stolen Generations' of First Nations people for previous government policies that removed Indigenous children from their families and placed them into white care. It was a highly mediatised event (see Johnston & Forde 2017).

References

Altheide, D & Snow, R 1979, *Media Logic*, Sage, Thousand Oaks, CA.
Arabena, K 2015, 'Achieving wellbeing for all through reconciliation action', in B Douglas & J Wodak, *Who Speaks for and Protects the Public Interest of Australia? Essays by Notable Australians*, Australia21, Canberra, pp. 38–39.
Asp, K 1986, *Mäktiga massmedier. Studier i Politisk Opinionsbildning* [Powerful Media. Studies in Political Advocacy], Akademilitteratur, Stockholm.
Asp, K. & Esaiasson, P 1996, 'The Modernization of Swedish Campaigns: Individualization, Professionalization, and Medialization', in DL Swanson & P Mancini (eds) *Politics, Media, and Modern Democracy: An International Study of Innovations in Electoral Campaigning and Their Consequences*, Praeger, Westport, CT.
Australian Bureau of Statistics 2011, *Estimates of Aboriginal and Torres Strait Islander Australians*, viewed 18 January 2017, www.abs.gov.au/ausstats/abs@.nsf/mf/3238.0.55.001.
Australian Bureau of Statistics 2013, 'Aboriginal and Torres Strait Islander Prisoners', *Prisoners in Australia 2013*, viewed 28 June 2014, www.abs.gov.au/ausstats/abs@.nsf/Lookup/4517.0main+features62.
Australian Bureau of Statistics 2016, *Census of Population and Housing – Counts of Aboriginal and Torres Strait Islander Australians, 2016*, viewed 27 October 2017, www.abs.gov.au/ausstats/abs@.nsf/Latestproducts/2075.0Main%20Features52016?opendocument&tabname=Summary&prodno=2075.0&issue=2016&num=&view=.
Australian Bureau of Statistics 2016a, *National Aboriginal and Torres Strait Islander Social Survey 2014–15*, released 27 May 2016, viewed 27 October 2017, www.abs.gov.au/ausstats/abs@.nsf/0/E8552A8B904A0469CA257FBF00113AD9?Opendocument.
Australian Reconciliation Barometer (ARB) 2010, 'Comparing the attitudes of Indigenous people and Australians overall', *Reconciliation Australia and Auspoll*, viewed

18 January 2017, www.reconciliation.org.au/wp-content/uploads/2014/05/Australia n-Reconciliation-Barometer-2010-full-report1.pdf.

Australian Reconciliation Barometer (ARB) 2012, 'An overview', *Reconciliation Australia and Auspoll*, viewed 19 January 2017, www.reconciliation.org.au/raphub/wp -content/uploads/2015/08/2012-Australian-Reconciliation-Barometer-Overview.pdf.

Australian Reconciliation Barometer (ARB) 2014, *Reconciliation Australia*, viewed 18 January 2017, www.reconciliation.org.au/wp-content/uploads/2015/10/RR7200-Ba rometer-Brochure_WEB.pdf.

Banerjee, SB 2003, 'The practice of stakeholder colonialism: National interest and colonial discourses', in A. Prasad (ed.), *Postcolonial Theory and Organizational Analysis: A Critical Engagement*, pp. 255–279.

Banks, G 2005, *Structural Reform Australian-style: Lessons for Others?* viewed 18 January 2017, www.pc.gov.au.

Bourdieu, P 1977, *Outline of a Theory of Practice*, Cambridge University Press, Cambridge.

Bozeman, B 2007, *Public Values and Public Interest: Counterbalancing Economic Individualism*, Georgetown University Press, Washington, DC.

Colvin, J 2014, *Targeting Greater Political Diversity*, Australian Institute of Company Directors, viewed 18 January 2017, www.companydirectors.com.au/director-re source-centre/publications/company-director-magazine/2014-back-editions/decembe r/feature-targeting-greater-political-diversity.

Commonwealth of Australia 2012, *Recognising Aboriginal and Torres Strait Islander Peoples in the Constitution Report of the Expert Panel: Report of the Expert Panel*, January, viewed 18 January 2017, ttps://antar.org.au/sites/default/files/expert_panel_ report_.pdf.

Cottle, S 2000, 'Media research and ethnic minorities: Mapping the field', in S Cottle (ed.), *Ethnic Minorities and the Media: Changing Cultural Boundaries*, Open Universities Press, Buckingham, pp. 1–31, viewed 21 June 2014, www.mheducation.co. uk/openup/chapters/0335202705.pdf.

Couldry, N & Curran, J 2003, 'The paradox of media power', in N Couldry & J Curran (eds), *Contesting Media Power: Alternative Media in a Networked World*, Rowman & Littlefield, Lanham, MD, pp. 3–15.

Dewey, J 1927, *The Public and its Problems*, Swallow Press, Athens.

Dodson, P 2015, 'Reframing the terms of engagement in Aboriginal affairs', in B Douglas & J Wodak, *Who Speaks for and Protects the Public Interest of Australia? Essays by Notable Australians*, Australia21, Canberra, pp. 36–37.

Douglas, B 2015, 'The case for a national public interest council', in B Douglas & J Wodak, *Who Speaks for and Protects the Public Interest of Australia? Essays by Notable Australians*, Australia21, Canberra, pp. 90–92.

Douglas, B & Wodak, J (eds) 2015, *Who Speaks for and Protects the Public Interest of Australia? Essays by Notable Australians*, Australia21, Canberra.

Dutta, M 2011, *Communicating Social Change*, Routledge, New York.

Dutta, M & Pal, M 2011, 'Public relations and marginalisation in a global context: A postcolonial critique', in N Bardham & K Weaver (eds), *Public Relations in a Global Cultural Context*, Routledge, New York, pp. 195–226.

Esser, F & Strömbäck, J (eds) 2014, *Mediatization of Politics: Understanding the Transformation of Western Democracies*, Palgrave, London.

Flathman, R 1966, *The Public Interest*, John Wiley & Sons, New York.

Forde, S 2011, *Challenging the News: The Journalism of Alternative and Community Media*, Palgrave Macmillan, Hampshire.

Forde, S, Foxwell, K & Meadows, M 2009, *Developing Dialogues: Indigenous and Ethnic Community Broadcasting in Australia*, Intellect Publishing, UK and University of Chicago Press, Chicago, IL.

Galtung, J & Ruge, MH 1965, 'The Structure of Foreign News: The Presentation of the Congo, Cuba and Cyprus Crises in Four Norwegian Newspapers', *Journal of Peace Research*, vol. 2, pp. 64–91.

Garnaut, R 2013, *Dog Days: Australia After the Boom*, Redback, Melbourne.

Goodin, R 1996, 'Institutionalizing the public interest: The defense of deadlock and beyond', *The American Political Science Review*, vol. 90, no. 2, pp. 331–343.

Grattan, M 2007, 'Foreword' in A Tiernan (ed.) *Power without Responsibility: Ministerial Staff in Australian Governments from Whitlam to Howard*, UNSW Press, Sydney.

Habermas, J 1984, *The Theory of Communicative Action*, vol. 1, Polity Press, Cambridge.

Habermas, J 1987, *The Theory of Communicative Action*, vol. 2, Polity Press, Cambridge.

Habermas, J 1996, *Between Facts and Norms: Contributions to a Discourse Theory of Law and Democracy*, MIT Press, Cambridge, MA.

Holland, I 2002, 'Accountability of Ministerial Staff?' *Research Paper* no. 19, 2001–2002, June, viewed 18 January 2017, www.aph.gov.au/About_Parliament/Parliamentary_Departments/Parliamentary_Library/pubs/rp/rp0102/02RP19#howmany.

Hunt, J 2013, Engaging with Indigenous Australia – Exploring the conditions for effective relationships with Aboriginal and Torres Strait Islander communities, Issues paper no. 5, *Closing the Gap*, October, Australian Government, www.aihw.gov.au/uploadedFiles/ClosingTheGap/Content/Publications/2013/ctgc-ip5.pdf.

Johnston, E 1991, *National Report Volume 1 and Volume 2: Royal Commission into Aboriginal Deaths in Custody*, Australian Government Publishing Service, Canberra.

Johnston, J 2013, *Media Relations: Issues and Strategies*, Allen & Unwin, Sydney.

Johnston, J 2016, *Public Relations and the Public Interest*, Routledge, London.

Johnston, J & Forde, S 2017, 'Mediatizing politics and Australian Indigenous recognition: A critical analysis of two landmark speeches', *Communication Research & Practice*.

Koch-Baumgarten, S & Voltmer, K (eds) 2010, *Public Policy and Mass Media: The Interplay of Mass Media and Political Decision-making*, Routledge, London.

Kristianson, G 1966, *The Politics of Patriotism: The Pressure Group Activities of the Returned Servicemen's League*, Australian National University Press, Canberra.

Laursen, B & Valentini, C 2014, 'Mediatization and government communication: Presswork in the European parliament', *The International Journal of Press/Politics*, vol. 20, no. 1, pp. 26–44.

Lippmann, W 1927, *The Phantom Public*, Harcourt, Brace and Co, New York.

Lloyd, B 2009, *Research Paper no. 23 2008–09, Dedicated Indigenous Representation in the Australian Parliament*, Parliament of Australia, March, viewed 19 January 2017, www.aph.gov.au/about_parliament/parliamentary_departments/parliamentary_library/pubs/rp/rp0809/09rp23#_Toc223150954.

Mansell, M 1992, 'Closing Remarks', in S McKillop (ed.) *Aboriginal Justice Issues, Proceedings of a Conference Held 23–25 June*, Australian Institute of Criminology, www.aic.gov.au/publications/previous%20series/proceedings/1-27/21.html.

McCallum, K, Meadows, M, Waller, L, Dunne Breen, M & Reid, H 2012, *The Media and Indigenous Policy: How News Media Reporting and Mediatized Practice Impact on Indigenous Policy: A Preliminary Report*, viewed 15 January 2017, from www.kooriweb.org/foley/resources/media/media-report_combined_final.pdf.

McCallum, K, Waller, L & Meadows, M 2012a, 'Raising the volume: Indigenous voices in news media and policy', *Media International Australia Incorporating Culture and Policy*, no. 142, pp. 101–111.

McCausland, R 2004, 'Special Treatment: The representation of Aboriginal and Torres Strait Islander people in the media', *Journal of Indigenous Policy*, pp. 84–98, viewed 28 December 2017, http://classic.austlii.edu.au/au/journals/JlIndigP/2004/16.pdf.

McNair, B & Swift, A 2014, 'Does the ABC deliver Australians good bang for their buck?', *The Conversation*, 30 April, viewed 29 December 2017, http://theconversation.com/does-the-abc-deliver-australians-good-bang-for-their-buck-25608.

Meadows, M 2000, *Voices in the Wilderness: Images of Aboriginal People in the Australian Media*, Greenwood Press, Westport, CT.

Meadows, M 2015, 'Blackfella listening to blackfella: Theorising Indigenous community broadcasting', in C Atton (ed.), *Routledge Companion to Alternative and Community Media*, Routledge, London, pp. 144–154.

Meyerson, D 2007, 'Why courts should not balance rights against the public interest', *Melbourne University Law Review*, vol. 31, pp. 801–830.

Molnar, H & Meadows, M 2001, *Songlines to Satellites: Indigenous Communication in Australia, the South Pacific and Canada*, Pluto Press, Sydney.

Moloney, K 2006, *Rethinking Public Relations*, Routledge, London.

Moreton-Robinson, A 2000, *Talkin' Up to the White Woman: Indigenous Women and Feminism*, University of Queensland Press, Brisbane.

Moreton-Robinson, A 2009, 'Imagining the Good Indigenous Citizen: Race War and the Pathology of Patriarchal and White Sovereignty', *Cultural Studies Review*, vol. 15, no. 2, pp. 61–79.

Moreton-Robinson, A 2015, *The White Possessive: Property, Power and Indigenous Sovereignty*, University of Minnesota Press, Minneapolis, MN.

Mosse, D 1998, 'Process-oriented approaches to development practice and social research', in D Moss, J Farrington & A Rew (eds), *Development as Process: Concepts and Methods for Working with Complexity*, Routledge, London, pp. 3–30.

Nakayama, TK & Krizek, RL 1995, 'Whiteness: A rhetorical strategy', *Quarterly Journal of Speech*, vol. 81, no. 3, pp. 291–309.

Nicoll, F 2001, *From Diggers to Drag Queens: Configurations of Australian National Identity*, Pluto Press, Sydney.

O'Mohoney, C 2014, 'If a constitution is easy to amend, can judges be less restrained? Rights, social change, and Proposition 8', *Harvard Human Rights Journal*, vol. 27, pp. 191–242.

Pease, B 2010, *Undoing Privilege: Unearned Privilege in a Divided World*, University of Chicago Press, Chicago, IL.

Plater, D 1992, 'Aboriginal People and the Media: Reporting' in S. McKillop (ed.) *Aboriginal Justice Issues, Proceedings of a Conference Held 23–25 June*, Australian Institute of Criminology, www.aic.gov.au/publications/previous%20series/proceedings/1-27/21.html.

Podger, A 2006, 'Directions for Health Reform in Australia', in *Productive Federalism, Proceedings of a Roundtable*, Productivity Commission, February.

Proudfoot, F & Habibis, D 2015, 'Separate Worlds: A discourse analysis of mainstream and Aboriginal populist media accounts of the Northern Territory Emergency Response in 2007', *Journal of Sociology*, vol. 51, no. 2, pp. 170–188.

Rawls, J 1971, *Theory of Justice*, Harvard University Press, Cambridge, MA.

Rennie, E 2014, 'National Indigenous Television', in B Griffen-Foley (ed.), *Companion to the Australian Media*, Australian Scholarly Publishing, Melbourne, pp. 292–293.

Rice, S 2015, 'The meaning(s) of public interest in law', in B Douglas & J Wodak (eds) *Who Speaks for and Protects the Public Interest of Australia? Essays by Notable Australians*, Australia21, Canberra, pp. 24–25.

Robertson, B, Demosthenous, H, Demosthenous, C & Soole, D 2005, 'On the contemporary position of Indigenous peoples of Australia', *Electronic Journal of Sociology*, vol. 7, pp. 3–15.

Sandel, MJ 1996, *Democracy's Discontent: America in Search of a Public Philosophy*, Harvard University Press, Cambridge, MA.

Sorauf, FJ 1957, 'The public interest reconsidered', *The Journal of Politics*, vol. 19, no. 4, pp. 616–639.

Strömbäck, J 2008, 'Four Phases of Mediatization: An Analysis of the Mediatization of Politics', *International Journal of Press/Politics*, vol. 13, no. 3, pp. 228–246.

Strömbäck, J & Dimitrova, D 2011, 'Mediatization and Media Interventionism: A Comparative Analysis of Sweden and the United States', *International Journal of Press/Politics*, vol. 16, no. 1, pp. 30–49.

Sullivan, P 2011, *Belonging Together: Dealing with the Politics of Disenchantment in Australian Indigenous Policy*, Aboriginal Studies Press, Canberra.

Tatz, S 2015, 'No parliament for old men: Young advisors rule now, Australian Broadcasting Corporation', *ABC*, August, viewed 17 January 2017, www.abc.net.au/news/2015-08-05/tatz-no-parliament-for-old-men/6673826.

Tiernan, A 2007, *Power without Responsibility: Ministerial Staff in Australian Governments from Whitlam to Howard*, UNSW Press, Sydney.

Tiernan, A 2014, *Government Productivity, Committee for the Economic Development of Australia Economic and Political Overview*, viewed 15 January 2017, www.ceda.com.au/research-and-policy/publications-and-resources/publications/epo.

Tiffen, R 1989, *News & Power*, Allen & Unwin, Sydney.

Weedon, C 2004, *Identity and Culture: Narratives of Difference and Belonging*, McGraw Hill, New York.

Wheeler, C 2006, 'The public interest: We know it's important, but do we know what it means', in R Creyke & A Mantel (eds), *AIAL Forum No. 48*, Australian Institute of Administrative Law, pp. 12–26, viewed 1 September 2013, http://150.203.86.5/aial/Publications/webdocuments/Forums/forum48.pdf.

8 Understanding the public interest puzzle in China's public relations

The role of balance and counterbalance based on Confucian Great Harmony

Jenny Zhengye Hou

Introduction

Public interest has been a long-standing yet unresolved puzzle in Western public relations research and practice (Edwards 2011; Stoker & Stoker 2012). Despite structural variances across Western democracy, a shared assumption underpinning public interest is that individuals have a 'responsible share' in forming group activities and participating in the affairs that sustain the 'great community' (Dewey 1927, p. 147). The public-private or state-society binary constitutes the foundation of Western public interest. Following the key spirit of common good, public interest is pursued through creating an equal and free 'marketplace of ideas' (Bivins 1993, p. 123), where individuals have access to information, and can freely debate public matters in the light of more inclusive interest than individual interest (Heath 1992; Mechling 1975; Sorauf 1957). Accordingly, the puzzle for public relations is how to fulfil an obligation of service in the public interest while continuing to advocate and subsidise organisational, especially corporate interests in representative forms (L'Etang 2004). To address this dilemma, the recent growing body of critical public relations scholarship (e.g. Johnston 2016) highlights the importance of cultural impacts, and calls for the examination of public interest communication under diverse and specific cultural microscopes.

In contrast to Western recognition and protection of individualism, China's authoritarianism – supreme state domination over individual interest – poses new challenges and interesting scenarios to understand the public interest in public relations. As 'the most salient difference between China and the West' (Chen 2004, p. 395), authoritarianism can be better understood in relation to Confucian 'Great Harmony' (*datong*). According to Callahan (2015), Great Harmony denotes twofold meanings: one describes a unified utopia (perfect world) where everyone enjoys an equal right to live harmoniously; and the other represents harmony-with-diversity (*he'er butong*) that encourages different opinions, norms and models while seeking to reach consensus. Nevertheless, a central tenet to Great Harmony is to respect the authority and legitimacy of a sovereign to rule Chinese society for overarching unity (Huang 2000). Rulers and elites are best situated to discern the common good because of their superior moral wisdom or technical knowledge (Nathan 2003). The ruled are obligated to submit individual interest to state and collective interests (Shue 2004). In this sense, the Western typical boundary between public and private where public debate and public interest originate is absent in China (Baxter 2011). Instead, the state system possesses rightness to determine what common good and public interest are (Chin 2012).

Even with today's marketisation, modernisation and globalisation, China's Great Harmony philosophy finds new space to flourish as a way of mitigating the clash between state and public interests. Noticeably, Chinese publics have become educated and assertive about public affairs ranging from the wealth gap between the rich and the poor, the inequity of resource allocation, and the deteriorative environment and food safety (Chen 2003). They no longer follow the authorities blindly, but attempt to articulate and strive for public interest actively (Yang 2005). In response, the Chinese government has, on the one hand, continued to earn legitimacy from economic growth. On the other hand, they keep reinvigorating the Great Harmony thinking in official lines such as 'Harmonious Society', 'Harmonious World', 'The China Model' and the recent 'China Dream' (Callahan 2015; Delury 2008), for the purpose of social control and cohesion. Instead of abolishing communism, the reinterpreted Great Harmony promotes large-scale nationalism and patriotism by mobilising publics to adhere to, and believe in, Chinese Communist Party (CCP) leadership in addressing new challenges and contradictions in transition (Callahan 2015). The state-centric intervention in society has been constantly legitimised to reconcile the socialist modernity and public interest pursuit. Consequently, core values like unity over difference, and the collective over the individual, continue to prevail in China (Lee 2010).

Against this backdrop, this chapter aims to explore how public interest is elaborated, negotiated and fulfilled (or not) in Chinese public relations practices under the authoritarian context. Going beyond the Western public-private binary, this research probes into the public interest among China's 'interest conflict complex' (Fulda et al. 2012, p. 679), such as state vs. collective, government vs. public, state vs. corporate, and business vs. public. This study aligns with Johnston's (2016) procedural framework, that is: 1 public interest is part of political process; 2 public relations practitioners have the capacity to navigate public interest, like journalists, lawyers and policy makers; 3 the public interest can be pursued through being integrated into strategic planning processes. This chapter particularly examines the dialectic interplay between the overarching Great Harmony philosophy and public relations practices in the public interest. The chapter now moves to review public interest in the West and in China, and then presents the findings of an empirical study which has theoretical and practical implications for Chinese public relations and communication.

The public-private binary: foundation of public interest in the West

Public interest is a concept originating from Western democracies. Although there is no unified definition, this concept is closely linked to values such as common good, community engagement and general welfare (Messina 2007). Public interest is considered essential to realising social justice and equity, and can be achieved by open discussions, reciprocity, social norms, and an ongoing process of validating truth claims (Weaver et al. 2006). Underlying a range of Western classic literature (e.g. Dewey 1927; Lippmann 1955; Habermas 1989) is a widely shared assumption that public interest arises from 'common good' over and above the interests of particular individuals (Feintuch & Varney 2006; van Cuilenburg & McQuail 2003). To that end, a prerequisite is to recognise and protect private civil rights and legal equality which could, in turn, aggregate to a common-good level. Individuals are acknowledged by law to have not only the right but also the obligation to participate in public matters of common concern and take collective action to pursue public interest (Dewey 1927). Therefore, in a normative sense, public interest in the West is mainly perceived in opposition to private interest, constituting the typical public-private binary.

Corresponding to this public-private binary, a dual challenge confronted by public relations is how to show faith to those whom they represent while meeting the obligation of serving the public interest (Lattimore et al. 2009). In search of a balance between the two conflicting demands, a growing number of public relations studies (e.g. Dodd et al. 2015; Ihlen & Verhoeven 2012; Yang & Taylor 2013) call to invoke sociological ideas such as Habermas's (1989) 'public sphere' and Putnam's (1996) 'civic engagement' to combat the dominant focus on private organisational interest. For example, Habermas's public sphere (or more recently spheres) – as an arena that exists outside the institutions of the state and mediates between society and the state – is deemed useful to bring back the public interest to the centre of public relations research (Holtzhausen 2010). To serve the public interest, public relations should aim to facilitate the construction of public spheres, where individual citizens are guaranteed access to information, and are able to openly and rationally weigh and evaluate various claims as to which are common good (Pojman & Fieser 2009; Stoker & Stoker 2012). Putnam's civic engagement is noted as another illuminating perspective to address the public interest challenge through implementing public relations functions of information production, relationship building, and creation of social capital (Dodd et al. 2015; Yang & Taylor 2013).

Further attempts to resolve the public-private interest paradox have revolved around how to deal with self-interest, which is viewed as a major obstacle to accomplish public interest. For example, Heath (1992, p. 318) proposed a 'negotiated self-interest model', through which the public good emerges from a controlled process of serving self-interest, but most interests are served through the 'logic of civil society' (Heath 2011). Edwards (2011) promotes a critical understanding of self-interest as one of a set of dynamics shaping organisational objectives, rather than rejecting it at the outset. Macnamara (2012) put forward a 'public diplomatic' model for public relations practitioners to go beyond the narrowly confined organisational interest but seek to create mutual benefits with publics. Johnston (2016) advocates two parallel public interest models: a service model (with service underpinned by the question: 'Will my decision hurt society, even if I benefit myself, my client, my employer or my profession?'), and an advocacy model (driven by social cause and a desire for change). Stoker and Stoker (2012) recommended 'superior individual interests' based on Dewey's (1927) public philosophy to reconcile multiple moral obligations to public relations practitioners themselves, client organisations, and the public. They argue that 'superior individual interests' refer to the deeper enlightened interests in both the long and short term, such as encouraging public inquiry, furthering public debate, and facilitating human and community improvement, and meanwhile valuing the rights and freedoms of individuals, private organisations and decision makers (Stoker & Stoker 2012, p. 41).

It can be summarised that public interest in the West remains an elusive concept and an unsettled issue in the public relations field. Although scholars adopt different philosophies and theoretical approaches, a focal discussion of public interest has been built on the public-private binary, specifically, exploring how to release and augment the public and social function of the predominantly self-serving public relations. Much attention has been given to either bringing back the community value to public relations, or constraining the private orientation of public relations services. Individualism is respected and encouraged as a critical base for the emergence and formation of public good. Civil society, instead of state government, is believed to play an important role in shaping and pursuing public interest. However, all of these conditions (e.g. democracy, rational individualism, community value) are missing in a non-Western, authoritarian context like China, where individualism is largely eroded by statism, and government dominates every aspect of public life. As Bond and Hwang (1986) emphasised, 'the Western starting point of the atomic individual is alien to Chinese considerations of man's social behaviour' (p. 215). Confucianism, especially the Great Harmony philosophy, has historically defined the relational order and interest system of Chinese society. Therefore, what follows next is a close examination of public interest in China's Great Harmony culture.

Confucian Great Harmony: the system of interests in Chinese culture

The Western binary that suggests opposition between public and private is inappropriate for China due to the often blurred boundary between the two and the weak sense of individualism in its collective culture (Huang 1993). In Chinese, the antonym of the word 'private/privacy' (*si*) is not necessarily 'public' (*gong*), but precisely, 'official' (*guan*), which indicates a strong authoritarian domination of public life, including the formation of public interest (McDougall 2004). At the macro level, authoritarianism refers to the government's absolute power and control over public resources and distribution, playing the roles of legislator, law enforcer and judge (Fan 2007). At the micro level, authoritarianism features a paternalistic decision-making mechanism, namely, the higher position, the more say the person has (Hou & Zhu 2012). To understand this hierarchical nature of Chinese authoritarianism, it is necessary to place it within the broad Confucian 'Great Harmony' context as illustrated below from both an historical perspective and its modern implications.

'The Great Harmony' (*datong*) is the title of a chapter in the *Book of Rites* (*Liji*), attributed to Confucius. The chapter begins with '*Tianxia weigong*' (literally, all under heaven is held in common) (McDougall 2004, p. 2). In this famous phrase, the '*Tianxia*' (heaven) system is defined as a Sino-centric hierarchical relationship among the unequal. The emperor is the son of heaven (*tianzi*), the medium between the divinities and people, and thus has divine rights to rule (Zhang 2004). Based on this 'asymmetrical worldview' (Huang 2000, p. 226), the Great Harmony world prescribes an important rule that the subordinates observe rituals such as presenting tributes to the emperor. In the golden age of harmony, the worthy and able would be promoted, people would care for each other whether they were relatives or not, thievery and rebels would not exist. The Confucian Great Harmony has, on the one hand, depicted an ideal political kingdom built on a stable social stratification; and on the other hand, and fundamentally, confers legitimacy upon political elites to rule and discern the common good (Peerenboom 2006; Shue 2004). Stated another way, *Tianxia* is not actually shared by all, but all that is ruled by the emperor (son of heaven) will be treated equally and properly because of the king's wisdom and benevolence. Nonetheless, the Great Harmony world is not an utterly closed and static system, but also promotes harmony-with-diversity (*he'er butong*). Harmony-with-diversity allows people to contribute different ideas and proposals to sustain the hierarchical solidarity of Chinese society.

Due to its defence of Chinese authoritarianism and inclusiveness of differences, the Confucian Great Harmony is still being applied as a political philosophy in China's socialist modernisation. For example, former President Hu Jingtao proposed 'a harmonious society' in 2005. He openly called for the use of harmony wisdom – allowing co-existence of similarities/agreements and differences/disagreements – to resolve social discord, ranging from the widened wealth gap, unequal resource allocation, and imbalanced development between *Han* and minority ethnic groups (Delury 2008). The Great Harmony thinking is also embedded in current President Xi Jinping's 'China Dream' (*zhongguomeng*). The China Dream, according to *Qiushi*, the CCP's theoretical journal, is to create a prosperous and harmonious China through the hard core of government authority (*wei*) surrounded by a soft pulp of benevolence (*de*). Dreyer (2015, p. 1020) comments that this strategy is 'astute statecraft in finding the right balance [between multiple interest conflicts]'. Guided by these repackaged political discourses, Lee (2010, p. 278) points out that Chinese intellectuals, albeit supposed to be the advocates of public interest, have actually echoed and reproduced the official line as 'insiders of a semi-official elite circle'.

Following the Confucian tradition and its modern tenets, China has consistently placed the state first, the collective second and the individual last, which conjointly shapes the conception and practice of public interest (Huang 1993). For instance, Article 51 of the 1982 Chinese Constitution stipulates that:

> the exercise by citizens of the PRC [People's Republic of China] of their freedoms and rights may not infringe upon the interests of the state, of society and of the collective, or upon the lawful freedoms and rights of other citizens.
>
> (Chin 2012, p. 901)

This provision reinforces subordinating the individual citizen's liberty, autonomy and rights to the tyranny of the majority at best, and at worst, to the Party-state dictatorship which monopolises the interpretation of public interests. The Chinese legal system provides discretionary power to government authorities to interpret public interest in ways that invade and ignore individual rights (Ren & Ji 2005). This is in sharp contrast to the public interest in the West, which essentially recognises and protects the individual civil right to access information, debate public matters and engage in political process.

The submission of public interest to the supreme state interest is also reflected in Chinese media systems. Chin (2012) identifies the five roles of Chinese media in the following order: first and foremost, the media must serve the CCP's interests, sustaining its legitimacy and capacity to govern; second, they must serve the collective or national interest as predominantly defined by the Party-state; third, they are required to serve the marketplace to grow economic capacity; fourth, they may serve individual cultural and social rights; finally, they are allowed to encourage civil free expression and political engagement only insofar as this does not interfere with higher priorities. The consistent maintenance of authoritarianism and the prioritisation of social cohesion and collectiveness over individual political rights have largely restricted the scope of public interest expression in China.

Even with the emergence and prevalence of social media as potentially emancipatory tools, the CCP's political superiority, its limited tolerance of dissenting voices, and the strict ideological control of policy-making (Esarey 2006) have made it difficult to articulate public interest in public spaces. Despite the recent growth of non-governmental organisations (NGOs) in China, which are devoted to improving the strained Party-state and society relationship, those NGOs are often viewed with suspicion and tightly monitored and controlled by the government (Tang & Li 2009). It can thus be argued that without a democratic basis, an equal social system and individual political participation, the major rival against public interest in China is not the private/corporate forces like in the West, but rather the Party-state.

An open-ended process approach to public interest in Chinese public relations

In order to provide an indigenous understanding of public interest communication in China, this chapter proposes an open-ended process approach to examining how public interest is interpreted and practised in China's public relations in the Confucian Great Harmony context. In this study, 'open-ended' refers to how the chapter rejects a 'false binary of public/private' (Baxter 2011, p. 8). Instead, it positions the public interest in a multi-interest conflict complex, in which state vs. collective, government vs. corporate, commerce vs. public are considered not as mutually exclusive but interwoven as potentially competing forces to shape the public interest in different directions (Yang & Arant 2013). Following Chapter 1, and other chapters in the book, 'process' means not to treat the public interest as an aggregated outcome that can be evaluated, but rather is a dialectic and iterative process which interplays with wider Great Harmony context. This context shapes and is being reshaped by the way of interpreting, articulating and pursuing public interest in Chinese public relations. This process is not one-off but cyclical, as a result of which the public interest is not a static concept but always in flux and negotiation.

As highlighted earlier, the essence of Confucian Great Harmony centres on following the state government authority to maintain hierarchical solidarity, while allowing for multi-way negotiation and contestation to achieve social consensus. In other words, the Confucian Great Harmony does not coerce pure bottom-up compliance or compromise, but actually opens up a space where domination, subordination, consensus, disputes, agreement and disagreement are negotiated, contested and/or restrained to allow 'all things in the universe to attain its way'; in Chinese, called 'the doctrine of the mean' (*zhongyong zhidao*) (Delury 2008). Within this framework, the central research question of this chapter is: *How does China's public relations as an industry interpret, articulate or contest the public interest in practice as it interplays with the overarching Great Harmony context?*

Primary data sources

This chapter draws from primary data sources collected from fieldwork in Beijing, China's capital city and the national political, economic and cultural centre. Beijing hosts the majority of professional public relations (PR) consultancies, large media organisations, multinational corporations (MNCs), emerging NGOs, and PR industrial associations such as China International Public Relations Association (CIPRA). The study adopted a qualitative approach in order to 'get at the inner experience of participants, to determine how meanings are formed through and in culture, and to discover rather than test variables' (Corbin & Strauss 2008, p. 12).

In-depth interviews were chosen as the main method of data collection. Through a purposive snowball sampling, 46 participants were recruited from five types of organisations: 1 professional PR consultancies; 2 corporations with in-house PR units; 3 NGOs or social interest groups; 4 media organisations; and 5 PR professional associations. Due to restricted access, no state/government participants were approached. All interviews were guided by an open-ended protocol with two foci: 1) How is public interest weighed, perceived and interpreted in China's Great Harmony context generally and in public relations practice specifically? 2) What strategies are used to negotiate, contest and pursue public interest in Chinese public relations practices? Because of the interview opportunities, the researcher was also given some background documents, from which typical case studies were identified as a complementary data source.

The central research question served to navigate the transcript reading until the larger themes appeared visible. Both interview and document data were analysed through an inductive, thematic analysis, as defined by Braun and Clarke (2006, p. 86) as 'searching across a data set … to find repeated patterns of meaning'. The researcher also focused on the latent meaning, namely, interpreting data based on the theoretical framework and linking data back to the contexts in which they were collected. In order to enhance the research validity, three verification techniques were applied: 1) member checking – all transcripts were reported back to participants for cross-validation; 2) constant comparison (Lindlof 1995) by developing alternative themes to arrive at the most parsimonious ones; and 3) attending to (rather than ignoring) anomalies, and integrating them into findings for nuanced understanding (Miles & Huberman 1994).

Three key themes emerged from the data. First, harmony as a means of balance: creative strategies of negotiating public interest. This refers to how harmony is creatively used as a means to negotiate and balance public interest with other conflicting interests (e.g. market growth, economic benefit, government domination). Second, harmony as a means of counterbalance: tacit rules and taboos. This indicates that harmony is reflectively observed as a principle to constrain the extent of negotiating the public interest to certain hidden rules and taboos. Third, harmony as an end of dynamic equilibrium: incremental changes and the public interest. These themes point to how harmony is regarded as an end featured by dynamic equilibrium between multiple negotiations and the accumulative changes in the public interest. The themes are now examined through the following narratives.

Harmony as a means of balance: creative strategies of negotiating public interest

When asked how public interest is weighted in Chinese public relations practice – whether this has been considered as one value orientation – it is widely shared among the participants that public interest is not pursued as a standalone mission, but embedded in organisational multi-interest complex (e.g., profit-making, social responsibilities). At best, public interest is interpreted by one participant as 'the ideal and the ultimate goal of all forms and stages of PR practice', while at worst, it is deemed by another participant as 'a lip service and a mission impossible when PR serves a particular organisation'. The public interest is associated with organisational goals for two reasons. On the one hand, it corresponds to the early stage of China's PR, which still struggles to help organisations achieve a market share in order to prove the value of PR. As a CEO from a PR consultancy explained, '[t]he first question for most Chinese organisations is market survival. This is where PR is needed most before taking public interest into consideration'. On the other hand, the downplayed public interest reflects the Chinese developing hybrid context characterised by a socialist market economy under an elite authoritarian regime. For example, a journalist commented: 'it is questionable whether China has a/the "public" in a Western sense, let alone the interest of publics.'

Nonetheless, it is undeniable that Chinese organisations (including government) are under growing pressure to fulfil public interest through responding to all-round economic, legal, ethical and discretionary expectations held by the wider society. Most of the participants felt a strong rise of the public in a Dewey (1927) sense, such as common concern over an issue, sharing information and taking collective action. For example, participants frequently mentioned 'media citizenship' or 'netizens' (*wangmin*) to describe the perceived rise of publics who have actively exercised citizenship in cyberspace through online discussions, petitions and protests on social and political issues of common concern. One PR manager from a state-owned enterprise (SOE) expressed: 'We feel now countless eyes watching our back as more and more people demand us to submit to rigorous rules about how public resources are used.' This is echoed by an official from the Chinese public relations association: 'We notice that concepts such as constitutionality, citizenship, and taxpayers' rights are being integrated into public values, which means Chinese organisations can no longer afford to ignore the public interest.'

Under the above circumstances, the data revealed a perceived imperative to negotiate public interest by using Confucian Great Harmony as a means to balance organisational multiple interest-seeking. To fulfil the public interest, the creative application of harmonious balance includes both a reactive strategy of logic resonance (*luoji gongzhen*), and a proactive strategy of networking with the First-in-Command (*yibashou*), who is the top/final decision maker. The reactive strategy of logic resonance was mainly identified from the group of corporate PR practitioners, supported by their agency partners. The idea is to resonate with and blend the public logic or concern into corporate social responsibility (CSR) initiatives, which is the most visible and effective way to fulfil public interest. For example, the participants explained the public concern about common good focusing on areas of education, health, sports, art and cultural rights, poverty reduction, disaster relief and risk management. One PR manager from an MNC in China illustrated:

> To address public interest is a complex and challenging task for PR as most of our efforts are directed to market. However, one tip is to incorporate public agenda in our CSR initiatives. For example, we've been volunteering in sponsoring China's Hope Project (a social cause to improve educational infrastructure in rural China) since the first day of entry to China. In doing so, we are recognised by both government and public, earned media coverage, and even established as a role model for other MNCs in China.

In the participant's words, this is a typical 'harmony philosophy' – seeking common ground (e.g., a public agenda) to align and reconcile competing interests and achieve multiple purposes (e.g., corporate reputation, media exposure, government recognition, public interest). This harmonious strategy of logic resonance is also confirmed in a PR agency training manual, stating that:

> Underlining a company's commitment and contribution to community and public agenda, for example, highlighting the company's social investment, environment concern, talent cultivation and charity donations is the key to represent public interest in their PR practices.
>
> (ACC Consultancy 2014, p. 2)

Compared to this reactive strategy of logic resonance which, in essence, treats public interest as instrumental (functional) to organisational objectives, the data have identified another proactive strategy to promote public interest as a main goal. This proactive strategy emerges from the interviews with PR people from NGOs – networking with the First-in-Command. According to the participants, this strategy also draws from the Confucian harmony thinking to acknowledge the paternalistic nature and supreme position of government authorities on the one hand, but to align with the First-in-Command and leverage their power to push forward a public policy on the other hand. To illustrate this point, the following section uses the Beijing-based Shining Stone Community Action (SSCA), a grass-roots NGO, as a case in point.

Since its foundation in December 2002, SSCA has been making efforts to push participatory urban community governance reform to replace government monopoly. Specifically, SSCA is promoting a new community model called 'community-building standardisation' to shift the government management of communities (*shequ guanli*) to community self-governance (*shequ zhili*), which entails: 1) participation from a greater plurality of actors; 2) more flexibility of processes and procedures; 3) leaner structures; and 4) internalisation of objectives (Beijing Municipal Government 2009). In practice,

SSCA experienced great difficulties at the outset until they devised a strategy of networking and aligning with the First-in-Command – the Department of Civil Affairs of the Dongcheng District in Beijing.

Through repeated meetings and lobbying government officials, by using rhetoric such as 'helping the government to achieve', 'serving as a bridge between different levels of hierarchy', and 'maximising public interest collaboratively', SSCA has not only gained trust from the local government to be registered as a 'people-run non-profit unit', but also borrowed influence from government to mobilise support from media and academia. One participant summarised the whole process as 'working with the government to change government thinking', which typically reflected their Confucian harmony philosophy to respect the authority first, but then leverage their influence to initiate cross-sector collaborations between government, social scientists, media and community residents. As a consequence, SSCA established the first successful model of participatory community governance, and subsequently helped to nurture and develop community-based organisations in other urban areas (Fulda et al. 2012).

Harmony as a means of counterbalance: tacit rules and taboos

The previous illustration of harmony as a means of balancing multiple interests to negotiate public interest is just one dimension. The other dimension emerging from the data is the harmonious counterbalance: namely, to what extent can the negotiation and contestation of public interest go? It seems clear to all participants that the bottom line is not the organisational economic survival, but political correctness in following and supporting the leadership of the CCP government. In spite of their growing desire for autonomy and flexibility, the participants' common awareness of the absolute authority of the Party-state has not only reflected but also reinforced the Confucian Great Harmony philosophy to sustain the hierarchical solidarity within Chinese society. It is therefore legitimate to claim that national (actually Party-state) interest always comes first, followed by collective interest and finally individual citizen rights which, however, are the basis of the Western conception of public interest.

The source of counterbalance force is not necessarily coming from a specific government body intervening in Chinese public relations, but instead systematic, ideological and historically institutionalised as cultural norms. Participants used different metaphors to describe how they felt about the counterbalance effect on their efforts to negotiate and pursue public interest. For example, the 'comfort zone' (adhering to the CCP leadership) is a compared framework within which they can negotiate public interest. One director from an NGO used the analogy of a 'birdcage' to elaborate how he felt both rigidity (control) and limited flexibility (tolerance) from the Party-state counterbalance with the NGO's attempts at public interest:

> The Party-state is treating our public interest pursuit like a bird in a cage. They are prepared to enlarge the cage as they see fit but a cage (dominance) is always there. This is to allow a sufficient scope to negotiate the public interest in non-critical realms while their consistency to control the critical realm is retained so that the improvement of public interest cannot pose a threat to the continuation of their rule.

Consequently, there are several tacit taboos identified by the participants in their negotiation process, one being state interpretations of the role of voting in popular culture. A typical example in this regard is the text-message voting system designed for a once popular TV show – *Super Girl (chaoji nvsheng)*. *Chaoji nvsheng*, a singing contest produced by Hunan Satellite TV between 2004 and 2006, with an audience of 400 million, adopted a text-message voting system to enable audiences to choose the best candidate. However, this text-message voting system drew attention from the top authority which forbade this initiative. The government issued an official document to restrict the broadcasting period of talent shows to less than two months. It also restricted the broadcast to between 7:30 pm and 10:30 pm at provincial and sub-provincial levels of satellite TV stations, and set up provisions on the language and behaviour of hosts, the professionalism of the judges and the guests, and the attire, hair and make-up of the candidates. The reasons for the prohibitions by the state were recalled and analysed by one respondent, a journalist, who said that she was not surprised about the official regulation because the concept of democracy was implied in the text-message voting mechanism. She commented:

> This is a warning for us to avoid [the expectation of a] 'vote' or 'right to vote' as political engagement. This is not deemed as a proper goal to pursue the 'public interest' in the eyes of the Party-state. Once people can choose their ideal candidate in a TV program through voting, people may also require choosing their national leader in the future, which is intolerant in the current regime.

Harmony as an end of dynamic equilibrium: incremental changes and the public interest

While the previous two sections explained how harmony was used as a *means* of balancing and counterbalancing multiple interests to pursue the public interest, this section illustrates how Chinese public relations actors have applied harmony as an *end* to determine what they want to achieve. When asked to specify what is meant by the end of harmony, participants tended to emphasise that the end is not a static status without any interest conflict, a final destination to arrive at, or the eternal priority of state interest over collective and public interests. Conversely, harmony as an end in itself was understood as in constant flux because of the multiple, iterative, and mutual accommodation and influence between the two competing sides (e.g., state vs. public). As a result, dynamic equilibrium can always be found in harmonious relationships. In one PR association official's words, '[t]he harmonisation (negotiation and balance) process is never ending'. Another journalist invoked 'the wisdom of Chinese *Yingyang*' to echo a similar view: '*Yingyang* means the two oppositions (e.g. state vs. public) are always in change – at one point or in one area, one may be stronger than the other, but at another time the weaker one could become stronger.'

Over the long term, incremental changes on both sides of the public interest and Party-state domination have been observed and recognised by the participants. Alternatively, although participants shared how the substance of the public interest remains ambiguous, unsure and abstract in China, what has gradually changed and improved is the awareness of the public interest: being 'public', not manipulative; and creating common good, not privileging a single party. This awareness enhancement has been embodied in the rhetorical changes as identified by participants. For example, one CEO from a local PR agency explained:

> Previously we tended to use 'mass people' (*renmin qunzhong*), emphasising the amount, collectiveness, and ideological consensus during Maoist era, but now we say 'public' (*gongzhong*) with an emphasis on the nature of being open, interactive and transparent, well, ideally, in communication.

This perceived rhetorical change is confirmed in D&S Consultancy's (2014) *30 Years' PR Development in China Report*, which identified such increasingly used buzzwords as 'public information right' (*zhiqing quan*), 'public hearing' (*tingzhenghui*), and 'public consultation' (*gongzhong zixun*). This rhetoric change signalled the awareness and emerging efforts to articulate the public interest in main political arenas. Another example of incremental changes in pushing the public interest is the increased involvement and public input from academics in policy-making process. For example, one interviewed PR professional association official who was also an academic working in a university, said 'I'll from time to time attend government expert panels to discuss public matters. My report can now be delivered directly to the state council (*guowuyuan*)'.

One incremental change as an outcome of the continuous negotiation is the growing authoritarian resilience, namely, government embraces both flexibility to negotiate fuzzy edges of regulatory frameworks and rigidity to keep the bottom line of the Party-state leadership. One director from an NGO commented that

> the government learned to adjust policies as appropriate, like in the case of the participatory community governance model. They make changes

to respond to public concern, but more importantly, to update their own political legitimacy in modern times.

However, the government hard-core policy of sticking to one-party leadership remains intact, as reflected by one journalist:

> The two hands are still there – one being hard and the other being soft. We can figure out where the public interest appeals work or not, so we should adjust our expectations and strategies accordingly.

It can now be recapped that the incremental changes are therefore somewhat synergetic, symbiotic and somehow commensurate with the essence of dynamic equilibrium and overall solidarity inherent in the Confucian Great Harmony philosophy. Both state and social actors, including public relations practitioners, understand the boundaries, the bottom line, and the 'rules of the game' in the process of pushing the public interest forward onto the government agenda. The extent of any negotiation is explained by one PR manager as: 'Going beyond the limit is as bad as falling short, and going too far is as bad as not going far enough (*guoyou buji*).' While it is clear that the public interest currently equates to state interest at this point in time, the transformative nature of the continuous harmonious negotiation, balance and counterbalance has the capacity to lead to an inclusive, responsive and supportive environment, where self-defined public interest can flourish in the wake of China's increasing democratisation and internationalisation.

Concluding remarks: harmony, the state and the public interest

This chapter has explored how public interest is interpreted, articulated and pursued in China's public relations practice within a Confucian Great Harmony context. Within this context, the Western socio-cultural conditions of informed publics, enlightened action, community values, and tolerance of free debate of different ideas are limited. Compared to the Western focus on the tension between public and private interests (Arendt 1998), this research has highlighted the dominance of the Party-state as the major rival, judge and influencer on the substance and manner of striving for the public interest in China. To contest public interest in China is mainly to attempt to loosen the state paternalistic control in the first instance. Within the Confucian Great Harmony context that enables both hierarchical solidarity and bottom-up negotiation, the process of seeking the public interest is like a game of balance and counterbalance among multiple competing interests. This process also leads to dynamic equilibrium and incremental changes on all of the involved parties. Chinese PR practitioners have reflectively navigated the Great Harmony philosophy as both a means and an end to inform and guide their public interest communication which, in turn, reshapes the established authoritarian polity.

Given the highly valued political stability and social cohesion in China, this study suggests that the way for Chinese PR practitioners to negotiate the public interest is not anti-state, or through radical challenges to the authority outright. Rather, it seems to work through collaborating with and influencing government subtly on the basis of following and maintaining their authoritative leadership. In doing so, it is argued that PR can indirectly reduce social conflicts and contribute to China's 'harmonious society' (Wexler et al. 2006). This is different from the Western civil society in which interest groups struggle to expand their scope of influence and resort to social disobedience in extreme cases, in order to constrain the tendencies of governments (Fulda et al. 2012).

Chinese PR practitioners creatively use a strategy of logic resonance to integrate the public interest into organisational CSR initiatives. They endeavour to pursue their understanding of the public interest, as demonstrated in the SSCA case study, by a strategy of networking with the First-in-Command to respect and leverage the power of government authorities to push the public agenda legitimately.

In parallel with the way Chinese PR practitioners negotiate the public interest is a counterbalance from the Party-state system to ensure the supreme priority of the state interest – upholding the CCP leadership – above all. Therefore, some tacit taboos are identified and avoided by Chinese PR practitioners (and media), such as not surpassing the ideological line and not touching on sensitive topics (e.g. democracy) publicly. Although the state has shown a growing desire and trend to articulate broader public interests, public voices are still weak and not being heard by the authorities. This includes the lack of voice afforded marginalised groups (Freeman 2010; Harold 2008). Public interest articulation in China is still fragmented and unorganised; the public voice is not strong enough to question and challenge the state. However, in considering the Chinese harmony culture, the government has also shown signs of allowing various strategies to interact with various social actors, depending on their perceived imperative and extent of conceding or counterbalancing public interest seekers.

The negotiating process between Chinese PR practitioners and state regulators (e.g., government) continues, using the Great Harmony philosophy, in seeking similarities and consensus while allowing for differences and disagreements. As such, the public interest cannot be seen as a static property that can be described or measured, but its substance is subject to the iterative interpretations, contestations and reconciliations within contextual specificities. As shown in this research, through balance and counterbalance between competing forces, the pursuit of public interest in China is a long-term, incremental process. The increased authoritarian resilience, an adjusted policy focus from pure economic growth to human interest, and the Party-state's willingness to concede certain civil liberties, could assist in improving the fulfilment of public interest. The future of public interest communication in China is still uncertain, but this study has placed it within a national context, enabling Chinese public relations practitioners to explore possible options and alternatives.

This chapter provides fresh alternatives to enrich the Anglo-centric knowledge of the relationship between public interest and public relations through substituting the public-private binary for a Chinese Great Harmony philosophy. This philosophy does not emphasise one-way compliance or conformity to the authorities, but rather opens up a space for mutual negotiation, accommodation and influence of all involved parties in order to achieve a dynamic equilibrium. The harmony-based approach to the public interest in China thus adds value to the existing repertoire of practical attempts to accomplish public interest in public relations, such as Heath's (1992, 2011) 'negotiated self-interest' and Stoker and Stoker's (2012) combining 'superior individual interest' with Dewey's public philosophy. Through presenting findings from primary sources, this study contributes to combating the tendency of theory-rich but data-poor public interest studies, offering possibly the first public interest communication study from China.

Moreover, the insights generated from this study provide implications for other Asian countries with similar institutional structures and cultural traditions where hierarchism and collectivism are supported, and community values of union, self-control and restraint are stressed (Zhang et al. 2005). Although Western ideas of the public interest public relations in Asian countries may be limited, cultural heritage empowers many Eastern countries to develop localised and robust approaches to defining, articulating and contesting the public interest as accepted within specific cultural, political, social and geographic contexts. Further research in this line of inquiry could include the voices from publics, interest groups and social organisations to assist in understanding how those organised or unorganised parties attempt to co-shape public interest, as well as how they wish to leverage the power of public relations to achieve their goals. Longitudinal case studies in emerging economies or authoritarian countries will also be beneficial to showcase how public interest has evolved with the overarching institutional changes such as modernisation, democratisation and globalisation.

References

ACC Consultancy 2014, *Media Training Manual*, Business Source Complete, Beijing, viewed 26 June 2015, pp. 1–45.

Arendt, H 1998, *The Human Condition*, 2nd edn, University of Chicago Press, Chicago, IL.

Baxter, L 2011, *Voicing Relationships: A Dialogic Perspective*, Sage, Thousand Oaks, CA and London.

Beijing Municipal Government 2009, *Community-building Standardisation Policy*, Government Printer, Beijing.

Bivins, TH 1993, 'Public relations, professionalism, and the public interest', *Journal of Business Ethics*, vol. 12, pp. 117–126.

Bond, MH & Hwang, KK 1986, 'The social psychology of Chinese people'. In MH Bond (ed.), *The Psychology of Chinese People*, Oxford University Press, New York, pp. 213–266.

Braun, V & Clarke, V 2006, 'Using thematic analysis in psychology', *Qualitative Research in Psychology*, vol. 3, no. 2, pp. 77–101.

Callahan, WA 2015, 'History, tradition and the China dream: Socialist modernization in the World of Great Harmony', *Journal of Contemporary China*, vol. 24, no. 96, pp. 983–1001.

Chen, N 2003, 'From propaganda to public relations: Evolutionary change in the Chinese government', *Asian Journal of Communication*, vol. 13, no. 2, pp. 96–121.

Chen, Y 2004, 'Effective public affairs in China: MNC-government bargaining power and corporate strategies for influencing foreign business policy formation', *Journal of Communication Management*, vol. 8, pp. 395–423.

Chin, YC 2012, 'Public service broadcasting, public interest and individual rights in China', *Media, Culture & Society*, vol. 34, no. 7, pp. 898–912.

Corbin, J & Strauss, A 2008, *Basics of Qualitative Research: Techniques and Procedures for Developing Grounded Theory*, 3rd edn, Sage, Los Angeles, CA.

D&S Consultancy 2014, *30 Years' PR Development in China Report*, pp. 1–36, Business Source Complete, Beijing, viewed 30 June 2015.

Delury, J 2008, '"Harmonious" in China', *Policy Review*, vol. 148 (April & May), pp. 35–44.

Dewey, J 1927, *The Public and its Problems*, Swallow, Chicago, IL.

Dodd, MD, Brummette, J & Hazleton, V 2015, 'A social capital approach: An examination of Putnam's civic engagement and public relations roles', *Public Relations Review*, vol. 41, pp. 472–479.

Dreyer, JT 2015, 'The "Tianxia Trope": Will China change the international system?' *Journal of Contemporary China*, vol. 24, no. 96, pp. 1015–1031.

Edwards, L 2011, 'Questions of self-interest, agency, and the rhetor', *Management Communication Quarterly*, vol. 25, no. 3, pp. 531–540.

Esarey, A 2006, *Speak No Evil: Mass Media Control in Contemporary China, Freedom at Issue. A Freedom House Special Report*, Freedom House, Washington, DC.

Fan, Y 2007, 'Guanxi, government and corporate reputation in China: Lessons for international companies', *Marketing Intelligence & Planning*, vol. 25, no. 5, pp. 499–510.

Feintuch, M & Varney, M 2006, *Media Regulation, Public Interest and the Law*, 2nd edn, Edinburgh University Press, Edinburgh.

Freeman, D 2010, 'Will China Google for freedom? The Chinese, the Internet and free speech', *BICCS Asia Paper*, vol. 5, no. 3, pp. 1–22.

Fulda, A, Li, Y & Song, Q 2012, 'New strategies of civil society in China: A case study of the network governance approach', *Journal of Contemporary China*, vol. 21, no. 76, pp. 675–693.

Habermas, J 1989, *The Structural Transformation of the Public Sphere*, Polity, Cambridge.

Harold, DK 2008, 'Development of a civil society online? Internet vigilantism and state control in Chinese cyberspace', *Asian Journal of Global Studies*, vol. 2, no. 2, pp. 26–37.

Heath, R 1992, 'Critical perspectives on public relations', in E Toth & R Heath (eds), *Rhetorical and Critical Approaches to Public Relations* (pp. 37–61), Lawrence Erlbaum Associates, Inc., Hillsdale, NJ.

Heath, RL 2011, 'External organisational rhetoric: Bridging management and socio-political discourse', *Management Communication Quarterly*, vol. 25, pp. 415–435.

Holtzhausen, DR 2010, 'Communication in the public sphere: The political context of strategic communication', *International Journal of Strategic Communication*, vol. 4, no. 2, pp. 75–77.

Hou, Z & Zhu, Y 2012, 'An institutional perspective of public relations practices in the Chinese cultural contexts', *Public Relations Review*, vol. *38*, no. 5, pp. 916–925.

Huang, CC 1993, '"Public Sphere"/"Civil Society" in China? The third realm between state and society', *Modern China*, vol. 19, no. 2, pp. 216–240.

Huang, YH 2000, 'The personal influence model and gao guanxi in Taiwan Chinese public relations', *Public Relations Review*, vol. 26, pp. 216–239.

Ihlen, O & Verhoeven, P 2012, 'A public relations identity for the 2010s', *Public Relations Inquiry*, vol. 1, no. 2, pp. 159–176.

Johnston, J 2016, *Public Relations and the Public Interest*, Routledge, London.

Lattimore, D, Baskin, O, Heiman, ST & Toth, EL 2009, *Public Relations: The Profession and the Practice*, McGraw-Hill, New York.

Lee, CC 2010, 'Bound to rise: Chinese media discourses on the new global order', in M Curtin & H Shah (eds), *Reorienting Global Communication: Indian and Chinese Media Beyond Borders*, University of Illinois Press, Urbana, IL, pp. 260–283.

L'Etang, J 2004, *Public Relations in Britain: A History of Professional Practice in the 20th Century*, Lawrence Erlbaum Associates, London.

Lindlof, TR 1995, *Qualitative Communication Research Methods*, Sage, Thousand Oaks, CA.

Lippmann, W 1955, *The Public Philosophy*, Transaction Publishers, New Brunswick.

Macnamara, J 2012, 'Corporate and organisational diplomacy: An alternative paradigm to PR', *Journal of Communication Management*, vol. 16, no. 3, pp. 312–325.

McDougall, BS 2004, 'Privacy in modern China', *History Compass*, vol. 2, pp. 1–8.

Mechling, TB 1975, 'Is public interest public relations practical and desirable? Report of a three year study project', *Public Relations Quarterly*, vol. 20, no. 2, pp. 10–22.

Messina, A 2007, 'Public relations, the public interest and persuasion: An ethical approach', *Journal of Communication Management*, vol. 11, no. 1, pp. 29–52.

Miles, MB & Huberman, AM 1994, *Qualitative Data Analysis: A Sourcebook of New Methods*, Sage, Thousand Oaks, CA.

Nathan, AJ 2003, 'Authoritarian resilience', *Journal of Democracy*, vol. 14, no. 1, pp. 6–17.

Peerenboom, R 2006, 'A government of laws', in S Zhao (ed.), *Debating Political Reform in China: Rule of Law vs. Democratisation*, ME Sharpe, Armonk, NY.

Pojman, LJ & Fieser, J 2009, *Ethics: Discovering Right and Wrong*, Wadsworth, Belmont, CA.

Putnam, RD 1996, 'Who killed civil America?' *American Prospect*, vol. 7, no. 24, pp. 66–72.

Ren, L & Ji, G 2005, 'The term of public interest in law' (in Chinese), *Journal of Nanhua University*, vol. 6, no. 1, pp. 76–78.

Shue, V 2004, 'Legitimacy crisis in China?' in PH Gries & S Rosen (eds), *State and Society in 21st Century China, Crisis, Contention and Legitimation*, Routledge Curzon, UK/NY, pp. 24–49.

Sorauf, FJ 1957, 'The public interest reconsidered', *The Journal of Politics*, vol. 19, no. 4, pp. 616–639.

Stoker, K & Stoker, M 2012, 'The paradox of public interest: How serving individual superior interests fulfill public relations' obligation to the public interest?' *Journal of Mass Media Ethics*, vol. 27, pp. 31–45.

Tang, L & Li, H 2009, 'Corporate social responsibility communication of Chinese and global corporations in China', *Public Relations Review*, vol. 35, pp. 199–212.

Van Cuilenburg, J & McQuail, D 2003, 'Media policy paradigm shifts: Toward a new communications policy paradigm', *European Journal of Communication*, vol. 18, pp. 181–207.

Weaver, K, Motion, J & Roper, J 2006, 'From propaganda to discourse and back again: Truth, power the public interest and public relations', in J L'Etang & M Pieczka (eds), *Public Relations: Critical Debates and Contemporary Practice*, Lawrence Erlbaum, Mahwah, NJ.

Wexler, R, Xu, Y & Young, N 2006, 'NGO advocacy in China: A special report from China development brief', *China Development Brief*, pp. 11.

Yang, A & Taylor, M 2013, 'The relationship between the professionalization of public relations, societal social capital, and democracy: Evidence from a cross-nation study', *Public Relations Review*, vol. 39, no. 4, pp. 257–270.

Yang, G 2005, 'Environmental NGOs and institutional dynamics in China', *The China Quarterly*, vol. 181, pp. 46–66.

Yang, J & Arant, D 2013, 'The roles and ethics of journalism: How Chinese students and American students perceive them similarly and differently', *Journalism & Mass Communication Educator*, vol. 69, no. 1, pp. 33–48.

Zhang, T 2004, 'Self-identity construction of the present China', *Comparative Strategy*, vol. 23, no. 3, pp. 281–301.

Zhang, YB, Lin, M, Nonaka, A & Beom, K 2005, 'Harmony, hierarchy and conservatism: A cross-cultural comparison of Confucian values in China, Korea, Japan and Taiwan', *Communication Research Report*, vol. 22, pp. 107–115.

9 Security, democratic legitimacy and the public interest

Policing and the communicative ritual in deeply divided societies

Ian Somerville and Scott Davidson

Introduction

In a world increasingly fractured by ethnic, religious and racial conflict the issue of security is increasingly a central concern. At the same time the task of producing democratic, equitable and effective policing is bound up with the task of developing approaches in which communication problems can be confronted and practical solutions formulated. This chapter examines contemporary communicative culture, where it is axiomatically 'good to talk' (Craig 2005), in relation to strategic communication initiatives deployed by police services in deeply divided societies. Two case studies are used to investigate and analyse the role of police public relations (PR): the ethno-religious divisions in Northern Ireland; and the racially divided context of Ferguson, Missouri, United States. Our study interrogates the metadiscursive framing that such human problems are caused by bad communication and can be solved by better communication (Craig 2005), particularly involving a specific and important kind of communication event, 'the communication ritual' (Katriel & Philipsen 1981). Models for democratic peace building and conflict resolution (deliberative democracy and agonistic pluralism) are explored in relation to how 'the public interest' is conceptualised and contested in divided societies and how this impacts on the issue of societal security and policing.

The public interest and political theory

A key theoretical problem explored in this chapter is how applications of notions of the public interest in public relations and wider communication scholarship tend to underestimate the levels of division and plurality in many communities. While, of course, there has been much theorising around dividing society into 'publics' in order to better target communication efforts, there has until recently been little PR scholarship which has engaged in empirical research into *deeply divided* societies (Somerville et al. 2017). The 'publics' in PR theory tend to represent differing socio-political perspectives, as in classic interest group theory, but typically they all belong to a more or less homogenous society where it makes sense to refer to building consensus, pursuing win-win solutions, etc. Finding the public interest in deeply divided societies is, to say the least, a more problematic endeavour.

Political theorists are divided on the public interest, with some arguing for the abolition of the concept, while for others its normative underpinning to pluralist capacities are central to the idea that a key role of government is about 'reconciling interests through deliberation and debate and about having procedures that can yield agreed – or certainly acceptable – policies and outcomes' (Anthony 2013, p. 127). There is not the space here to engage fully with this debate and the reader is directed to Chapter 1 of this book for an overview, and elsewhere for an introduction to key perspectives (see, for example, Anthony 2013; Bozeman 2007; Cochran 1974; Johnston 2016; Simm 2011).

Ultimately our position is that in any consideration of the public interest it is difficult to completely abandon normative principles. As Simm (2011) notes, the idea of attempting to accommodate various societal interests while at the same time upholding certain fundamental values (e.g. basic human rights) has been advocated as a resolution to the question of the public interest by philosophers from Hobbes and Hume to Rawls. On this view, 'the public interest is what emerges from deliberative processes that occur within democratically legitimated institutions' (Anthony 2013, p. 128). At the same time, it must be recognised that conflicting values and divergent interests in society mean that no one definition can ever be viewed as final, the public interest 'only comes into existence and is consequently defined when we voice and debate our concerns and views' (Simm 2011, p. 560).

The public interest and deliberative turns

While the cultivation of a public service ethos has been a minor theme in the field of public relations (Johnston 2016), there has been a deliberative turn in the field. This change is largely grounded in assumptions of the ethical superiority of dialogic forms of communication. Indeed, it has been described as ubiquitous in public relations literature by Theunissen and Wan Noordin (2012), with both critical and functionalist paradigms converging on variations of dialogic communication as constituting the most ethical or civic-friendly form of practice.

There have been occasional attempts at incorporating the work of Habermas within this turn. Successful communication would be validated through evaluating levels of consensus achieved through an emphasis on rationality and consent (Burkart 2007). A rules-based approach to dialogue was applied by Meisenbach (2006) that sought to apply an assumption that organisations should use deliberative methods to understand if their policies or values were accepted as valid by stakeholders. This approach is also extolled for enshrining a principle of the public holding a right to participate and to hold communicative relationships with organisations and institutions. This is necessary to enact civil society (Taylor 2009). More recently, Edwards (2016) has drawn on models of rational deliberation to propose a framework for critically assessing the role of public relations in democratic societies.

These themes and assumptions are resonant of similar assumptions expressed in other fields of scholarship. Most pertinent to our study, Keller-Hirsch (2012) notes the turn in scholarship focused on societies that have experienced traumatic conflict and equation of transitional justice with the co-creation of shared senses of belonging; a vision of communitarian social harmony where conflict is substituted by 'overlapping consensus of community' (Keller-Hirsch 2012, p. 2). The focus on dialogue has heralded the growth of a ritualised and formulaic consultation industry that markets itself as guaranteeing the generation of 'the public view' in an easily digestible format for policy-makers and managers (Kashefi & Mort 2004, p. 300).

The dialogic turn in public relations is now running into the conceptual and practical difficulties experienced in other fields. The use of consensus as a regulative ideal is constantly confronted with a reality that elements of reasonable disagreement, or outright dissent, will remain with contestable conceptions of just norms in relationships between groups ineliminable (Tully 2008). Recently there has been a period of increasing deployment of public participation initiatives. During this same period there 'has been a rapid expansion in socioeconomic inequality and political polarization' (Walker et al. 2015, p. 8). Indeed, the age of organisational dialogue has palpably failed to generate a sense of public trust, suggesting that the emphasis on rationality and consensus may be having the unintended consequence of entrenching power inequalities between groups. Critical studies reveal how some dialogic initiatives are primarily designed as a legitimising exercise for organisational interests who use the process to co-opt activist groups and neutralise their more transformative demands (Ganesh & Zoller 2012).

One valuable framework for critiquing and reforming dialogic models is Mouffe's (2005) political philosophy of agonistic democracy. Shavit and Bailey (2015) succinctly encapsulate this distinction between the rational deliberation of Habermas's and Mouffe's agonistics:

> While Habermas seeks to recover the moral foundations of democracy as public debate that upholds consensus according to universal principles of rationality, Mouffe rejects the ideal of rational consensus and conceptualizes democracy as domesticated warfare, in which adversaries make necessary compromises in the form of tentative suspension of hostilities.
>
> (p. 104)

Agonists diverge from communitarian or dialogic approaches through their assumptions that no forms of rational thinking or values exist that can be universally applied to adjudicate between all issue or power conflicts. Indeed, they further diverge from the privileging of consensus by instilling a positive disposition toward conflict and struggle within democratic societies. For organisational communication, the agonistic assumption will be that all organisations inevitably favour some values or groups over others, and that safeguarding the public interest requires the nurturing of the ability of citizens generally to contest decisions, and in particular, marginalised groups to challenge any rationalisation of harmful social relationships (Davidson 2016). Mouffe argues that the existence, or creation, of any group identity always implies the formation of socially grounded differences with *us-them* relationships permanently susceptible to declining into *friend-enemy* antagonism (Mouffe 2005). The agonistic aspiration is that the experience of active participation in public forums helps foster an identity as a citizen and accordingly reduces the possibility of resorts to violence. Unlike much of the dialogic turn which places consensus as the central organising concept, agonism privileges a sense of open contestation that renders other identities visible not as strangers but as potential allies or respected opponents (Tully 2008).

Social interaction and the communication ritual: 'It's good to talk'

Shavit and Bailey (2015) note that Habermas and Mouffe rely on very different philosophical arguments about the nature of language and communication to conceptualise democratic participation. Bogen (1999) identifies the reliance on Searle's speech act theory in Habermas's work, a perspective on communication which privileges the formal-analytic propositional meaning of utterances, and downplays the role of social and cultural context and the importance of 'in-the-moment' interaction. Mouffe borrows 'forms of life' from Wittgenstein to describe the importance of exploring how the *particular* social and historical contexts of public participation rather than a *universal* notion of consensus and rationality shape and enable democratic interaction (Mouffe 2000, p. 13). Clearly, if we acknowledge the importance of social and historical context in any democratic communicative encounter we must acknowledge that there are more elements at play than merely deliberative procedures that prioritise rational argumentation. Goffman used the term the 'interaction order' to refer to the social organisation of face-to-face encounters and argued: 'Face-to-face interaction has its own regulations; it has its own processes and its own structure' (Goffman 1964, p. 136). Shavit and Bailey (2015) argue that there is an important congruence between Mouffe's argument regarding 'forms of life' and Goffman's 'interaction order':

> In this view, the interaction order can be seen as a fundamental 'form of life,' that is, a ritual organization of social encounters that transforms individuals into morally accountable human beings … the ongoing, working consensuses of face-work in which self and others are treated, at least temporarily, as valued, has strong parallels to Mouffe's notion of 'agonistic pluralism'.
>
> (p. 110)

Unsurprisingly Habermas (1984) dismissed Goffman's 'presentation of self' in the interactional encounter as a type of strategic action: 'the dramaturgical qualities of action are in a certain way parasitic; they rest on a structure of goal-directed action' (Habermas 1984, p. 90). However, two points could be made in response to Habermas's criticism; firstly, Goffman is surely correct to insist that merely analysing the *propositional content* of the language deployed in actual communicative situations may tell you very little about the actual interactions in those situations; and secondly, as Rawls (1987) noted, Habermas's analysis fails to acknowledge the moral element of 'face work' (Goffman 1967) demonstrated in Goffman's ethnographic study of the interaction ritual. Shavit and Bailey (2015, p. 110) emphasise this point that 'face-work, a dimension of the interaction order, is social actors' ritual treatment of the social personas of self and other as valued'. It could be argued that much of the talk, based on the 'ritual order', that is central to deliberative encounters can perhaps be better explicated as 'face work' than as Habermas's communicative rationality, and moreover perhaps represents the interactional basis for the mutual recognition that Mouffe and others see as a necessary starting point for democratic agonistic pluralism (Shavit & Bailey 2015).

Craig (2005) observes that contemporary Western culture is particularly self-conscious and reflexive about communication and indeed generates large quantities of metadiscourse about it. It is a culture dominated by

> the idea that communication is important, the idea that human problems are caused by bad communication and can be solved by better communication, ... the idea, in short, that it is 'good to talk'.
>
> (Craig 2005, p. 660)

This idea that communication is important for more than just the transmission of information arguably involves thinking about communication using a different kind of metaphor than in much contemporary theorising about communication. A transmission view of communication foregrounds 'imparting', 'sending', 'transmitting' or 'giving information to others', whereas the ritual view of communication conceptualises 'language as an instrument of dramatic action, of thought as essentially situational and social' (Carey 2009, p. 18). It would be wrong to assume this means we should underplay the importance of the processes of information transmission or indeed attitude change brought about by communication; rather, Carey (2009, p. 7) is suggesting that 'one cannot understand these processes aright except insofar as they are cast within an essentially ritualistic view of communication and social order'. Thinking about the role of communicative interaction in deeply divided societies throws into sharp relief Carey's (2009) point that communication is not a neutral process or conduit for transmitting information but 'a symbolic process whereby reality is produced, maintained, repaired, and transformed' (p. 23). Moreover, in contexts where repairing or transforming 'reality' is particularly important we can see more clearly the kinds of interactional events which involve a more explicit demonstration of what Katriel and Philipsen (1981) described as 'the communication ritual'. While ordinarily we think mostly about communication from within the transmission metaphor, at certain times and in certain circumstances the ritualistic view of communication asserts itself. Engaging in overtly ritualistic communication events indicates that the participants are involved in the serious business of resolving communication failures or even resolving conflict. It is one of the arguments of this chapter that theorising communication as ritual is essential especially in the kinds of interactions whose purpose is engaging in repairing deep societal division and demonstrating a deliberative legitimacy in developing a common view of the public interest.

Policing and the public interest: communication and legitimisation

The criminal justice system is an arena where many citizens encounter governmental authority most directly and forcefully within their local communities (Fyfe 2001). It is for this reason that the police, as the most public-facing manifestation of criminal justice, tend to be found at the centre of conflicts over legitimacy (Hays 2012). Hays (2012, p. 562) notes:

> if the police do not establish legitimacy in the eyes of those who are subject to their authority, they will encounter both passive resistance and open defiance as they seek to enforce the laws.

Reiner (2000) suggests that a police service seeks to derive legitimacy both from their professionalism and from their responsiveness to citizens. Hays (2012) notes that Reiner also makes an important point about what he terms 'revisionist' critics of policing who would argue that the

> police cannot form true partnerships with members of disadvantaged communities, because the intent of policing is not to benefit these communities but to control behavior that might threaten the security and property of higher-status groups.
>
> (p. 563)

We don't need to fully accept the revisionist argument to nevertheless acknowledge that in many societies, the police have been explicitly used by the dominant or majority group to reinforce privilege and oppress minority groups through harassment and at times selective enforcement of the laws. Policing can very easily become a very potent symbol of the government acting in the interest of one societal group rather than in the public interest. This revisionist analysis can obviously be extended beyond the class inequalities which Reiner (2000) focuses on to police relationships with ethnic, racial or religious minorities. It is unsurprising that campaigns by minority groups for equal protection and fair application of the law frequently focus on police behaviour and how citizens can exert local control over policing their communities (Weitzer & Tuch 2006). The following part of our chapter assesses the use of communication fora/rituals in attempts to establish public interest policing by drawing on two case studies which highlight communicative efforts to resolve sectarian distrust (Northern Ireland) and racial tension (Ferguson, St Louis).

Policing, communication and engagement in Northern Ireland

This case study analyses the development of policing in Northern Ireland since the end of the sectarian conflict in 1998. It discusses the recommendations of the Independent Policing Commission (IPC) and focuses particularly on the Partners and Communities Together (PACT) model of police/community engagement (for a list of acronyms connected with policing and the peace process in Northern Ireland see Table 9.1). The case study draws on qualitative data from reports and scholarly studies on this process to illustrate how participants and researchers have understood the issues of communicative engagement and the concept of policing in the public interest.

Northern Ireland is a deeply divided society. It comprises two main rival ethno-political blocs: unionists/loyalists who are pro-British and mainly Protestant, and nationalists/republicans who are pro-Irish and mainly Catholic. For almost 50 years, since the partition of the island in 1921, Protestants monopolised power in Northern Ireland in part due to their fear of being subsumed into a Catholic-dominated Southern state. However, grievances of the Catholic minority eventually led in the late 1960s to civil rights demonstrations, civil unrest and the armed campaign of the Irish Republican Army (IRA) aimed at removing British rule from Ireland. A key outcome of the Belfast Agreement (10 April 1998), which formally brought to an end the violent conflict in Northern Ireland, was the devolution of powers to a consociational (i.e. mandatory power-sharing) government. An important feature of the Belfast Agreement was the focus on the reform of policing and justice in Northern Ireland.

On 4 April 2002 the Police Service of Northern Ireland (PSNI) officially took over from the Royal Ulster Constabulary (RUC). This symbolic change of name arose from the changes emanating from the Belfast Agreement and the resulting recommendations of the IPC. Policing in Northern Ireland changed its structure, its community representation (50:50 recruitment from Protestant and Catholic communities) and its accountability, with the goal of becoming more acceptable to the whole Northern Ireland community (Quinn & Hargie 2004). One of the main recommendations of the IPC was that a more nodal approach to the delivery of policing be introduced, one that explicitly established partnership policing structures: 'Below district level, local communities and police should be encouraged to develop consultative forums on lines that suit them and their neighbourhood. We recommend that it should be the aim of every police beat manager to have such a forum in his

Table 9.1 List of abbreviations of bodies and organisations in Northern Ireland

Abbreviation	Organisation or body
CSP	Community Safety Partnerships
DPP	District Policing Partnerships
IPC	Independent Policing Commission
IRA	Irish Republican Army
NPT	Neighbourhood Policing Team
PACT	Partners and Communities Together
PCSP	Policing and Community Safety Partnerships
PSNI	Police Service of Northern Ireland
RUC	Royal Ulster Constabulary

or her patrol area' (*IPC Report*, Section 6, p. 35). Brunger (2011) notes that the PACT model was 'explicitly promoted as fostering a more nodal approach to local police decision making by engaging with a more diverse range of groups ... Therefore, enhancing the accountability and legitimacy of the PSNI at the local level' (p. 105).

Neighbourhood Policing Teams (NTPs) were established in 2003 and they were tasked with developing the PACT model. At the same time there were other responses to the IPC report. A key initiative (and the one which has attracted much more academic scrutiny) was the setting up of District Policing Partnerships (DPPs) in each of the 11 Police Districts in Northern Ireland. We will discuss the PACT initiative in detail below but it is also important to examine DPPs which operated as follows: 'Each DPP must hold six community forums each year – the Policing Board monitors this. They also monitor equality issues. The DPPs identify issues to be brought to the Policing Board' (Policing Board staff member, cited in Hays 2012, p. 575). Hays (2012) suggests, however, that from the start DPPs did not really address citizen concerns about police responsiveness to community needs. His findings highlight the distance between the activities of DPPs and the concerns of ordinary citizens as well as 'the representativeness of the DPP process and the functioning of the police within it' (p. 575). As one participant stated, 'DPP meetings are a complaining forum ... Police must respond to all questions raised but they sometimes do so in ways that are not helpful – they appear to be stonewalling. Only community activists attend these meetings' (nationalist community representative, cited in Hays 2012, p. 576).

Byrne and Topping's (2012) research also reports interviewees complaining that these public meetings generally failed to connect with the needs of local communities and tended to be dominated by bureaucracy, focusing on facts and figures:

Basically the DPP meetings are not community friendly ... they can be full of statistics and very formal and actually intimidate those maybe less confident or not as well educated as those sitting at the top table.
(community representative, cited in Byrne & Topping 2012, p. 72)

Lack of faith in DPPs wasn't just limited to local community representatives. In Topping's study one senior PSNI officer confided that initially many serving police officers themselves were resistant to the whole notion of DPP community forums: 'the likes of the people [community organisations] they were talking about involving were horrifying the "old school" RUC/PSNI establishment' (PSNI officer, cited in Topping 2008, p. 786). Acknowledging the problems of 'both the representativeness of the DPP process and the functioning of police within it' (Hays 2012, p. 575), the PSNI, along with Local District Councils in Northern Ireland, introduced Community Safety Partnerships (CSPs) to run alongside DPPs as another forum where citizens could voice concerns about community policing issues. However, this initiative didn't appear to resolve the problem of remoteness and alienation felt by local citizens. One respondent suggested that the 'administration and running of community safety partnerships should be based in the community and not in council buildings removed from community settings' (community representative, cited in Byrne & Topping 2012, p. 74). In 2011 DPPs and CSPs were amalgamated but the problem of 'representation' on these bodies remained 'a major concern in the view of working class loyalists' (loyalist community representative, cited in Byrne & Topping 2012, p. 90).

Partners and Communities Together (PACT)

In post-conflict Northern Ireland, therefore, attempts at district-level police/community partnership and engagement have met with limited success, but what of the neighbourhood-level engagement which was tasked to NPTs? The PACT model adopted by NPTs was designed to provide a fixed point of contact between the local patrol level PSNI areas and the public. According to Brunger (2011, p. 105), the model was meant to represent 'the new beginning to the governance of policing in Northern Ireland and how public policing in particular is more accountable to the public'. PACTs were organised at a much more grass-roots level than DPPs/CSPs had been, thus for example Belfast had one CSP but has 12 PACTs. PACTs are explicitly promoted as 'neighbourhood focused' and 'neighbourhood owned', and providing a mechanism that will provide a 'focus for identifying community concerns', thus 'encouraging communities and neighbourhoods to identify and solve problems alongside the PSNI' (official PACT guidance documentation 36, p. 12, cited in Brunger 2011, p. 107). The PACT partnership model involves PACT public meetings which take place together at two-month intervals with the public meeting format providing NPT officers with the 'opportunity to communicate with local people' and 'enable low level, localised policing issues to be addressed together, through partnership with communities' (official PACT guidance documentation 36, p. 2, cited in Brunger 2011, p. 107). Brunger (2011, p. 108) notes that:

> PACT public meetings are based upon an 'open' format, which places emphasis on encouraging public discussion, where the agenda is directed by the audience. Any issues raised are then prioritised and taken forward to the PACT panel, which assembles after the public meeting. ... [I]t is up to the panel members to decide upon how, based upon the efficacy, reasonableness and operational viability, the issues proposed should be prioritised by the NPT or other agencies if so required.

Maintaining this ethos of 'community ownership' means that the events are chaired by a member of the public, whose role it is to manage the meetings and encourage the participation of the audience. Brunger (2011) makes a number of interesting observations in respect to PACT events. Firstly, they serve the function of providing a forum for the public to bring low-level disorder issues to the attention of the PSNI with the aim of solving these issues in partnership with them. Secondly, however, attendance can be low at these meetings and therefore it is not always easy to tell how representative they are of the local community. For Brunger (2011, p. 106), however, the key contribution of PACT:

> lies in its symbolic role of fostering greater community involvement ... This symbolic role is further amplified and consolidated through the meanings and representative practices that take place within the operation of the public meetings.

There is little doubt that PACT provides a great deal of symbolic capital for the PSNI but there is also clearly genuine buy-in to the initiative by the police themselves and local community representatives. A PSNI officer, serving at the patrol level, noted:

> They are very welcome, they are helping us to communicate with local people and keep them informed with what we are doing in their locality. If I am honest, I place a lot of importance on the PACT initiatives.
> (PSNI officer, November 2009, cited in Brunger 2011, p. 110)

A PACT panel member stated: 'I think, to put it simply, PACT provides an example of a local, community-led partnership that is addressing community problems and delivering mutually agreed programmes of intervention' (November 2009, cited in Brunger 2011, p. 110).

Brunger suggests that PACT meetings frequently provide PSNI officers a space 'where they can engage in dramaturgical performances, from which their message can be conveyed to the assembled audiences' (Brunger 2011,

p. 106). What he means is that rather than using meetings to merely transmit information to a passive audience they involve the 'dramatisation of the experiences of crime by elaborating extreme case studies' to other participants in the group (Brunger 2011, p. 117). This of course does contain dangers (raising fear levels, etc.), but it is reflective of a very different communication approach at the local, situational level and Brunger (2011) argues that overall PACTs have been a positive development for community policing in Northern Ireland because they have helped foster a more community-focused, decentralised and accountable police service. Arguably if we think about a PACT event as a specific kind of communicative ritual designed, not just to tackle local crime issues but, more broadly, to foster a view of policing as a public service for all of Northern Ireland's citizens, we can construe it as a significant and particularly salient development in the context of a Northern Ireland which has a history of wariness in respect to the role and the legitimacy of policing.

Citizen-police interaction in Ferguson, St Louis

This case study focuses on the attempts by state and local government and policing authorities to instigate dialogic responses to a fundamental breakdown in relationships between the police and African American residents of St Louis. It analyses the events and conduct of the first public meeting of the Ferguson Commission which was established to study and make recommendations on citizen-police interactions. At its initial stages the commission represents an attempt to deploy the ritualised assumptions of the deliberative turn to deeply divided urban communities. Institutional responses to the situation in St. Louis are multi-faceted and ongoing, but this chapter focuses on the structure of the first official attempts at dialogue.

The ongoing issue of antagonistic police-community relationships reached a tipping point in August 2014 in Ferguson, a neighbourhood in greater St Louis with its own separate local government administration. The crisis was sparked when an unarmed black teenager, Michael Brown, was shot dead by a white police officer in the street. Immediately following Brown's death there was a prolonged period of street protests. Some of these protests descended into violent exchanges between the police and protestors (*The New York Times* 2015). These events took place in front of a growing media circus of news crews from across the United States and abroad. A state of emergency was called prior to the grand jury's consideration of the actions of the police officer who shot Brown. When the jury decided not to support charges against the officer, there was a renewed period of protests and street-level confrontation, not just in Ferguson but in urban areas across the United States which became a driver for a wave of new community activism under the aegis of Black Lives Matter (Boyles 2015).

Brown's death was an exemplar of a pattern of police shootings in other US cities, with Zimring (2017) estimating there are over 1,000 police killings of civilians per year. This situation was racially aggravated by a predominantly white police service frequently using firearms when patrolling predominantly African American neighbourhoods. At the time of the shooting, 60 per cent of Ferguson's population was African American, but only four out of 50 police officers covering the town were, and no city officials were African American (Mirzoeff 2016). The breakdown in consensual policing was for many explicitly intertwined with economic inequality. As economic deprivation within the region shrunk the local government tax base, the City of Ferguson council was accused of aggressively seeking court fines and collecting court costs as a source of alternative income. The significance of this practice as an income stream is illustrated by estimates that Ferguson and its neighbouring municipality Florissant collected $3.5 million in 2013 (ArchCity Defenders 2014). The federal-level investigation into the events in Ferguson concluded that local courts were abusing their authority by seeing their role as advancing the city's financial interests, and that within the local police, '[o]fficers appear to see some residents, especially those who live in Ferguson's predominantly African-American neighborhoods, less as constituents to be protected than as potential offenders and sources of revenue' (USDOJ 2015, p. 2). Control of the communicative responses to these events were removed from the local police authority's hands by wider political jurisdictions – the governor of Missouri who enacted the Ferguson Commission and the federal attorney general in Washington, DC, who used powers to order police reform through community engagement.

The announcement by Governor Nixon to establish the Ferguson Commission set the tone and scope of its work. In doing so Nixon underlined the value of the Ferguson Commission as a case study in deliberative communication guided by a particular interpretation of the public interest. That interpretation, at least initially, deployed a simplified reception of the norms of the deliberative model as identified by Edwards (2016) that all affected by the issue should be accorded equal status and access to the dialogue; participants must set aside their own interests in favour of the common good with arguments based on reason to be privileged over contributions grounded in pathos. Speaking to the media to announce the commission, Nixon emphasised 'shouting' and 'outsiders' were not welcome to participate in the public dialogue (CNN Transcripts 2014). The goals set for the commission were summarised as a process of collecting information on social and economic conditions, drawing on sources of expertise before formulating technical recommendations (Ferguson Commission 2014). Nixon publicly associated himself with the assumptions that there were technical solutions to the issues confronting Ferguson, and that these could be revealed through dispassionate and rational fact finding.

The transcript of the first public meeting of the Ferguson Commission (2014a) is a valuable documentary record of issues that arise when trying to apply deliberative solutions to breakdowns in police-community relationships. Close analysis of the session reveals the tensions between the approach used by its organisers and the participatory expectations of local citizens who attended.

A significant proportion of the first meeting was devoted to explaining the rules-based approach to the dialogue. This connected to the strong theme running throughout the session that the legitimacy of the commission would be linked to its adherence to a set of rules and values. At the meeting the assistant attorney general of Missouri provided a long verbal briefing on the state's transparency laws ('sunshine law'), detailing requirements on issues such as open meetings, record keeping, and even exact instructions on how many commission members receiving an email from another member would trigger a requirement for its contents to be declared publically. Commission members were all asked to speak about themselves and why they had 'answered' the 'call to serve' (Ferguson Commission 2014a, p. 41). After a set of contributions of varying length all the members were then asked to speak individually again, this time about their aspirations and hopes for the commission. After this the commission members were asked to perform a group exercise involving sheets of paper with suggested guiding principles and ordering these into a top five. Once these had been agreed there was a 45-minute discussion of the principles on this list. It is at this point the format of the meeting begins to be openly challenged by audience members: 'I would like to know when the community is going to get to talk and it's already 3.30 and the meeting was supposed to be over at five' (Ferguson Commission 2014a, p. 120). After a prolonged set of challenges by clearly frustrated audience members the meeting returns to its pre-set agenda and invites audience members to vote by keypad on which part of the governor's work programme for the commission should begin first. Audience members were also asked to fill out green sheets of paper with their own priority issues of concern. The final part of meeting was the only opportunity for audience members to speak freely, rather than listen to commission members or rank some pre-selected options.

The format of the meeting followed what was clearly a localised interpretation of the rituals of the deliberative turn. It was introduced and presented to the audience with optimistic language littered with lofty ideals, and yet on various levels, for a significant number of citizens who participated, it clearly disappointed their expectations of how a public space should function. Two major themes of these challenges were the legitimacy of the commission's membership to represent the concerns and lived experiences of local residents, and a querying of how the dialogue was seen as de-politicising issues.

Representation and legitimacy

In the meeting there was dissensus amongst participants on the decision to accord privileged status and commission membership to an appointed group of so-called community leaders. Although not explicitly stated in its executive orders from the governor, the Ferguson Commission can arguably be viewed as an attempt to establish a form of a deliberative mini-public. Mini-publics are attempts to construct forums whose membership are broadly representative of public interests while de-linking deliberation from the strategic communicative action associated with electoral politics or interest group campaigning (Warren 2009). A group small enough to enable in-depth dialogic interaction between its members while, crucially, holding some democratic legitimacy through its composition being representative of wider communities (Goodin & Dryzek 2006). But instead of the traditional approach where a group of citizens considered demographically representative of the affected community is recruited, the Ferguson Commission comprised a cross-section of a less well-defined demographic – community leaders: 'as a commission ... we as leaders are committed to lasting, positive change for St. Louis' (co-chair McClure, Ferguson Commission 2014a, p. 12). In the meeting co-chair McClure was anxious to emphasise the representative 'cross-section' (Ferguson Commission 2014a, p. 76) diversity of its members: 'You are all accomplished leaders in your own right and in your spheres of influence, and we come from many different perspectives and from diverse opinions' (Ferguson Commission 2014a, p. 13). The claims of being representative were challenged before and during the meeting. Before the meeting one local newspaper, the *St. Louis Post-Dispatch*, described the members of the commission as a 'mix of lawyers, CEOS, former and current police officials and educators – along with one 20 year-old protestor' (Deere 2014). When audience members began to question the format of the meeting, the composition of the committee became a prominent issue. As one audience member stated: 'You do not understand and you do not go through the things the people in the community are going through ... how can you fix what's going on in the community when you don't even include the community?' (Ferguson Commission 2014a, p. 124). This view was echoed by another audience member: 'we are honoured that you all have credentials and you're educated, but you do not reflect the community that we live in' (Ferguson Commission 2014a, p. 129). Indeed, the long section of the meeting aimed at bolstering the leadership and representative credentials of the commission members was also forthrightly challenged: 'The fact of the matter is we sat for hours and listened to your resumes. We sat for hours and listened to your pedigree. We don't care' (audience member, Ferguson Commission 2014a, p. 144).

De-politicisation

A second major theme in how some audience members challenged the structure of the dialogue centred on a rejection of the attempts to de-politicise the issues of racial inequality and policing. This is a central concern of agonistic writers when considering the impact of the deliberative turn as exemplified by Mouffe's critique of Habermas. For Mouffe it is a mistake to portray difficult social issues as merely technical conundrums awaiting a solution to be provided by experts, but policy decisions always involve to some degree a choice between conflicting alternatives. Public dialogues serve democracy when they enable a transparent struggle between opposing conceptions of what constitutes the public good. To this end, public dialogue should not be seeking to eradicate disagreement, but constantly encouraging the mobilisation of citizens to scrutinise or challenge hegemonic orders (Mouffe 2005, 2013). The deliberative turn is accused of wanting to de-politicise public forums because too often it is assumed the practical function of dialogue is to consolidate communities by squeezing out spaces for dissensus or struggle between competing projects (Honig 1993).

The commission presented its vision of a rules-based dialogue that sought to include rational, non-partisan, consensus-oriented exchanges that excluded explorations of difference and dissensus. Co-chair Wilson told the meeting: 'We ask ourselves … to maintain an open mind' (Ferguson Commission 2014a, p. 7), and that 'we'll find common ground in ways that we never thought possible' (Ferguson Commission 2014a, p. 16). Co-Chair McClure underlined the depoliticised tone of the commission's workings: 'so we're going to work to tackle these issues in a way that doesn't take sides, that doesn't place blame for misunderstanding' (Ferguson Commission 2014a, p. 13). This approach was challenged from within by one commission member, Traci Blackmon, who in a dissonant note based on her experience of civil rights campaigns in Alabama told the meeting, '[w]e rushed too quickly to healing. We rushed too quickly to Band-Aids' (Ferguson Commission 2014a, p. 64), and argued the dialogue would need to focus on racial and economic disparities in a manner that was 'uncomfortable' if it were to hold value. From the exchanges in the meeting it was apparent that many members of the audience were hoping to hear platforms or policies to transform the economic situation and relationships with the police – and the opportunity to evaluate competing conceptions of the common good. Audience members made direct appeals to commission members: 'how do you feel you can fix it?' (Ferguson Commission 2014a, p. 125). Another audience member asked: 'what can we do to fix the problem, you guys didn't even have a thing to fix the problem' (Ferguson Commission 2014a, p. 131). The absence of any platforms or political mobilisation within the structure of the dialogue drew strongly sceptical contributions from some audience members as to the political strategy behind the commission. 'This is pacifying' (Ferguson Commission 2014a, p. 149), said one audience member, while another stated: 'What we don't want you to do is become just another bureaucracy, just taking the information and doing nothing and turning it against us' (Ferguson Commission 2014a, p. 150).

Conclusions

The turn to dialogue places consensus as the regulative ideal in public interest communication. This implies the public interest is best served by agreements forged through interactions with the people affected, rather than through internal decision-making mechanisms followed by dissemination of policies through publicity. The ritual of dialogue can be understood as a symbolic commitment to democracy in increasingly pluralistic societies. As seen through the two case studies, communicative deliberation rituals are both a pragmatic response by institutions to meet the norms of inclusion and diversity in police-community relations and a symbolic response to the requirement that policing be seen to be in the public interest. The public commitments to a fostering of dialogue and participation are conscious enactments of progressivism, what Tully (2008) would view as a willing obligation to engage with institutional self-reflection and 'other-understanding' of differing identities within local communities. Yet, this chapter has explored how dialogue, and in particular its interpretation in everyday practice, only offers an incomplete answer to the question of how police-community relations should serve a democratic ethos. Institutions advocating for increased public participation clearly hold progressive promise, but the translation into practice frequently runs into the entrenched divisions and inequalities explored in this chapter. Ultimately deliberation will fail to meet its progressivist goals unless it is conducted in conjunction with other modes of participation that centre on protest or contestation (Walker et al. 2015).

Alongside consensus as a regulative ideal, the deliberative turn also places dispassionate rationality as a participative norm. This is problematic in deeply divided communities, where citizens are frequently motivated to participate based on us/them identities. There is a particular peril to presenting policies and policing norms as some kind of common-sense aggregation of the best arguments. Groups and identities who believe themselves to be disempowered by local socio-political relationships may respond to a presentation of this state of affairs as being a rational outcome by withdrawing from democratic engagement, leading to us/them relationships declining into antagonism or violence. Indeed, if dialogue is purely based on a dominant group's conception of logic and legitimacy then there is the prospect of dialogue being seen as a vehicle to negate the ability of marginalised groups to achieve progressive change.

Rather than judging if police-community relationships serve the public interest purely through the maintenance of consensus between major stakeholders, attention also needs to be directed to evaluating if programmes are fostering a propensity for non-violent discursive exchanges and a belief in the efficacy of exchanging views with other citizens. Evidence of a willingness by groups to continue their economic or cultural rivalry within shared public spaces would be one indicator of successfully serving the public interest. This implies a willingness by institutional communicators to cede control of the dialogue and not fear the enactment of passionate disagreement.

Furthermore, while dialogue organisers might be tempted to initiate public engagement by using optimistic or uplifting cues based on shared positive experiences, as we saw in the Ferguson case study, when engaging with divided communities there needs to be recognition that it is often lack of trust, disappointment, or dissensus that prompts participation and engagement. The temptation to suggest that historical inequalities, based on institutional racism and a denial of civil rights within a community can be quickly overcome through 'better' communication needs to be avoided if trust is to be maintained. It would also be remiss not to acknowledge the reality of a post-conflict society where the importance of existing political realities and cultural memories make societal transitions, including in relation to policing, especially difficult for some communities. If ultimate decision-making power remains with institutional elites, then the transformative power of public discussion forums should not be over-stated. This links directly to the issue of representation on police-community forums. Who precisely is engaged in these interactions, in the 'face work' (Goffman 1967), and how are their interactions constructing an agreed definition of the public interest? This was an important issue for participants cited in both case studies and the Northern Ireland context highlighted that the attempts to engage at what we might call the intermediate or district level were characterised by failure and alienation. This is a crucial point. Despite good intentions the district-level meetings were viewed by ordinary citizens primarily as information transmission events whereas arguably the PACT meetings were characterised much more by communication as a symbolic process which was making a contribution to repairing and transforming the reality of life in a deeply divided society. Neighbourhood PACT interactions were viewed by citizens as much more satisfactory both in regard to distribution of power and representation (they were chaired by ordinary citizens). They were also, as Brunger (2012) noted, seen as significant 'dramaturgical' events for the police, and indeed, perhaps they can be viewed as important dramaturgical events or communication rituals for all involved. These more micro-level engagements attracted the most favourable comments from community participants and imply that, as far as policing in the public interest goes, in the context of deep societal division it is 'good to talk' as long as you do it first at the neighbourhood level.

References

Anthony, G 2013, 'Public Interest and the Three Dimensions of Judicial Review', *Northern Ireland Legal Quarterly*, vol. 4, no. 2, pp. 125–142.

ArchCity Defenders 2014, *Municipal Courts White Paper*, November.

Bogen, D 1999, *Order without Rules Critical Theory and the Logic of Conversation*, State University of New York Press, Albany, NY.

Boyles, A 2015, *Race, Place, and Suburban Policing*, University of California Press, Oakland, CA.

Bozeman, B 2007, *Public Values and Public Interest*, Georgetown UP, Georgetown, DC.

Brunger, M 2011, 'Governance, accountability and neighbourhood policing in Northern Ireland: Analysing the role of public meetings', *Crime, Law and Social Change*, vol. 55, no. 2, pp. 105–120.

Burkart, R 2007, 'On Jürgen Habermas and public relations', *Public Relations Review*, vol. 33, no. 3, pp. 249–254.

Byrne, J & Topping, J 2012, *Report for Belfast Conflict Resolution Consortium*, University of Ulster.

Carey, JW 2009, 'A Cultural Approach to Communication', in *Communication as Culture: Essays on Media and Society*, Routledge, New York, pp. 11–28.

CNN Transcripts 2014, 'CNN Newsroom: Missouri News Conference', 21 October, viewed 8 April 2018, http://edition.cnn.com/TRANSCRIPTS/1410/21/cnr.05.html.

Cochran, C 1974, 'Political Science and "The Public Interest"', *The Journal of Politics*, vol. 36, no. 2, pp. 327–336

Craig, RT 2005, 'How We Talk About How We Talk: Communication Theory in the Public Interest', *Journal of Communication*, vol. 55, no. 4, pp. 659–667.

Davidson, S 2016, 'Public Relations Theory: An agonistic critique of the turns to dialogue and symmetry', *Public Relations Inquiry*, vol. 5, no. 2, pp. 145–167.

Deere, S 2014, 'Nixon announces members of Ferguson Commission', *St. Louis Post-Dispatch*, November 19, viewed 10 March 2017, www.stltoday.com/news/local/govt-and-politics/nixon-announces-members-of-ferguson-commission/article_018cc5a3-d3db-5296-a581-75ca49921153.html.

Edwards, L 2016, 'The Role of Public Relations in Deliberative Systems', *Journal of Communication*, vol. 66, pp. 60–81.

Ferguson Commission 2014, 'Gov. Nixon to create commission to address issues raised by events in Ferguson', Press statement, October 21, viewed 20 March 2017, https://stlpositivechange.org/content/gov-nixon-create-commission-address-issues-raised-events-ferguson.

Ferguson Commission 2014a *Record of Proceedings*, December 1, viewed 25 September 2017, https://stlpositivechange.org/sites/stlpositivechange/files/meeting_attachments/ferguson-commission-meeting-transcript-12-1-14.pdf.

Fyfe, J 2001, 'Good policing', in RG Dunham & GP Alpert (eds), *Critical Issues in Policing: Contemporary Readings*, Waveland Press, Prospect Heights, IL, pp. 161–180.

Ganesh, S & Zoller, HM 2012, 'Dialogue, activism, and democratic social change', *Communication Theory*, vol. 22, no. 1, pp. 66–91.

Goffman, E 1964, 'The Neglected Situation', *American Anthropologist*, vol. 66, no. 6, pp. 133–136.

Goffman, E 1967, *Interaction Ritual*, Anchor Books, New York.

Goodin, R & Dryzek, J 2006, 'Deliberative Impacts: The Macro-Political Uptake of Mini-Publics', *Politics & Society*, vol. 34, no. 2, pp. 219–244.

Guelke, A 2012, *Politics in Deeply Divided Societies*, Polity Press, Cambridge.

Habermas, J 1984, *The Theory of Communicative Action Vol. 1* (trans. T McCarthy), Beacon Press, Boston, MA.

Hays, RA 2012, 'Policing in Northern Ireland: Community Control, Community Policing, and the Search for Legitimacy', *Urban Affairs Review*, vol. 49, no. 4, pp. 557–592.

Honig, B 1993, *Political Theory and the Displacement of Politics*, Cornell University Press, Ithaca, NY.

Horowitz, D 2000, *Ethnic Groups in Conflict*, University of California Press, Oakland, CA.

Independent Commission on Policing in Northern Ireland 1999, *A New Beginning: Policing in Northern Ireland – The Report of the Independent Commission on*

Policing in Northern Ireland, September 9, viewed 15 May 2017, http://cain.ulst.ac.uk/issues/police/patten/patten99.pdf.

Johnston, J 2016, *Public Relations and the Public Interest*, Routledge, London.

Kashefi, E & Mort, M 2004, 'Grounded Citizens' Juries: A tool for health activism?', *Health Expectations*, vol. 7, pp. 290–302.

Katriel, T & Philipsen, G 1981, 'What we need is communication', *Communication Monographs*, vol. 8, pp. 301–317.

Keller-Hirsch, A 2012, 'Introduction: The Agon of Reconciliation', in A Keller-Hirsch (ed.), *Theorizing Post-Conflict Reconciliation*, Routledge, London, pp. 1–10.

Meisenbach, RJ 2006, 'Habermas' discourse ethics and principle of universalization as a moral framework for organizational communication', *Management Communication Quarterly*, vol. 20, no. 1, pp. 39–62.

Mirzoeff, N 2016, 'The Murder of Michael Brown: Reading the Ferguson Grand Jury Transcript', *Social Text*, vol. 34, no. 1, pp. 49–71.

Mouffe, C 2000, *The Democratic Paradox*, Verso, London and New York.

Mouffe, C 2005, *On the Political*, Routledge, New York.

The New York Times 2015, Q&A: What happened in Ferguson?, *The New York Times*, 10 August, viewed 28 September, www.nytimes.com/interactive/2014/08/13/us/ferguson-missouri-town-under-siege-after-police-shooting.html?ref=ferguson.

Parkins, J & Mitchell, R 2005, 'Public participation as public debate: A deliberative turn in national resource management', *Society and Natural Resources*, vol. 18, no. 6, pp. 529–540.

Pearson, R 1989, 'Beyond ethical relativism in public relations: Coorientation, rules, and the idea of communication symmetry', in J Grunig & L Grunig (eds), *Public Relations Research Annual*, vol. 2, LEA, Hillsdale, NJ, pp. 67–86.

Phillips, L 2012, *The Promise of Dialogue: The Dialogic Turn in the Production and Communication of Knowledge*, John Benjamins, Amsterdam.

Quinn, D & Hargie, D 2004, 'Internal communication audits: A case study', *Corporate Communications: An International Journal*, vol. 9, no. 2, pp. 146–158.

Rawls, AW 1987, 'The Interaction Order Sui Generis: Goffman's Contribution to Social Theory', *Sociological Theory*, vol. 5, no. 2, pp. 136–149.

Reiner, R 2000, *The Politics of the Police*, Oxford Univerity Press, Oxford.

Shavit, N & Bailey, BH 2015, 'Between the Procedural and the Substantial: Democratic Deliberation and the Interaction Order in "Occupy Middletown General Assembly"', *Symbolic Interaction*, vol. 38, no. 1, pp. 103–126.

Simm, K 2011, 'The Concepts of Common Good and Public Interest: From Plato to Biobanking', *Cambridge Quarterly of Healthcare Ethics*, vol. 20, pp. 554–562.

Somerville, I, Hargie, ODW, Taylor, M & Toledano, M 2017, 'Introduction: Public Relations in Deeply Divided Societies', in I Somerville, ODW Hargie, M Taylor & M Toledano (eds), *Public Relations in Deeply Divided Societies: International Perspectives*, Routledge, London.

Taylor, M 2009, 'Civil society as a rhetorical public relations process', in R Heath, EL Toth & D Waymer (eds), *Rhetorical and Critical Approaches to Public Relations II*, Lawrence Erlbaum, Mahwah, NJ, pp. 76–91.

Theunissen, P, Wan Noordin, WN 2012, 'Revisiting the concept "dialogue" in public relations', *Public Relations Review*, vol. 38, no. 1, pp. 5–13.

Topping, JR 2008, 'Diversifying from Within: Community Policing and the Governance of Security in Northern Ireland', *British Journal of Criminology*, vol. 48, pp. 778–797.

Topping, J & Byrne, J 2012, 'Paramilitary punishments in Belfast: Policing beneath the peace', *Behavioral Sciences of Terrorism and Political Aggression*, vol. 4, no. 1, pp. 41–59.

Topping, J & Byrne, J 2016, 'Shadow policing: The boundaries of community-based policing in Northern Ireland', *Policing and Society*, vol. 26, no. 5, pp. 522–543.

Tully, J 2008, *Public Philosophy in a New Key*, vol. 1, Cambridge University Press, Cambridge.

USDOJ 2015, *Investigation of the Ferguson Police Department*, United States Department of Justice, Civil Rights Division, March 4.

Walker, E, McQuarrie, M & Lees, C 2015, 'Rising participation and declining democracy', in C W Lees, M McQuarrie & E Walker, *Democratizing Inequalities: Dilemmas of the New Public Participation*, New York University Press, New York, pp. 3–26.

Warren, M 2009, 'Governance-Driven Democratisation', *Critical Policy Studies*, vol. 3, no. 1, pp. 3–13.

Weitzer, R & Tuch, SA 2006, *Race and Policing in America: Conflict and Reform*, Cambridge University Press, New York.

Zimring, F 2017, *When Police Kill*, Harvard University Press, Cambridge, MA.

10 Lobbying for life

Violence against the press and the public interest

Julieta Alejandra Brambila and Jairo Lugo-Ocando

Introduction

Over the years, transnational advocacy and non-governmental organisations (NGOs), activists, journalists and other civic allies have adopted a series of communication strategies in order to bring public attention to specific issues, impact public opinion and shape policy making. This repertoire of strategies could be seen as part of what has been called 'public interest-forming practices' (see Chapter 1 of this book), which are the way in which communication practices and campaigns interact with policy making and implementation, social development and social change. Nowhere has proven to be a more fertile ground for the use of public interest-forming practices than the field of human rights (Sikkink 1993). In part, this is because human rights are the basis for public interest work and civic advocacy (Putnam 1993). In recent years, we have seen an increasing adoption of public communication techniques by civic organisers in order to mobilise the public towards increasing awareness, political action and policy impact (Lugo-Ocando & Hernández-Toro 2015). In doing so, we argue, activists, NGOs and close allies have created civic networking coalitions, defined as a set of collective actors distinguished largely by a primary interest in defending human rights and by the use of public interest-forming practices (among others activities) in their public interactions.

Despite the increasing relevance of civic networking coalitions in the protection of the safety of journalists in Latin America (Waisbord 2013, p. 166; Relly & González de Bustamante 2017; Segura & Waisbord 2016), insufficient attention has been given to them in the academic literature. This chapter is an attempt to analytically investigate the relationship between civic networking coalitions and public interest communication, and an opportunity to explore how the aforementioned coalitions produce 'public interest-forming practices'. The key argument is that: when members of the journalistic community, civic actors and transnational organisations perceive a grievance[1] regarding journalists' safety (for instance, a violent killing or forced disappearance of a professional colleague), they could articulate a civic networking coalition aimed at raising awareness, attracting public support and influencing policy making. In that sense, the purpose of this chapter is to examine the ability of civic networking coalitions to act and, next, to investigate which elements need to be in place in order for them to succeed (for instance, the legitimacy of the perceived grievance and solidarity, setting specific goals, and gaining international support). Additionally, we are also interested in analysing the main public interest-forming practices that civic networking coalitions deploy in order to achieve their goals (such as campaigning, community-advocacy journalism, public demonstrations and media activism).

We aim to investigate this argument by examining two case studies of lobbying and campaigning that have taken place in Mexico. These two civic networking coalitions were articulated in order to resist and denounce anti-press violence. We offer a detailed account about how these two civic networking coalitions, in 2006 and 2010, adopted public interest-forming practices intended to create specific measures to increase the safety of reporters in the country. These two cases are: first, the creation of the Office of the Special Prosecutor for Crimes against Journalists; and second, the statutory mechanism to protect journalists and human rights defenders. The selection of these two case studies aims to illustrate the wide range of possible circumstances in which civic coalitions use public interest-forming practices to foster a more robust institutional framework for the protection of journalists in Mexico.

Our analysis is framed within the public security crisis which has impacted upon Mexican society since 2006, when the government launched a military strategy to weaken drug cartels, which have resulted in more than 110,000 people being murdered and 30,000 'disappeared' in cartel-related violence (Schedler 2016, p. 1050). This situation is commonly referred to in news media reports as 'Mexican war on drugs'. Since the Mexican government launched this military strategy, more than 80 journalists have been killed and 25 have been forcibly 'disappeared' (presumed dead) in possible connection to their work (CNDH 2016).

This chapter is organised as follows: first we provide a theoretical foundation for our analytical framework. We then examine the safety of journalists within the Mexican context and present an examination of two civic networking coalitions, developed in response to the position of journalists in Mexico. Finally, we draw some conclusions about the relationship between these civic forming coalitions, journalism and public interest-forming practices.

Social movements and human rights campaigning

Campaigning and lobbying are considered to be the quintessential activities for which public relations (PR) is recognised as a professional discipline (Edwards 2016). This is because PR, as a political social practice, is based upon a series of communication and relational strategies that are used to inform and persuade audiences in order to allocate or re-allocate legitimacy and power. Consequently, power in the context of PR needs to be analysed as communicative action, since power is 'normative-symbolic' and belongs to those who can command the attention of the media (Etzioni 1964). In this sense, we agree with Castells (2007, p. 242) when he suggests, 'the media are not the holders of power, but they constitute by and large the space where power is decided'.

For Castells, wherever power exists, there is always resistance. He calls this form of resistance 'counter-power', which is defined as 'the capacity by social actors to challenge and eventually change the power relations institutionalised in society' (Castells 2007, p. 248). According to Castells (2007), counter-power has been present in every civilisation; however, in contemporary hyper-connected and globalised societies, where traditional political institutions are in crisis, counter-power has taken the form of social movements[2] or civic networks. With the rise of digital technologies and mass-self communication – which refers to 'private senders and public or semi-public and private recei-vers' (Castells 2007, p. 246), social movements and civil networks have deployed a hybrid repertoire of both collective and connective actions in pursuing their goals. In this context, one of the primary goals for social movements and civil networks is the expansion of democratic expression and contestation of domination (Castells 2007). Among the family of social movements, Segura and Waisbord (2016, p. 3) have identified 'media move-ments' as 'civic initiatives aimed at transforming media policies to promote pluralism in public communication'. They argue that media movements may have many goals, including: the regulation of official advertising in the press; strengthening public and community broadcasting; Internet regulation; and stopping violence against journalists.

In this line of thinking, we argue that civic networking coalitions are a type of media movement that focuses on defending human rights, using public interest-forming practices, among other activities, in their public interactions. In this context, a campaign is made up of a series of actions that allow civic networking coalitions to politically mobilise segments of the public and to set and direct the public agenda towards a specific goal. In the case of human rights activism and media advocacy, this is done in order to facilitate social change, promote collective action and influence policy formation (Segura & Waisbord 2016).

In order to advance their agendas, civic networking coalitions deploy cam-paigning strategies which include organised efforts that seek to inform stake-holders and community groups about decision-making processes, while allowing the necessary feedback for broad consultation and effective action. In many cases, these campaigns incorporate lobbying in order to create external (international) or internal (domestic) pressures towards political intervention (Rice & Atkin 1989). These might include a media presence, street protests and convincing legislators to make decisions that help address certain issues and political agendas. These campaigns need to convey a sense of legitimacy in order to be effective. The entity organising the campaign must convince its stakeholders that its actions and objectives are desirable and appropriate to the challenge. The campaigns equally need to establish the degree of urgency to which stakeholders' claims call for immediate action. These are considered in terms of being time-sensitive, such that any delay in attending the claims made by the campaign can be deemed unacceptable by the public.

In what follows, we will explore human rights activism, social movements and civil coalitions in contemporary Mexico in order to provide a context to presenting and discussing our two case studies.

Background: Mexican political context

After Mexico concluded a long process of democratisation with elections in 2000, the country rapidly moved towards a bloody and chaotic war to weaken drug-trafficking organisations in 2006. That year, in the middle of a political crisis derived from allegations of electoral fraud (Meyer 2015), Mexican President Felipe Calderón (2006–2012) declared a formal military operation to weaken drug cartels just ten days after he took office (Meyer 2015). The so-called 'Mexican war on drugs' (as Calderón labelled his own militarisation policy) was declared with neither a parallel effort to re-build the judicial apparatus that had been historically corroded by corruption and inefficacy, nor with integral efforts to shield local police corporations (Enciso 2017; Schedler 2015). In 2012 the new government, led by Enrique Peña Nieto, decided to continue the militarisation strategy, although in public he and his cabinet maintained silence on the issue (Schedler 2015, p. 15). In the ten years from 2006, more than 110,000 were killed in cartel-related violence, but the perpetrators of those crimes have gone unpunished (Schedler 2016, p. 1050). The number of cartel-related crimes – homicides, kidnappings and extortion – increased dramatically in this period, especially within subnational regions of the country (Hope 2015). Furthermore, with the military in the streets fighting openly against drug cartel cells, human rights violations by the military (or other state authorities such as local police groups) also boomed in the same period (Enciso 2017; Anaya 2014). Significantly, Mexican journalists – as witnesses to these events, and in many cases first responders to these atrocities (Brambila 2017a) – did not escape this spiral of criminal violence. Before we examine the impact on journalists at this time, we will devote some space to elucidating why violence against the press is a public interest issue.

Violence against journalists

We define anti-press violence as physical attacks, verbal intimidation and threats against news journalists and media outlets that arise as a result of their work (Brambila & Hughes 2018, p. 91). Although violence in society is relevant in its own right as a focus of analysis for social scientists, for us anti-press violence particularly matters because these actions limit journalistic professional practice, which is largely considered to be a *sine qua non* condition for news journalism to fulfil its professional values, including its democratic role (Löfgren Nilsson & Örnebring 2016, p. 881; Brambila & Hughes 2018). Furthermore, media scholars have proven that violence against the press has broad consequences, not only for the journalists and news media that directly receive such attacks, but also as a chilling effect on other colleagues and civil society in general, with such acts jeopardising access to valuable public information and limiting freedom of the press (Brambila & Hughes 2018). Finally, anti-press violence constitutes a public interest issue, especially because it is widely considered a public health problem (Riddick et al. 2008).

Mexico's epidemic of anti-press violence

Although violence against the press was part of the repertoire of manipulation implemented by Mexico's public officials during the extensive authoritarian regime (especially at a local level), killing and forced disappearances of journalists did not constitute a regular means of coercion during Mexico's one-party rule (1928–2000). In fact, as in other one-party regimes, but contrary to brutal military dictatorships in South America, Mexican autocrats (mostly civilians) favoured clientelism and co-optation over violent means as the main form of press control (Lawson 2002). However, violence against the press did occur. Political historian Benjamin Smith documented around 200 violent attacks against local journalists and newspapers between 1940 and 1960, and around 20 journalists killed between 1944 and 1970 (Smith 2018). Furthermore, in 1984, the violent killing in Mexico City of the very influential journalist and political columnist for the national newspaper *Excelsior*, Manuel Buendía, was one of the more relevant crimes against the press during the one-party regime. Later, in the 1990s and 2000s, a dozen journalists were killed either for political purposes, or by public officials colluding with organised crime or drugs traffickers, including Héctor Félix Miranda, co-founder of muckraking magazine *Zeta* in Tijuana, Baja California (Simon 1997). In fact, according to the Committee to Protect Journalists, an independent press freedom advocacy organisation based in New York, during the last decade of the Institutional Revolutionary Party's (PRI) domination of the party arena and electoral system (from 1988 to 2000), 16 journalists were killed (Waisbord 2002).

However, these numbers pale in comparison to the more than 100 journalists who have been killed in the country since 2000. According to the London-based international news safety organisation Article 19 México, 26 journalists were killed during the first six years of the first federal government elected via democratic and free elections (2000–2006). From 2007 onwards, when Felipe Calderón declared the military strategy to weaken drug cartels, lethal attacks on the press increased even more. Since then, more than 80 journalists have been killed and there have been 25 disappearances (presumed dead), according to Article 19 México (2016). To these numbers, we can add a high level of intimidation tactics and acts of aggression suffered by journalists in this period. From 2010 to 2015, for every journalist killed per year, there were (on average) at least 35 acts of verbal intimidation and physical aggression against the press documented by Article 19 México (2016). It is possible that the real number is far higher than this. Further data from this non-profit organisation show that in the last decade the vast majority of victims were local beat journalists or investigative reporters working on common crime (called *nota roja*), corruption, organised crime, drugs and human rights violations in the country's interior. Finally, when it comes to the prosecution of crimes against the press, the Human Rights Commission (CNDH 2016, p. 47) reports that almost 90 per cent of crimes committed against journalists as a result of their jobs go unprosecuted. In cases related to the forced disappearance of journalists and attacks against media facilities, few of the perpetrators have faced any legal consequences (CNDH 2016, p. 48).

In an attempt to try to document and explain this violent wave of attacks against the Mexican press, both international and Latin American academic literature has embraced the so-called 'Mexican war on drugs' (Holland & Rios 2017). However, as academic research on the Mexican media system has suggested, other structural factors at a subnational level have also played a role in fostering the conditions in which attacks against the press have risen – factors including many cases of violations of human rights by public security bodies, poor performance of democratic institutions, and rampant social inequality (Hughes et al. 2017a; Brambila 2017a, 2017b; Relly & González de Bustamante 2014).

When civic coalitions meet public interest

This section explores how civil society organisations, in conjunction with international and national news safety organisations and advocacy coalitions of journalists, deploy public interest-forming practices to raise awareness and demand justice on the issues of journalists' safety and impunity in crimes against the press in Mexico. In the process, we argue, these civic coalitions have also engaged in lobbying processes and institutional building that have resulted in a more robust legal and operational framework to guarantee the exercise of freedom of the press in the country. Although these efforts have not yet materialised in a structural change in the conditions that limits anti-press violence in the country – just between 2016 and 2017 as many as 16 journalists were violently killed in Mexico (Vázquez 2017) – these experiences illustrate how a group of civic coalitions have used 'public interest-forming practices' to advance their objectives and influence social engagement and public life.

We argue that among other strategies, civic coalitions use strategic communication and public relations techniques – including but not restricted to social mobilisation and advocacy journalism – to capture public attention, raise awareness and influence policy making. However, even when the civic coalitions deployed in these processes share some common elements, they also show important differences, especially in terms of composition, demands and resources. We will examine two cases in which different actors have created civic coalitions that successfully led to the building of institutional frameworks to implement their specific demands.

The first example focuses on the role played by independent journalists and media owners, national and international news safety organisations, as well as Latin American organisations of publishers and international bodies, brought together to raise awareness of the issue of crimes against the press and demand the creation of a special prosecutor with the capacity to address federal courts in these cases. The special prosecutor, the Office of the Special Prosecutor for Crimes Against Freedom of Expression, part of the Attorney General's Office, was established in 2006 by presidential mandate. The second example considers the communication and public relations strategies and lobbying tactics developed by national NGOs, independent groups of journalists and international bodies to push for the creation of a special law to protect journalists with the aim of establishing protocols for national and local authorities following attacks and aggression towards the press. The new *Law of Protection for Human Rights Defenders and Journalists* was approved by both chambers of Congress and passed into legislation in July 2012.

The following section will analyse how these two networked civic coalitions have deployed public interest-forming practices in order to create specific measures to increase the safety of reporters in the country, namely, the creation of the Office of the Special Prosecutor for Crimes Against Journalists (later changed to the Office of the Special Prosecutor for Crimes Against Freedom of Expression), and the statuary mechanism to protect journalists and human rights defenders.

Special Prosecutor for Crimes Against Freedom of Expression

Mexican journalist Alfredo Jiménez Mota, a specialist in organised crime reporting for the legacy newspaper *El Imparcial*, went missing as he was about to meet with one of his sources on the night of 2 April 2005 in the city of Hermosillo, in the north-western state of Sonora. He has not been seen since. According to the Committee for the Protection of Journalists his abduction was linked to his reporting on drug-trafficking organisations operating in Sonora and the links between them and close allies among local authorities (Campbell & Salazar 2008). Mota's disappearance is emblematic of contemporary violence against the press and is regarded by journalists in Sonora as an example of what could happen to any colleague who investigates organised crime links in that state. In the first days immediately following his disappearance, newspapers in Sonora (including *El Imparcial*) and the neighbouring state of Sinaloa (where Mota worked for newspapers *El Debate* and *Noroeste*) called for citizens' help in finding Mota (Baldenegro 2005).

Despite the continued problem of a lack of professional solidarity, journalists from different media outlets held social protests in the state of Sonora demanding the return of their colleague (Article 19 México 2008, p. 16). Two weeks after his disappearance, on 18 April, around 500 people marched in silence in Hermosillo, the capital city of Sonora, to protest the lack of results in the case (García et al. 2005). Around the same time, a group of 60 local journalists from Sonora sent a letter to Mexican President Vicente Fox demanding justice for the missing journalist. On 19 April, in Hermosillo, Fox announced that he would use 'all State forces' to find Mota (Granados Chapa 2006).

In the days immediately following Mota's disappearance, the Inter American Press Association (IAPA), a transnational organisation of the more influential newspapers and media outlets in Latin America and Mexico, was very active in fostering different strategies to advance legal investigations (IAPA 2010). As Juan Fernando Healy, owner of *El Imparcial*, belonged to IAPA, the organisation designated a special group of journalists to investigate the case on 6 April 2005. Months later, as the judicial case showed no sign of substantial progress, the IAPA members held meetings with President Fox, congressmen, and members of the Supreme Court. On 14 April, the IAPA asked federal authorities to create a special prosecutor's office to investigate crimes against the press (IAPA 2010). On 30 August 2005, the IAPA held a 'meeting of newspaper editors and publishers from Mexico's northern border' and national newspapers in Hermosillo (IAPA 2010). Attending the meeting were owners and representatives of some of the country's most influential newspapers, such as national newspapers *El Universal* and *Milenio*, as well as local newspapers such as *El Diario de Yucatán* (from the southern state of Yucatan), magazine *Zeta* (from Baja California), *Noroeste* and *Debate* (from Sinaloa), *Norte* and *El Diario de Chihuahua* (from the northern state of Chihuahua), *El Mañana* (from Tamaulipas), and *El Siglo de Torreón* (from Coahuila) (IAPA 2010). This was a meeting without precedent in the recent history of the Mexican press. Following the meeting, the group published the so-called 'Declaración de Hermosillo' (Hermosillo Declaration), in which they demanded that the Mexican authorities clarify Jiménez Mota's disappearance, as well as other brutal crimes against Mexican journalists. 'This claim included, with all firmness, the Executive, Legislative and Judicial powers, with the purpose to coordinate all their powers to create greater guarantees for the freedom of expression', stated the Declaration. After this, in December 2005, the Chamber of Deputies in conjunction with the Federal Attorney's Office set up a working group to follow up attacks on journalists (Cambio 2005).

After the historical 'Declaración de Hermosillo', in January 2006, the IAPA, in conjunction with organisations like the International Federation of Journalists, held another meeting in Mexico, this time in the border city of Nuevo Laredo, Tamaulipas, the city undergoing at that time the highest rates of lethal crimes against the press (mainly perpetrated by organised crime groups) (IAPA 2005). Following this meeting, the group set up the so-called

'Phoenix Project' (Proyecto Fénix), which created a special group of journalists to investigate the forced disappearance of Mota, a joint effort not seen before in the recent history of Mexican journalism. The John S. and James L. Knight Foundation funded the campaign led by the IAPA, which aimed to put an end to the impunity in crimes against journalists in Mexico and Latin America. Among other things, the campaign included the use of advertisements to bring impunity to the public's attention (IAPA 2006). The campaign also included special training for journalists working in hazardous areas (IAPA 2006). Dario Fritz, an investigative reporter and former member of the Rory Peck Trust in Mexico, recalled that this initiative was revolutionary in the Mexican context: 'there has never been anything like it (…) this was the first time that somebody did something like that here [in Mexico]' (Fritz 2015). Furthermore, the group also agreed to publish a map of risks to document cases and raise public awareness of the issue (IAPA 2006). Fritz also participated in this initiative. He recalled: '[we wanted to] look at the more emblematic cases; investigate them; make a map; and generate awareness and diffusion of all these cases' (Fritz 2015). The Map of Risks was published in January 2006. The investigation in Mexico, led by investigative journalist María Idalia Gómez, documented testimonies from dozens of reporters, editors, publishers, photographers, cameramen and officials in 15 cities in six out of the 32 Mexican states (IAPA 2006).

One year after Mota went missing, in April 2006, a dozen Mexican newspapers simultaneously published the first results of the Phoenix Project made up of a group of journalists from various news media in Mexico and sponsored by the IAPA (2006). In that publication, journalists pointed out: 'The most relevant fact of this story is that a year has passed since the reporter was kidnapped and the attorney general's office has no information as to his whereabouts' (Watson 2006).

Finally, amidst continuing national and international pressure around the issue of violence against the press and impunity, on 15 February 2006 the Mexican government created the Office of the Special Prosecutor for Crimes Against Journalists, to examine cases concerning freedom of expression at the federal level. In July 2010, the office was replaced by the Office of the Special Prosecutor for Crimes Against Freedom of Expression, which was granted powers to bring to federal court any crime against freedom of expression in the country. However, after more than ten years in existence, the results of the special prosecutors are lacking, and the Mota case has not been resolved (CNDH 2016). This case is not an exception – as noted earlier, 25 journalists have disappeared since 2005 and are still missing. The perpetrators of these crimes have gone unpunished (CNDH 2016).

Special task force to protect journalists

Similar to the institutional creation of the Special Prosecutor's Office, the special protection mechanism for journalists, which is a statutory mechanism, was the product of a long process which included lobbying, contestation, and strategic communication and public relations tactics led by a heterogeneous civic coalition, which included human rights advocacy organisations and international bodies (Campa 2014, p. 21).

As noted earlier, since 2006, when the Mexican president announced the military strategy to weaken organised crime in Mexico, acts of aggression against journalists had reached unprecedented levels. From 76 acts of aggression against journalists documented by 2003, the number increased to 244 in 2009, according to the annual report published by Article 19 México (2011, p. 7). However, acts of aggression not only increased in number but also in their intensity and brutality. The London-based advocacy organisation reports that from 2006 to 2012, 57 journalists were violently killed as a result of their job (Article 19 México 2016). Furthermore, cases like Jiménez Mota's forced disappearance became more common. In the same period, 17 journalists went missing (mainly in subnational states like Tamaulipas, Michoacán and Veracruz). Also, in the same period, 43 media facilities (headquarters) were violently attacked, the majority of them in the northern states of Nuevo Leon, Coahuila and Tamaulipas (Article 19 México 2016).

In this context, a group of civil society organisations came together to draft a National Protection Mechanism to protect journalists and human rights defenders (Joloy 2013, p. 492). Like journalists, human rights defenders had been another vulnerable group increasingly targeted by aggression during this violent period (Joloy 2013). In February 2010, a group of organisations linked to the so-called Civil Society Space (Espacio de la Sociedad Civil) held meetings with representatives of international bodies and Mexican public officials on the issue of aggression against journalists and human rights advocates. The meeting was held in a special venue in Tlatelolco, Mexico City, just a few blocks from the famous square where the military and paramilitary groups massacred dozens of students on 2 October 1968. The meeting was sponsored by the Ministry of the Interior, the Human Rights Commission (CNDH), and the Mexican representative of the Offices of the High Commissioner for Human Rights (Campa 2014, p. 22). Colombian experts who, years before, had designed similar mechanisms in Colombia, were also invited to the meeting (Joloy 2013, p. 492). This is relevant because according to an investigative journalist from the muckraking magazine *Proceso*, Homeron Campa, 'the idea to create a special mechanism for the protection of journalists was largely inspired by the Colombian experience' (Campa 2014, p. 22).

Days later, on 26 July 2010, three journalists were kidnapped in the city of Gómez Palacio in the state of Durango while covering a protest by inmates and relatives at a local prison. They were Jaime Canales Fernández from Grupo Multimedios, and Héctor Gordoa Márquez and Alejandro Hernández Pacheco, head of information and camera operator, respectively, both from media outlet Televisa. The criminals forced media companies 'to broadcast videos of interrogations carried out by alleged collaborators of a rival group'

(Cepet 2010). Grupo Multimedios met the demands of the kidnappers. On 30 July, Mexican journalist Denise Mearker decided, together with Televisa and her production team, not to air her programme 'Punto de Partida' in protest at the kidnapping of one of its investigative team. This was one of the few public acts ever held by Televisa to protest against the attacks that their journalists and professional team had received due to their work.

This series of events marked the beginning of a round of public contestations and collective indignation led by a group of independent journalists. An investigative reporter, founder of the journalists' professional organisation Periodistas de a Pie (Journalists on Foot) and one of the many journalists behind this movement, Daniela Pastrana, recalled: 'I think everything exploded with that event (…) We gathered together. We worked and made a Facebook page' (Pastrana 2014). They labelled the movement Los Queremos Vivos (We Want Them Alive), and generated a protest in Mexico City, in which around 2,000 people participated, including independent journalists, citizens and students (Baltazar & Pastrana 2011), a show of solidarity never before seen around this issue. Similar mobilisations took place in another 14 cities throughout the country. According to Pastrana, one of the successes of these social mobilisations was that nobody took particular advantage of them: 'what we decided from the beginning was to not allow logos, because we wanted to avoid any conflict among different organisations (…) I think that the great success of this demonstration was that every kind of journalist came together'. In the long term, the Facebook page of Los Queremos Vivos became a space of digital denunciation of crimes and aggression against the press. Through this digital space journalists and civic organisations from all over the country continually share information on anti-press violence and have raised awareness of these issues with colleagues (Baltazar & Pastrana 2011).

Just a few days after these cycles of civil contestation, in August 2010, following campaigning by news safety organisation Article 19 México, alongside a collective of national and international organisations, two international figures on freedom of expression visited Mexico on a joint official visit: Frank la Rue, the United Nations Special Rapporteur for Freedom of Opinion and Expression, and Catalina Botero, the Special Rapporteur on Freedom of Expression for the Inter American Commission of Human Rights. In their respective meetings with Mexican authorities, they emphasised the necessity of implementing a special task force for the protection of journalists (Campa 2014, p. 22). During their time in Mexico, Botero and la Rue held meetings with several news advocacy organisations, academics and think-thanks (Reforma 2010). For many news safety organisations in the country, these visits opened a window of opportunity to bring attention to the issue of the special mechanism and increased pressure on the Mexican government. 'We hope their visit will induce the State to provide the answers that have been constantly denied to victims and their relatives', said Darío Ramírez, chief representative of Article 19 México. In the public report made at the end of their joint visit, they suggested that the Mexican state '[e]stablish a special national mechanism to protect journalists' (United Nations 2010).

From that moment, policy making took two different, albeit related, roads (Campa 2014). On the one hand, the Mexican government (via the minister of the interior) signed an agreement of collaboration to implement a set of actions to protect journalists. Later they began public consultations about this issue with several NGOs. While this first round of consultations did not gain support from more important civil organisations in the country and abroad, in a parallel policy-making arena, a group of civil society organisations (numbering more than 200) started working on this issue in the Mexican Congress (Joloy 2013, p. 494). This group included international organisations like Amnesty International and Peace Brigades International, as well as the Office of the High Commissioner for Human Rights (OHCHR) in Mexico (Joloy 2013, p. 494). According to Daniel Joloy, the involvement of these international bodies 'permitted the construction of a solid base of trust amongst civil society organizations themselves' (Joloy 2013, p. 496). In this context, Congressman Rubén Camarillo from the National Action Party (PAN) began public consultations to create a special mechanism for the protection of journalists. From November 2011 to March 2012 his office in the Senate organised approximately 20 public consultations with prominent NGOs, including Espacio OSC, Cencos, Casa de los Derechos, Agustin Pro, and Comisión Mexicana Protección Derechos Humanos (Joloy 2013). In such meetings the organisations agreed to the creation of the special mechanism to protect journalists and discussed its legal design. As Campa (2014, p. 20) suggests in his academic work on this matter, '[c]ivil organisations and international bodies of human rights exercised direct pressure on Congress and the Mexican government'. After several weeks of consultation and intense lobbying, the Mexican government higher chamber (the Senate) approved the new legislation on 24 April. Two months later, Mexican President Calderón approved the Law for the Protection of Human Rights Defenders and Journalists on 25 June 2012. However, as with the development of the Special Prosecutor's Office, discussed previously, despite the creation of a special mechanism to protect journalists, after more than three years, the law has not yet resulted in a significant decrease in crimes against journalists. Among other things, critics suggest a lack of material and human resources, as well as a lack of confidence in federal authorities from journalists and human rights defenders (CNDH 2016).

Conclusion

In general terms the development of the two case studies discussed in this chapter show how media movements in the form of civic networking coalitions can successfully use public interest-forming practices, such as campaigning, community-advocacy journalism and media activism, both off- and online in order to disrupt the public space, set the agenda and enhance civic collaborative efforts. The two cases reviewed in this chapter exemplify the rich and diverse spectrum of public communication strategies that media movements can deploy in order to make their voices heard. Also, the two cases illustrate how, in times of conflict, civic networking coalitions are capable of making a real impact on the political process and in the public policy agenda in what might be described as public interest-forming practices.

Additionally, these two examples suggest that in a world that is becoming more connected and interdependent every day (Castells 2007), the role of international actors (from regional organisations to international advocacy groups and global bodies) can play a determining role in setting the media agenda and enhancing public awareness inside national states (Relly & González de Bustamante 2017). This is especially true in the Mexican case, where campaigns developed by civic networking coalitions have been seen as a counter-narrative to the official account deployed by the Mexican authorities through expensive international public image campaigns, developed to improve the country's image abroad during the so-called 'war on drugs' (Brambila 2014).

The two civic networking coalitions examined here in their different ways suggest that networking interactions between national civil society organisations and international bodies and groups, as well as independent journalists and human rights advocacy groups, can deploy tactics that contribute towards enhancing solidarity within the network, bringing public attention to their own agendas and engaging in policy formation practices (Relly & González de Bustamante 2017; Segura & Waisbord 2016). However, as we suggested at the beginning of the chapter, it is worth considering that the two cases are framed in a specific historical situation and actually occurred in two related but different moments of Mexico's epidemic of violence. On the one hand, the institution-building process of the Special Prosecutor's Office happened at the beginning of this wave (between 2005 and 2006), when independent coalitions and advocacy networks of independent journalists and news safety organisations were scarce in the country. At that time, in order to foster a common agenda, the civic networking coalition was led by a regional association of publishers and owners (the IAPA) that took on one symbolic case – the forced disappearance of journalist Jiménez Mota – in order to form a common agenda. On the other hand, the approval of the Law for the Protection of Human Rights Defenders and Journalists occurred in the middle of the country's epidemic of violence, between 2010 and 2011. At that time, national organisations and international bodies were more aware and indeed more organised around the broader issue of violence in the country. However, as we have shown, even when civil society awareness and civic density were improved, the civic networking coalition needed to go through a learning process of empathy and solidarity in order to present a common agenda and successfully impact on public policy.

Additionally, the two examples illustrate how a civic networking coalition is made up of a heterogeneous variety of actors, suggesting that there is no one best way to create and boost a common public agenda. In the first example, the coalition was made up of different national and international organisations that advanced their specific agenda through different contestation cycles and lobbying tactics. On this point it is important to mention that the regional association of publishers and owners, IAPA, played a pivotal role from the beginning. However, joint efforts from different media owners (including close competitors in the media market), in order to mitigate acts of aggression against the press, have been scarce since then. This is especially important because in a comparative perspective, one of the key factors in increasing the awareness about the protection of journalists during the more violent years in Colombia, during the late 1980s and 1990s, was the public commitment and professional solidarity among some of the most emblematic journalistic figures and media owners in the country (Hughes et al. 2017b). In Mexico, however, this possibility seems less plausible, not only because the more relevant media companies have close relationships with Mexican political elites (Guerrero 2010), but also because Mexican journalists widely perceive a lack of support from many of their own organisations (Article 19 México 2016).

The second example suggests that civic network coalitions can be made up of a larger number of international and domestic civil society organisations that articulate their concerns in specific demands to Mexican authorities. One important element here is that the involvement of certain international actors with proven reputations in the process, like 'Amnesty International (...) and the OHCHR permitted the construction of a solid base of trust amongst civil society organizations themselves' (Joloy 2013, p. 496). Additionally, it is important to note that institution-building did not end when particular demands materialised in certain institutions, but remain a continuous process in which established and new civic networking coalitions need to routinely maintain pressure in order to increase effectivity and mitigate remaining problems. In the end, we believe that civic networking coalitions can successfully engage in institution-building practices by advancing their own agendas with grass-roots lobbying techniques that engage different civil organisations groups including international bodies, as well as national organisations working directly with victims. Finally, we conclude that the Mexican experience has not yet materialised in qualitative improvements either in regard to the protection of journalists or in terms of the effectiveness of judicial prosecution of crimes against the press. The lack of results suggests that civil society mobilisation and international awareness are not enough to change structural and institutional conditions, such as weakness in rule of law enforcement, high levels of societal and criminal violence, widespread corruption and scandalous collusion between corrupt public officials and criminals that prevail inside the broken Mexican state. As such, public interest-forming practices alone, as illustrated in this chapter, are insufficient to effect meaningful change.

Notes

1 According to Snow (2013), grievances are the common feelings that agglomerate a social movement. This condition could be associated with feelings like dissatisfaction, fear, indignation, resentment, and moral shock.
2 Tarrow (2011, p. 5) has defined social movements as 'collective challenges by people with common purposes and solidarity in sustained interaction with elites, opponents and authorities'.

References

Anaya, A 2014, *Violaciones a los derechos humanos en el marco de la estrategia militarizada de lucha contra el narcotráfico en México 2007–2012*. Working paper. Mexico, Aguascalientes, CIDE, viewed 30 April 2017, http://ppd.cide.edu/docum ents/302668/0/Libro%204.pdf.

Article 19 México 2008, *Libertad de prensa en México: La sombra de la impunidad y la violencia*. Asociación Mundial de Radios Comunitarias, Comité para la Protección de los Periodistas, Federación Internacional de Periodistas, Fundación para la Libertad de Prensa, Fundación Rory Peck Trust, Instituto Internacional para la Seguridad de la Prensa, Instituto Internacional de la Prensa, International Media Support, Open Society Foundation, Reporteros sin Fronteras, Sociedad Interamericana de Prensa, and UNESCO, viewed 28 April 2017, www.mediasupport. org/wp-content/uploads/2012/11/ims-press-freedom-México-ES-2008.pdf.

Article 19 México 2011, *Silencio forzado: El Estado, cómplice de la violencia contra la prensa en México*, Articulo 19 México, viewed 28 April 2017, www.ifex.org/México/ 2012/03/20/article19informe2011.pdf.

Article 19 México 2016, *Informe 2015. M.I.E.D.O. (Medios, Impunidad, Estado, Democracia, Opacidad)*, Articulo 19 México, viewed 28 April 2017, http://México. indymedia.org/IMG/pdf/305133218-informe-anual-de-violencia-contra-la-prensa.pdf.

Baldenegro, S 2005, 'Exigen en Sonora reforzar busqueda', *Reforma*, April 10, viewed 28 April 2017, https://reforma.vlex.com.mx/vid/exigen-sonora-reforzar-busqueda -193753255.

Baltazar, E & Pastrana, D 2011, 'The Mexican press: At the crossroads of violence', *Nieman Reports*, 20 April, viewed 28 April 2017, http://niemanreports.org/articles/ the-mexican-press-at-the-crossroads-of-violence/.

Brambila, J A 2014, 'Imagen de México y medios de comunicacion (2006–2012)', *Revista Internacinalistas, Imagen de México en el Mundo*, no. 4, viewed 28 April 2017, https://ja brambila.com/2014/12/04/imagen-de-México-y-medios-de-comunicacion/.

Brambila, J A 2017a, 'Forced silence: determinants of journalist killings in México's states, 2010–2015', *Journal of Information Policy*, vol. 7, pp. 297–326.

Brambila, J A & Hughes, S 2018, 'Violence against journalists', in T Vos (Ed.), *The International Encyclopedia of Journalism Studies*, Wiley, London.

Brambila, J A 2017b, 'Challenges to Media Openness in Contemporary México', in M Friedrichsen and Y Kamalipour (eds), *Digital Transformation in Journalism and News Media*, Springer International Publishing, Berlin, pp. 397–408.

Cambio 2005, 'Acuerdan instalación de mesa que revise crímenes de periodista', *Cambio*, 1 December, viewed 28 April 2017, www1.sipiapa.org/casosimpunidad/a cuerdan-instalacion-de-mesa-que-revise-crimenes-de-periodistas/.

Campa, H 2014, *Cuando el mecanismo falla*, Master's dissertation, CIDE, viewed 28 April 2017, http://repositoriodigital.cide.edu/bitstream/handle/11651/452/127777. pdf?sequence=1.

Campaña Permanente de Protección de Periodistas (Cepet) 2010, 'Secuestra el narco-tráfico a cuatro periodistas mexicanos; exige a medios difusión de sus mensajes', 1 August, viewed 10 April 2018, https://libexmexico.wordpress.com/2010/08/01/secues tra-el-narcotrafico-a-cuatro-periodistas-mexicanos-exige-a-medios-difusion-de-sus-m ensajes/.

Campbell, M & Salazar, M 2008, 'The Disappeared in Mexico', 30 September, viewed 10 April 2018, https://cpj.org/reports/2008/09/mexico-08.php.

Castells, M 2007, 'Communication, power and counter-power in the network society', *International Journal of Communication*, vol. 1, no. 1, pp. 238–266.

Center for Journalists and Public Ethics 2010, 'Four journalists released after being held for six days by criminals', 3 August, viewed 28 April 2017, www.ifex.org/ México/2010/08/03/journalists_released/.

Comision Nacional de Derechos Humanos (CNDH) 2016, *Recomendación general 24. Sobre el ejercicio de la libertad de expresión en México*, CNDH, 8 February, viewed 28 April 2017, http://dof.gob.mx/nota_to_doc.php?codnota=5429312.

Edwards, L 2016, 'The role of public relations in deliberative systems', *Journal of Communication*, vol. 66, pp. 60–81.

El Universal 2010, 'Maerker suspende emision de programa por secuestro', 30 July, viewed 28 April 2017, http://archivo.eluniversal.com.mx/notas/698645.html.

Enciso, F 2017, *Violencia y Paz. Diagnósticos y propuestas para México*, Mexico City, Instituto Belisario Dominguez, viewed 28 April 2017, http://bibliodigitalibd.senado. gob.mx/bitstream/handle/123456789/3689/violenciapaz_final%20%281%29br.pdf?se quence=1&isAllowed=y.

Etzioni, A 1964, *Modern Organization*, Prentice Hall, Englewood Cliffs, NJ.

Fritz, D 2015, Personal communication, 9 December.

García C, Figueroa, C & Sanchez, M 2005, 'Marcha en Sonora por la lenta búsqueda de reportero desaparecido', *La Jornada*, 19 April, viewed 28 April 2017, www.jorna da.unam.mx/2005/04/19/index.php?section=estados&article=035n1est.

Granados Chapa, M 2006, 'Alfredo Jiemenz Mota', *Reforma*, 6 April.

Guerrero, E 2017, 'Un decenio de violencia', *Nexos*, 1 January, viewed 28 April 2017, www.nexos.com.mx/?p=30923.

Guerrero, M A 2010, 'Los medios de comunicación y el régimen político', in Loaeza & Prud'homme (Coords.), *Instituciones y procesos políticos*, El Colegio de Mexico, Mexico City, pp. 231–300.

Holland, B E & Rios, V 2017, 'Informally governing information how criminal rivalry leads to violence against the press in México', *Journal of Conflict Resolution*, vol. 61, no. 5, pp. 1095–1119.

Hope, A 2015, 'De narcos a mafiosos, del tráfico de drogas al saqueo ciudadano', *Animal Politico*, 23 October, viewed 28 April 2017, http://narcodata.animalpolitico. com/de-la-droga-a-la-extorsion-texto/.

Hughes, S 2006, *Newsrooms in Conflict: Journalism and the Democratization of México*, University of Pittsburgh Press, Pittsburgh, PA.

Hughes, S, Mellado, C, Arroyave, J, Benitez, J L, de Beer, A, Garcés, M & Márquez-Ramírez, M 2017a, 'Expanding influences research to insecure democracies: How violence, public insecurity, economic inequality and uneven democratic performance shape journalists' perceived work environments', *Journalism Studies*, vol. 18, no. 5, pp. 645–665.

Hughes, S, Garcés, M, Márquez-Ramírez, M & Arroyave, J 2017b, 'Rethinking professional autonomy: Autonomy to develop and to publish news in Mexico and Colombia', *Journalism*, vol. 18, no. 8, pp. 956–976.

Hutton, J G 1999, 'The definition, dimensions, and domain of public relations', *Public Relations Review*, vol. 25, no. 2, pp. 199–214.

Inter American Press Association (IAPA) 2005, *La SIP entrena periodistas mexicanos para prevenir riesgos frente al narcotráfico*, IAPA, 30 November, viewed 28 April 2017, www1.sipiapa.org/iapa-trains-mexican-journalists-sip-entrena-periodistas-mexicanos/.

Inter American Press Association (IAPA) 2006, *Risk Map for Journalists. Brazil, Colombia, Mexico*, IAPA.

Inter American Press Association (IAPA) 2010, *Alfredo Jiménez Mota, a Case that Shook the Mexican Press and which Led to Change*, 28 July, viewed 28 April 2017, http://en.sipiapa.org/notas/1143392-alfredo-jimenez-mota-case-that-shook-the-mexi can-press-and-which-led-to-change.

Joloy, D 2013, 'Mexico's national protection mechanism for human rights defenders: Challenges and good practices', *Journal of Human Rights Practice*, vol. 5, no. 3, pp. 489–499.

Lawson, C 2002, *Building the Fourth Estate: Democratization and the Rise of a Free Press in Mexico*, University of California Press, Los Angeles, CA.

Löfgren Nilsson, M & Örnebring, H 2016, 'Journalism under threat: Intimidation and harassment of Swedish journalists', *Journalism Practice*, vol. 10, no. 7, pp. 880–890.

Lugo-Ocando, J & Hernández-Toro, M 2015, 'Public relations and humanitarian communication: From persuasion to the creation of a community of equals', in J L'Etang, D McKie, N Snow & J Xifra (eds), *The Routledge Handbook of Critical Public Relations*, New York, Routledge, pp. 226–234.

Meyer, L 2015, 'Felipe Calderon o el infortunio de una transicion', *Foro Internacional*, vol. 55, no. 1, pp. 16–44.

Nerone, J 1994, *Violence against the Press: Policing the Public Sphere in US History*, Oxford University Press, Oxford.

Ortiz, R E n.d., 'Alfredo Jimenez Mota', *Nuestra Aparente Rendición*, viewed 28 April 2017, www.nuestraaparenterendicion.com/tuyyocoincidimosenlanocheterrible/index. php/component/k2/item/58-jose-alfredo-jimenez-mota#.WPX32JN_Oko.

Osofsky, H J, Holloway, H & Pickett, A 2005, 'War correspondents as responders: Considerations for training and clinical services', *Psychiatry: Interpersonal and Biological Processes*, vol. 68, no. 3, pp. 283–293.

Pastrana, D 2014, Personal communication, 31 December.

Personal communication 2015, Journalist from the state of Sonora, 9 September.

Putnam, R 1993, *Making Democracy Work: Civic Traditions in Modern Italy*, Princeton University Press, Princeton, NJ.

Reforma 2010, 'Denuncian ante ONU ataques a periodistas', *Reforma*, 11 August, viewed 28 April 2017, www.clasesdeperiodismo.com/2016/06/23/denuncian-ante-la -onu-%E2%80%8Bamenazas-contra-el-periodismo-en-bolivia/.

Relly, J E & González de Bustamante, C 2014, 'Silencing Mexico: A study of influences on journalists in the northern states', *The International Journal of Press/ Politics*, vol. 19, no. 1, pp. 108–131.

Relly, J E & González de Bustamante, C 2017, 'Global and domestic networks advancing prospects for institutional and social change: The collective action response to violence against journalists', *Journalism & Communication Monographs*, vol. 19, no. 2, pp. 84–152.

Rice, R E & Atkin, C H 1989, *Public Communication Campaigns*, Sage, Thousand Oaks, CA.

Riddick, L, Thomson, G, Wilson, N & Purdie, G 2008, 'Killing the canary: The international epidemiology of the homicide of media workers', *Journal of Epidemiology and Community Health*, vol. 62, no. 8, pp. 682–688.

Schedler, A 2015, *En la niebla de la Guerra: Los ciudadanos ante la violencia criminal organizada*, CIDE.

Schedler, A 2016, 'The criminal community of victims and perpetrators: Cognitive foundations of citizen detachment from organized violence in Mexico', *Human Rights Quarterly*, vol. 38, no. 4, pp. 1038–1069.

Segura, M S & Waisbord, S 2016, *Media Movements: Civil Society and Media Policy Reform in Latin America*, University of Chicago Press and Zed Books Ltd., London.

Sikkink, K 1993, 'Human rights, principled issue-networks, and sovereignty in Latin America', *International Organization*, vol. 47, no. 3, pp. 411–441.

Simon, J 1997, 'Tijuana brass: Cloud over a crusader', *Columbia Journalism Review*, vol. 36, no. 1, pp. 21–22.

Smith, B 2018, *Stories from the Newsroom, Stories from the Street: The Mexican Press, 1940–1976*, The University Press of South Carolina, Columbia.

Snow, D A 2013, 'Grievances, individual and mobilizing', in Snow, Porta, Klandermans and McAdam (eds), *The Wiley-Blackwell Encyclopedia of Social and Political Movements*, Sage, London.

Tarrow, S G 2011, *Power in Movement: Social Movements and Contentious Politics*, Cambridge University Press, Cambridge.

United Nations 2010, *Visita Oficial Conjunta a México*, UN, 26 August, viewed 28 April 2017, www.cinu.org.mx/prensa/comunicados/2010/PR213CIDH.htm.

Vázquez, J 2017, 'México, guardián de la impunidad', *Animal Político*, viewed 28 April 2017, www.animalpolitico.com/blogueros-altoparlante/2017/11/06/mexico-guardian-la-impunidad/.

Waisbord, S 2002, 'Antipress violence and the crisis of the state', *Harvard International Journal of Press/Politics*, vol. 7, no. 3, pp. 90–109.

Waisbord, S 2013, *Reinventing Professionalism: Journalism and News in Global Perspective*, John Wiley & Sons, London.

Washington Office on Latin America 2015, *The Mechanism to Protect Human Rights Defenders and Journalists in Mexico: Challenges and Opportunities*, WOLA, viewed 28 April 2017, www.wola.org/sites/default/files/MX/Jan%202015-The%20Mechanism%20to%20Protect%20Human%20Rights%20Defenders%20and%20Journalists%20in%20México.pdf.

Watson, J 2006, 'Missing Mexican reporter's case in spotlight', *The San Diego Union Tribune*, 4 April, viewed 28 April 2017, http://legacy.sandiegouniontribune.com/uniontrib/20060404/news_1n4México.html.

Index

Printed in the United States
by Baker & Taylor Publisher Services